Geographies of Embodiment

SOCIETY AND SPACE SERIES

The Society and Space series explores the fascinating relationship between the spatial and the social. Each title draws on a range of modern and historical theories to offer important insights into the key cultural and political topics of our times, including migration, globalisation, race, gender, sexuality and technology.

These stimulating and provocative books combine high intellectual standards with contemporary appeal for students of politics, international relations, sociology, philosophy, and human geography.

Series Editor: Professor Stuart Elden, University of Warwick

Migration, Ethics & Power: Spaces of Hospitality in International Politics by Dan Bulley

Geographies of Violence by Marcus A. Doel

Surveillance & Space by Francisco R. Klauser

The Data Gaze by David Beer

The Making of Migration by Martina Tazzioli

Geographies of Embodiment

Embodiment

Critical Phenomenology
and the World of Strangers

Kirsten Simonsen
Lasse Koefoed

$SAGE

Los Angeles | London | New Delhi
Singapore | Washington DC | Melbourne

⑤SAGE

Los Angeles | London | New Delhi
Singapore | Washington DC | Melbourne

SAGE Publications Ltd
1 Oliver's Yard
55 City Road
London EC1Y 1SP

SAGE Publications Inc.
2455 Teller Road
Thousand Oaks, California 91320

SAGE Publications India Pvt Ltd
B 1/I 1 Mohan Cooperative Industrial Area
Mathura Road
New Delhi 110 044

SAGE Publications Asia-Pacific Pte Ltd
3 Church Street
#10-04 Samsung Hub
Singapore 049483

© Kirsten Simonsen and Lasse Koefoed 2020

First published 2020

Editor: Robert Rojek
Assistant editor: Eve Williams
Production editor: Katherine Haw
Copyeditor: Catja Pafort
Proofreader: Camille Bramall
Indexer: Avril Ehrlich
Marketing manager: Susheel Gokarakonda
Cover design: Francis Kenney
Typeset by: C&M Digitals (P) Ltd, Chennai, India

Library of Congress Control Number: 2019943597

British Library Cataloguing in Publication data

A catalogue record for this book is available
from the British Library

ISBN 978-1-5264-6358-6
ISBN 978-1-5264-6359-3 (pbk)

Contents

About the Authors

Lasse Koefoed is Associate Professor in Cultural and Political Geography at Roskilde University, Denmark. His research interests relate to critical urban studies, cities and ethnic minorities, nation and nationalism, postcolonialism, cross-cultural encounters and everyday life. He has been involved in several major research projects financed by the Danish Research Council for Social Science like the latest project 'Paradoxical Spaces: Encountering the other in public space'. His recent focus has been on developing an extended phenomenological reconceptualization of the political through the concept of everyday politics and politics of hospitality. He has published widely in international journals like *Mobilities*, *Ethnicities*, *Cities* and *Antipode*.

Kirsten Simonsen has been Professor in Social and Cultural Geography at Roskilde University since 1996. She has published extensively (both journal articles and edited books) in the fields of urban studies, philosophy of geography, space and place, practice theory, minorities and everyday life. Following earlier work on practice theory and everyday urban practices, her recent research has increasingly been focusing on the body and embodied identities. This has led to an interest in phenomenology as a critical theory and its application to the life of ethnic minorities in the city. Her latest research projects, all financed by the Danish Research Council for Social Science, are 'The Stranger, the City and the Nation' and Paradoxical Spaces: Encountering the other in public space' (with Lasse Koefoed).

Acknowledgements

This book has been written on both a long-time and a short-time basis. First, it is based on research performed by us (individually and together) over a number of years both in the form of empirical research and through a gradually developed common approach. This development has happened through four research projects all supported by the Social Science Research Council of Denmark. We are very grateful for their support. Secondly, the formulation and writing-up of the book gave us the possibility both to unify this work and to use it to take our approach a step forward. We thank the editors and production team at SAGE (Robert Rojek, John Nightingale, Eve Williams and Katherine Haw) for that opportunity and especially the *Society and Space* series editor, Stuart Elden. Stuart's interest and encouragement in the early stages of the project has been invaluable to the process.

Successive parts of the work have been presented at different conferences: Nordic Geographers Meetings, International Critical Conferences of Geography, Aegean Seminars, Annual Meetings of the Association of American Geographers, RGS-IBG Annual International Conference in Edinburgh (2012) and European Urban and Regional Studies Conference in Crania (2016). The same has been the case on seminars at the University of British Columbia, Glasgow University, Radboud University Nijmegen, Martin Luther University Halle-Wittenberg, Stockholm University, Uppsala University, Malmö University, Tromsø University, Trondheim University, Tampere University and Aalborg University. We are grateful for all the comments we received on these occasions.

We would also like to thank friends and colleagues from our research group on mobility, space and urban studies (MOSPUS) and researchers on intercultural studies at our neighbour department, all at Roskilde University, for working as an encouraging research environment. In particular we want to thank David Pinder who generously commented on Chapter 4. Beyond Roskilde we want to thank Kye Askins, Guy Baeten, Lawrence Berg, Luiza Bialasiewicz, Gunnel Forsberg, Derek Gregory, Henrik Gutzon Larsen, Peter Hopkins, Olivier Kramsch, Martin Lemberg Pedersen, Carina Listerborn, Anders Lund Hansen, Irene Molina, Chris Philo, Divia Tolia-Kelly, Dina Vaiou and Helen Wilson for support and valuable discussions.

Introduction

Before *producing* effects in the material realm (tool and objects), before *producing itself* by drawing nourishment from that realm, and before *reproducing itself* by generating other bodies, each living body *is* space and *has* its space: it produces itself in space and it also produces that space. (Lefebvre, 1991a: 170)

The aim of this book is to argue for an approach to social life and the production of space based on an understanding of space as genuinely embodied space. From a practice-orientated re-reading of phenomenology, it will explore the relationship between bodily practices, socio-cultural encounters and spatial formations rooted in what we will embark upon as a *critical phenomenology*. We shall return to this term in our first chapter and now just say that we consider critical phenomenology to consist of a starting point in phenomenology combined with critical social theory of different orientations. Throughout the book, the arguments will be illustrated by way of empirical material from four research projects in which one or both of us have participated. They have all, in some sense, been dealing with everyday life, the habitability of different spatial formations, cross-cultural urban encounters, and cultural and political processes in contemporary urbanism.

One might ask: why start with phenomenology? Primarily, we start here because phenomenology opens up the possibility of practising critical analysis through (first-person) experience, seeing life as lived embodiment rather than simply thematizing bodies as objects or texts. It allows social processes to be understood simultaneously from within and without; for example, to explore estrangement not only as a systemic phenomenon, but also through the way it suffuses the experiences of those who have to live through situations of estrangement. Secondly, phenomenology in some sense opens a door to the meaning of 'the stranger'. It understands consciousness as consciousness *of* something, something *other* than itself, whether human or non-human, in this way providing a basis for an understanding of the encounter with an approaching 'stranger'. Then, the stranger is only a category within a specific context; as an outsider inside, it takes on a spatial function by establishing relations of *proximity* and *distance* within the home(land) (Ahmed, 2000). The stranger has a place by being the one 'out of place' at home. In this way, the distinction between friends and strangers is not only categorical but also political; the proximity of the stranger is seen as a risk of the coherence of the community of home or nation, thus raising both ethical and political questions.

More generally, phenomenology can also be seen as a starting point of another theme that runs throughout the book as a whole: the spatiality (and temporality) of social life. The relation between practice and space is crucial here. It is not simply that we act *in* space. Spatial relations between subjects and others (human or non-human) are produced through actions that make some objects reachable and others beyond reach. The space of a room or a city is shaped by a decision (it is constructed to hold specific practices), which subsequently shapes what actions are allowed to 'happen' in there. All practices, then, involve an intimate coexistence of bodies and objects. However, that does not mean that living bodies are just objects alongside other objects. Bodies and objects are not the same, exactly because of their different relations to space. As Merleau-Ponty (1962) tells us, our bodies' existence in space is not, like the one of things, a relation of position; we *inhabit* space, and this inhabitation is a bodily situation that shapes our horizons and our point of view of the world. Our moving bodies are reaching out to the environment but also affected by the 'where' of that movement. It is both about our 'finding our way' and our 'feeling at home' in the world. As Lefebvre (1991a: 170) said, each living body produces itself in space and simultaneously produces that space.

Questions on critical phenomenology reside on the borderline between philosophy and social science, a border that cannot be anything but fluid since the process of interrogating the conditions, institutions and assumptions of intercorporeal lived experience is their shared field. Our book locates itself on this borderline and its aims develop out of quests for understanding problems met in concrete empirical research. Still, none of us resides within the discipline of philosophy. It is of course a risk to read philosophers as a non-philosopher, since we do not have the resources fully to locate them in the intellectual histories from which they emerge. Still we read them, because they help us solve problems we meet in our empirical work. It is deliberately a pragmatic reading, oriented towards establishing a more solid and nuanced ontological and theoretical framework when approaching our research questions. When it comes to our empirical work, it is all conducted in Denmark, which unavoidably gives the project a somewhat Eurocentric flavour. However, recognizing the contextuality of all knowledge production, we do not make any claims on universality, but maybe still on the ontological level some human equivalence.

The four research projects that have provided empirical material to the book, throughout which the theoretical approach has matured, were all run in urban areas in Denmark. They all take their starting point in everyday practices and everyday constructions of meaning with the aim of getting a differentiated and nuanced understanding of individual and collective life, but also in order to use that understanding as a critical corrective to contemporary social relations and tendencies. The first one was called 'The multiple faces of the city – construction of the city in practice and narrative' (Simonsen, 2005b, 2008b) and presented a research problem set against tendencies in urban literature to generalize the features of urban life by creating a binary opposition between seeing the urban as a collection of local communities or as a continuous fluidity and mobility. Through an analysis of everyday practices and urban narratives, it identified a range of different modes of life in contemporary Copenhagen. The second project focused on nationalism and was called 'Glocal nationalisms. Globalization, everyday life and narratives of Danish identity' (Koefoed, 2006; Koefoed and Simonsen, 2007). Through an analysis of banal, everyday nationalism in Hundested (a Danish provincial town), it explored the dominant appearance of an increasing nationalism in Denmark, but also a differentiation in competing forms of nationalism constituting an 'identity struggle' over the definition of Danish identity. The third project, 'The stranger, the city and the nation' (Koefoed and Simonsen, 2010, 2011, 2012), is about life as ethnic minority in Denmark. We asked: What are the experiences and possibilities of ethnic minorities to 'feel at home' in different socio-spatial formations? How do they construct their city and their nation in practice and narrative? The analysis basically was about habitability for 'the strangers' (in this case, people of Pakistani heritage) on different socio-spatial scales, but it also emphasized the differences among answers to the questions in order to give a nuanced understanding of their conditions of life. Finally, we have the project 'Paradoxical spaces: cross-cultural encounters in public space'.[1] (Koefoed et al., forthcoming; de Neergaard et al., 2017; Simonsen et al., 2017, 2019). This project differs somewhat from the others both in research question and in method, since we focus more directly on concrete encounters in public spaces and how they are performed, which also means that the dominant method was of a more ethnographic character, even though it naturally also involved interviews. We focused on three different modes of encounters (collective planned encounters, encounters with authorities and everyday encounters). The aim was to understand both how 'the stranger' is encountered and what these meetings can tell us about possibilities and limitations on co-existence in the city.[2]

THE STRUCTURE OF THE BOOK

The book consists of five chapters, of which the opening one outlines the approach that will be developed and put to work throughout the whole text. It is a purely theoretical chapter, while the next four include illustrations from empirical studies. In Chapter 1, 'Figuring the Ground', we start with the direct question: what is critical phenomenology? We begin by exploring different definitions of the term, which arose in different fields during the 2010s. We then try to pin down our own understanding of the term taking our starting point from Maurice Merleau-Ponty and his embodied phenomenology, but also taking inspiration from feminist theory, critical race theory and postcolonial thinking. The second part of the chapter consists of a discussion of the possibility that insights from critical phenomenology could contribute to the development of a 'new humanism' that avoids the rationalist and self-righteous claims of the old ones.

In Chapter 2, 'Bodies and Embodiment', we show what it means to us to work on geographies of embodiment. Again, our starting point is Merleau-Ponty's embodied phenomenology. His understanding of corporeality is based on a non-dualist ontology of the body and its environment. The body concerned is not just an object in the world, neither is it a mere assemblage or juxtaposition of its parts; it is a *phenomenal, lived body* in continuous interaction with its environment. Within that thinking, we discuss habituation and corporeal agency, orientation and disorientation, intercorporeality and reversibility, and bodies and power. 'Embodied identities' refers to the connection between identities and everyday practices and to visible identities in the form of identities marked on and through the body – both issues are illustrated by practices, experiences and identity-construction performed in everyday life in Copenhagen. The theme of the temporality and spatiality of the body is developed from both Merleau-Ponty and Henri Lefebvre and is seen as a question of both inhabitation and social conflict. It is illustrated by a case that we call 're-scaling identities', analyzing the habitability of different spatial formations for ethnic minorities. The chapter is rounded off by theorizing the associated issues of affectivity and emotions.

In Chapter 3, 'Encountering the Other', we turn more directly to the question of intercorporeal and intercultural meetings. It is written against the background of our latest project described above, which focuses on encountering the Other in public space. We elaborate on the concept of encounter and thence relate our work to much of the literature around this issue appearing within geography in the 2000s and 2010s. It is in this chapter that we devote most attention to postcolonial thinking. However, the greater part of the chapter deals with empirical analysis and interpretive theorization of the three different modes of encounter that we isolated, exemplified by 'multicultural' festivals, encounters with the police and mobile encounters on a public bus, respectively. The analysis showed how concrete encounters give rise to a range of different emotions and practices residing in an interspace between 'cosmopolitan hope' and 'postcolonial melancholia'.

In Chapter 4, titled 'Urban Perspectives', we offer an understanding of 'the urban' that emerges from our approach to critical phenomenology. It is collected under two headings: 'The flesh of the urban' and 'The urban as a world of strangers'. The first part focuses on the chiasmatic relationship between bodies and cities, seeing it as a dynamic and turbulent materiality of urban existence. The approach holds that the urban, as a phenomenon, functions not only as physical horizons for urban bodies, but also as an imaginary horizon for individuals and collectives. These two can be described as chains of operations done on and with the surroundings, and in their temporality and spatiality they serve as the background for the notions of 'the embodied city' and 'the narrative city', respectively. Difference and strangers are the main issues of the second part of the chapter. It starts from the 'figure' of the stranger, which is used as a background for discussing the conditions of 'becoming the stranger' in contemporary European urban environments. Throughout the chapter, empirical material from our projects is used as illustrations, and our conceptualizations engage in dialogue with contemporary concepts of the urban such as 'cosmopolitan urbanism', 'multicultural cities', 'planetary urbanization' and 'postsecular cities'.

Finally, Chapter 5 turns towards 'Political Perspectives'. We argue that the take on phenomenology in which we reside definitely has a political perspective. Already Merleau-Ponty delivered on this front with an understanding of politics rooted in existence and coexistence. When developing our take on what we call 'everyday politics', however, we turn to Hannah Arendt. She blended historical and phenomenological approaches in her critique of totalitarianism and developed her notion of politics in response to its destruction of the human condition of plurality. She sees the political as a human activity with plurality as its condition and centring on the spaces where humans interact and take responsibility for their shared world. Building on Arendt's views enables us to develop an understanding of everyday politics that emphasizes experience, difference and coexistence. This understanding is illustrated by two cases. One is about banal everyday nationalism. Through narrative interviews it explores the upsurge of nationalism in Denmark/Europe, simultaneously showing a plurality of nationalisms and an increasing Orientalism within the dominant form. The other case is about the 'politics of hospitality' and tells the story of a local non-governmental organization (NGO) caring for refugees arriving around 2015 during the so-called 'immigration crisis' in Europe. Together, these cases expose the complexity and ambiguity of everyday politics.

NOTES

1. Two other people have participated in this project: postdoc Maja de Neergaard and research assistant Mathilde Dissing Christensen, who will also appear as co-authors in publications associated with the project.

2. The empirical material from these projects will be used as illustration through-
    out the book. A considerable amount of that will take the form of extracts from
    in-depth interviews. In all of these cases, the text consists of translations made by
    us from interviews originally carried out in Danish.

Figuring the Ground

We remain physically upright not through the mechanism of the skeleton or even through the nervous regulation of muscular tone, but because we are caught up in a world. If this involvement is seriously weakened, the body collapses and becomes once more an object. (Merleau-Ponty, 1962: 254)

This shows us how the world itself is more 'involved' in some bodies than others [...]. It is thus possible to talk about the white world, the straight world, as a world that takes the shape of the motility of certain skins. (Ahmed, 2006: 159–60)

WHAT IS CRITICAL PHENOMENOLOGY?

'Critical phenomenology' is a term that currently and more or less simultaneously is turning up in many different connections and different disciplines – it involves in all cases, in one way or another, seeing thinking as a practice that is *embodied* as well as socially and politically situated. Let us here just illustrate the range of ideas that are connected to the term by way of introducing a few of those authors specifically using the term. For example, Jérôme Melançon (2014) localizes this thinking in the shared field of philosophy and social sciences. Taking his starting point as the work of Maurice Merleau-Ponty and Pierre Bourdieu, he emphasizes reflexivity, that is, thinking about our own situation and those of the people who surround us by a constant confrontation of what unites and separates us, from our body to our most abstract thoughts – a radical attempt to understand our lives through those of others. The geographer George Revill (2015) sees it as an approach that theorizes the spatio-temporal specificity of experience, the ontologically generative qualities of that experience and the politics articulated by particular distributions of the sensible. Eric Mohr (2014) connects the term to phenomenology's relevance for ideology critique. For him, critical phenomenology means putting the findings of phenomenology to work for the sake of social critique. For this purpose he draws on the German value phenomenologist Max Scheler to develop an ideology critique as a critique of the ways in which social organization institutionalizes value-delusions and/or value-inversions. Finally, Lisa Guenther offers a longer definition worth quoting in its entirety:

> By critical phenomenology, I mean both a philosophical practice of reflecting on the transcendental and material structures that make experience possible and meaningful, and also a political practice of 'restructuring the world' in order to generate new and liberatory possibilities for meaningful experience and existence. As a philosophical practice, critical phenomenology rejects the absolute priority of a singular transcendental ego, both to the world and to a more complex sense of transcendental intersubjectivity. It also questions the priority of the transcendental to the material, without foregoing a transcendental analysis of experience altogether. As a political practice, critical phenomenology is a struggle for liberation from the structures that privilege, naturalize, and normalize certain experiences of the world while marginalizing, pathologizing, and discrediting others. (2017: 49)

We can assent to all these definitions and also find inspiration in them. For us, then, critical phenomenology involves specific choices within a phenomenological literature, seeking definitions that are open to social analysis and politics but also a combination of phenomenology with other critical social theories. The starting point is taken from a group of phenomenologists whose work has been known as 'asubjective' and second- or third-generation phenomenology and which addresses questions of intersubjectivity, ethics and politics. That includes authors such as Merleau-Ponty, Patočka, Waldenfels, Levinas and Arendt, amongst whom our starting point is Merleau-Ponty and his embodied phenomenology. The version of critical phenomenology we embark on, however, also has strong affiliations to feminist theory, critical race theory, postcolonial thinking and the unorthodox Marxism of Henri Lefebvre. These choices rely on our theoretical reflections but also on the empirical field in which we have been working. Combining phenomenology with feminist theory and postcolonialism is of course not a new exercise (see Fanon, 1967a; de Beauvoir, 1972; Alcoff, 1999, 2006; Ahmed, 2000, 2006; Young, 2005, just to mention a few). The basis for the connection is the common interest in embodiment and embodied experiences, and it is in this connection that the critical potential of phenomenology in particular has been exposed. Our initial reflections on critical phenomenology can then be summarized in three points:

First, it is a critical theory that emphasizes experience.[1] Most critical theory focuses on inequalities and oppression as rooted in structural and systemic relations – and in many cases for good reasons. There is, however, more to it than that. It is insufficient to describe the world's general structures without also attending to the way they are experienced from within – that is, including the experiences of those who are finding themselves in and suffering from situations of oppression. This is where Merleau-Ponty's phenomenology has an invaluable role to play. It offers an epistemology and a descriptive method that eschews rationalism and objectifying mind–body dualisms, and instead invites a focus on embodied, situated and often more affective forms of experience. In phenomenology, the account of the world is not an objective one; it is the way it is experienced. Phenomenologically speaking, 'a world' is a taken-for-granted, context-giving horizon from within and against which our lived experiences emerge: 'The world is not what I think, but what I live through' (Merleau-Ponty, 1962: xvi–xvii). Merleau-Ponty describes our existence and our lifeworld in the light of the fact that we are experiencing bodies.[2] In his thinking, the question of the world is far from any solipsistic ideas of private worlds; he advocates a radical intersubjectivity, which he theorizes as an opening onto otherness and into a common space where our worlds overlap and intertwine – in this way seeing the world as an 'intermundane space' (1968: 269). Furthermore, he was adamant that phenomenology eschews any return to experience in some naïve and uncritical sense. It is exactly because experience is already infused with layers of cultural sedimentation, saturated with habit and inertia, and interwoven with power and obfuscation, that it must be ceaselessly interrogated and opened up to experiments (Coole, 2001: 20). In this way, he anticipates and escapes later 'poststructuralist' critique claiming that experience is presumed to be 'authentic' and offering a self-evident truthfulness.

This point also means that phenomenology is not a return to a simple level of description. It sticks close to experience, but experiences and events have to be interpreted as they emerge within the tissue of ideal and material connections of existence. This is an interpretive and creative act as well as a discovery. In critical analysis it also involves particular knowledge interests. For this part we have drawn inspiration from what Sandra Harding (1998) calls *borderlands epistemology*. She characterizes it as a form of standpoint epistemology using practices and experiences in 'borderlands' as starting points for analysis. Harding further traces the intellectual background of standpoint epistemologies to a specific reading of Hegel's ideas about the master/slave relationship. It emphasizes how knowledge about the relationship achieved from the standpoint of the slave's life is preferable to the more distorted understanding available from the master's perspective. From the latter, everything the slave does appears to be a consequence either of the master's will or of the slave's brutish nature – s/he does not appear fully human, while the same activities from the slave's perspective can be understood as human (tactical) actions performed in relation to his/her conditions of life. These reflections have since informed Marxism as well as feminism, anti-racism and postcolonialism.

Harding maintains that borderland epistemologies are not only about experiences of marginal lives. Research has to start off from such positions in order to understand the relationship between those lives, and other social and cultural relations. The approach is 'grounded', but not conventionally so. It is not just neutral conceptualizations, but theoretical reflections around them. What the borderlands thinking claims is that all knowledge attempts are socially situated and some of these positions are better than others as a starting point for knowledge production.

Second, critical phenomenology is a phenomenology that is sensitive to difference. The principal figures in the phenomenological tradition (Husserl, Heidegger, Sartre, Merleau-Ponty and various others) have been targets of criticism for not paying adequate attention to the question of difference, not least formulated within feminist literature. Much of this critique has been aimed at Merleau-Ponty, probably because his work is, at the same time, attractive to feminism. His ontology, with its emphasis on human embodiment and lived experience, is very obviously congenial to any approach interested in embodied difference. On closer inspection, however, the critique is not that straightforward; it actually covers two (connected) discussions.

The first discussion concerns ontological and ethical questions and has come from authors such as Levinas, Foucault and Derrida, who shared the suggestion that in affirming context, phenomenology (including Merleau-Ponty) allows the other to disclose only that which the subject has prepared for (Reynolds, 2004) – that it pays only minimal attention to the other conceived of as irremediably different and thereby precludes the possibility of something being 'absolute other'. Levinas (1987) tightens up this assertion with the phrase 'imperialism of the same'. As regards Merleau-Ponty, this critique partly seems unfair and partly a question of genuine disagreement. First, many of his discussions actually do emphasize how interaction with others can both result in appreciation of their alterity and allow us to surprise ourselves and move beyond our horizons. Surprise and disorientation disrupt already acquired meanings and expectations. In other words, his understanding of others on the one hand does not reduce them to the same. On the other hand, however, neither does it see their alterity as so radical that it precludes all mutual understanding. This latter point in particular appears in *The Visible and the Invisible* (1968) in which he advances an ontology of a field where self and other are understood as emergent singularities within an interworld and as both equivalent and non-identical. Self and other are at the same time intertwined and divergent, and alterity is something that is created *in* encounters; accordingly, there can be no such thing as 'absolute' alterity.

The second discussion has a more social character and is about gender/sex/race differences. 'The other' is criticized for being abstracted from particular others. This critique hits phenomenology broadly (including Levinas, see Ahmed, 2000), but the feminist critique of Merleau-Ponty can be seen as seminal. For example, Iris Marion Young shows that his formulations can be read as taking as norm a masculine style of inhabiting lived space, and that the traditional western style of feminine bodily comportment, viewed in the light of this norm, can be defined as an 'inhibited intentionality' and an 'ambiguous transcendence'

(Young, 1990a). Similarly, Judith Butler (1989) criticizes him for naturalizing his own historical situation of gender relations by taking the traditional masculine, heterosexual experience as paradigmatic of normal bodily intentionality. Both arguments are parallel to the earlier work of Franz Fanon on race, in which he implicitly charges Merleau-Ponty's theory of a normative corporeal schema with being based upon European man, a white man (Fanon, 1967a; Mahendran, 2007).

If we look at Merleau-Ponty's specific examples, he might be found guilty as charged. However, even if he did not make deep explorations of differences in terms of class/gender/race relations, later developments have shown that there is nothing within his larger phenomenology that precludes such reformulations. Amongst his contemporaries, it had already been done by Simone de Beauvoir on gender and Franz Fanon on race. In *The Second Sex* de Beauvoir insists on the experiential realities of sexual difference. Citing Merleau-Ponty, she writes: 'I am my body' and 'if the body is not a thing, it is a situation: it is our grasp of the world and the outline for our projects' (2010: 46). De Beauvoir's argument has been attractive because, by in this way conceiving the body as lived and as one's phenomenal 'situation', she escapes the objectivist reduction of sex to 'raw biological material' without entering into the opposite reduction of sexual difference to a mere structural or discursive effect (see also Moi, 1999; Kruks, 2012, 2014). In *Black Skin White Mask* (1967a), Fanon, as mentioned, criticizes Merleau-Ponty's phenomenology of perception, but he also appropriates it in his critical theorizing of race and racism. He discloses how colonization shapes not only the social and political structures of a society, but also the psychic life and lived experience of both the colonized and the colonizer. He also develops a phenomenological account of the lived experience of 'the black man' who comes to experience himself as fixed and objectified in the ubiquitous white racist gaze. For Fanon, this gives rise to a feeling of 'non-existence' of the black man (1967a: 139). He does not and cannot exist as a black man – only as a failed white or honorary white – as long as colonial structures remain in place.[3]

In the wake of these works a bulk of literature taking a phenomenological approach to difference has appeared, in particular in the twenty-first century, when there seems to be a renewed blossoming of phenomenological thinking. A range of axes of difference has been treated – such as class, gender, race, sexuality, age, disability and religion – even if gender and race seem to be the dominant ones. Iris Marion Young has been a ground-breaking feminist phenomenologist. Her essay *Throwing like a girl* appeared in 1990 and was followed by other texts addressing experiences emanating from the facticities of female physiology and analysed as 'normatively disciplined expectations imposed on female bodies by male-dominated society' (2005: 5). Others explore more than one axis of difference. Linda Alcoff in *Visible Identities* (2006), for example, employs phenomenology to grasp the nature of gendered and racialized identities, claiming that 'They are most definitely physical, marked on and through the body, lived as a material experience' (2006: 102). And Sara Ahmed in *Queer Phenomenology: Orientations, Objects, Others*

(2006) takes up the phenomenological notion of 'orientation' to explore both queer and non-white experience. Finally, as a preliminary illustration of the growth of this phenomenology of alterity and difference, we shall draw attention to two edited collections (published in 2011 and 2017, respectively). The first is called *Phenomenologies of the Stranger: Between Hostility and Hospitality* (edited by Richard Kearney and Kascha Semonovitch, 2011), the second one *Body/Self/Other: The Phenomenology of Social Encounters* (edited by Luna Dolezal and Danielle Petherbridge, 2017). As the titles suggest, both books collect papers that explore both the lived experience of our relations with others and the importance of phenomenology when considering questions of social justice and critique that hinge on the textures of lived experience and ethical and political relations growing out of them.

This leads us to the third and final point in our characterization of critical phenomenology; it is that *it involves a politics that emphasizes co-existence.* Again, we can start from the political thinking of Merleau-Ponty. It might seem surprising because, even if his embodied phenomenology has attracted increasing attention in the aftermath of the linguistic turn of many social sciences, few have engaged in the political aspects of his thinking. Exceptions are Sonia Kruks (1977, 1981) and Diana Coole (2001, 2007a). As they show, there are strong political elements in Merleau-Ponty's thinking, which is closely connected to his participation in political discussion in the France of his age. He identified a crisis of modernity rooted in a common dualistic structure within Cartesian ontology, modern epistemologies and political regimes: the rationalist regimes were existentially violent, failing to realize their own ideals, and rationalism's failure to grasp the dialectics of collective life rendered potentially progressive action impotent. In the two books *Humanism and Terror* (1969, orig. 1947) and *Adventures of the Dialectic* (1974, orig. 1955), Merleau-Ponty used this insight to criticize the dominant political ideologies of his time: liberalism and communist Marxism. Even if these publications were a picture of the period, the ideas they were built on have more lasting relevance. As Coole argues:

> Since we still inhabit the ruins and crisis of a faltering modernity that calls for interpretation and intervention, his critique and his method of undertaking it retain considerable resonance, especially in the light of the political dead end of so-called postmodernism. (Coole, 2007a: 9)

Merleau-Ponty basically thought about politics as a set of practices and processes within everyday life in which *coexistence* ineluctably involves power and conflict as well as reason and communication. For him, politics was primarily about collective life and he rooted it in an ontology of the interworld, conceived as a thick intersubjectivity or a field of forces where struggles for coexistence are performed. Methodologically, he argued for an interpretive work beginning from a feeling for one's times, their lacunae and possibilities. Specific political regimes should be *understood* and judged on the ways in which they tackle the dilemma of coexistence, and this is how he himself approached the comparison of liberal and communist alternatives. In this way, Merleau-Ponty's political thinking can provide the background for renewed criticism of the current direction that politics and coexistential relations are taking, as well as for experiments of co-existence and small, everyday resistances that open fissures and new opportunities for progress.

Two other thinkers we find inspiring when it comes to the political-ethical side of phenomenology are Emmanuel Levinas and Hannah Arendt (see also Topolski, 2015). They both found inspiration in existential phenomenology with its emphasis on concrete lived experience, and they both (like Merleau-Ponty) put forward a social or relational ontology, emphasizing alterity and plurality, respectively. In this sense, they both explored 'the political' seen as the realm of human coexistence. For Levinas, ethics is the primary element of philosophy (and precedes ontology), and his ethics is an ethic of *responsibility*. It does not prescribe a set of codes, norms or rules of conduct, but it still has a normative basis; it differentiates better from worse ways of being with (or, more precisely, *for*) others (Ahmed, 2000: 140). In this way responsibility is intrinsically relational. When Levinas so strongly emphasizes the idea of absolute otherness, it is connected to an urge to avoid two different reductions: the reduction of the other to the same and the reduction of the other to an object or concept. A traumatic image that illustrates the latter is the tattoos of Auschwitz, the reduction of human particularity to a number.

Hannah Arendt also made her starting point mid-twentieth-century European totalitarianism, a context she herself had experienced and lived through. Just like both Merleau-Ponty and Levinas, she began with critique of a political phenomenon of her own time. In *The Origins of Totalitarianism* (1973, orig. 1954), she intertwines an analysis of nineteenth-century anti-Semitism, European imperialism, the rise of totalitarianism and the destruction of the Jewish people, and she offers a phenomenological account of these different experiences of dehumanization. Subsequently, her reconceptualization of the political centres on exactly the aspect of the human condition that she thought totalitarianism had destroyed – that is, *human plurality*. In *Human Condition* (1958) she declared plurality the basic condition for political action, but not as a question of consensus; it involves a productive (agonistic) tension between equality and distinction – or plurality and particularity. The political realm is to her the space in which we co-create the shared world as a realm of difference and distinction. Political experience allows each person to appear as a particular individual in a shared public space and to distinguish herself through word and deed (Topolski, 2015).

These three authors together, then, can inspire by their political thinking including intersubjectivity, co-existence and human experience, but also because their concrete analyses involve elements that we can trace again now in the first decades of the twenty-first century.

CRITICAL PHENOMENOLOGY AS A 'NEW HUMANISM'

> Even those amongst us who today revive the word 'humanism' do not support the *shameless humanism* of our ancestors any more. It might characterize our time that it dissociates humanism from the idea of a self-righteous humanity and not only reconciles, but considers indivisible the awareness of human values and that of the infrastructure that gives them existence. (Merleau-Ponty, 1960: 224–5, our translation)

This quote discloses how humanism (seen in relation to anti- and posthumanism) has been subject to discussion at least from the middle of the twentieth century – in philosophy and subsequently in a range of social sciences – and that Merleau-Ponty was deeply involved in this discussion. In particular, he would be critical of all abstract conceptions of 'rational man' possessing reason and an autonomous, rational will (see also Simonsen, 2012).

Here, our interest concentrates on more recent criticism coming primarily from poststructuralism and posthumanism that encompasses a range of different perspectives sharing the critique of humanism and the effort to displace 'the human' as the centre of social enquiry. Anti-humanism in the form of poststructuralism and deconstruction took off by implying the absence of human agency by means of the illustrative phrases such as 'the end of man' or 'the death of the subject'. Posthumanist thinking continues this line but also departs from it in significant ways. It refrains from the prioritization of epistemology over ontology and introduces new ontologies as part of the theoretical project, and it radicalizes the displacement of the 'human' through critique of an anthropocentrism allegedly shared by humanism and anti-humanism. Some of the common ground of these approaches is informatively summarized by Braun (2004a, b). He distinguishes between three different ways of proposing the 'posthuman': (1) posthumanism as deconstructive responsibility that focuses on the construction of the *figure* of the human and the way in which it is established as an *identity* differentiated from other categories of being; (2) posthumanism as ontology including 'cyborg' ontology and different ontologies dealing with the *making* of humans and non-humans alike as relational effects of anonymous, generative forces; and (3) posthumanism as non-anthropocentrism, less radically claiming the 'social' world is a 'more than human' one and consequently admitting into the 'social' all manner of non-human entities and actors.

Within geography, these issues are addressed far beyond the writings that strictly follow the involved philosophical trajectories, but it can be represented by two 'movements' within the subject. First, 'the cultural turn' within human geography ushered in a number of approaches emphasizing the representational dimension of social and cultural processes. It occurred when deconstruction and (French) poststructuralism entered the scene, emphasizing dominant discourses and representations and giving room to important issues such as difference, otherness and identity politics. Secondly, and in reaction to the former, a re-materialization occurred, partially based on posthumanist philosophies and opening up to a renewed animal geography or broader approaches such as actor-network geographies, 'more-than-human' geographies and non-representational theory (Anderson and Harrison, 2010). These developments have indisputably delivered analytical and normative gains regarding, on the one hand, representation and difference and, on the other, inclusion of materiality, the bio-sphere and technology. They do, however, also demonstrate remaining problems as to the fate of the human in human geography, sometimes even verging on a renewal of geography's old problem of naturalism. They have a troubled relationship to issues of lived experience, notions of subjectivity and agency, and (in its strongest forms) also those of responsibility and politics.

Our claim is that a critical phenomenology offers resources for reconstitution of a form of humanism that eliminates the theological, rationalist and Eurocentric presuppositions that have marred the old ones; that it can anticipate much of the critique raised by anti- and posthumanism without reaching the excesses of posthumanism. Let us as a first step take a closer look into the position of Merleau-Ponty in the route from humanism to posthumanism.

We could summarize the advances of anti-humanism and posthumanism as (1) a path from the self-containing subject towards subjectivities as relational effects of arrangements or assemblages, and (2) an emphasis of materiality or, more broadly, the 'non-human' or 'more-than-human'. Phenomenology, and in particular Merleau-Ponty, does, however, travel quite a distance down that lane. Phenomenology in general can be characterized as a turn towards objects; rather than consciousness being seen as directed towards itself, it is understood as having objects in its view, as being shaped by that which appears before it in 'this here and now' (Ahmed, 2006: 25). It is from this position that dichotomies such as subject/objects, mind/body and meaning/matter are contested. In this effort, Merleau-Ponty sought an ontology giving room to nature, man, spirit and history without reducing one to the other. This project had to be 'presented without any compromise with humanism, nor moreover with naturalism, nor finally with theology [...] to show that philosophy can no longer think according to the cleavage: God, man, creatures' (Merleau-Ponty, 1968: 274). Merleau-Ponty is more sympathetic to romantic and vitalist approaches (see Merleau-Ponty, 2003). Yet he is concerned that their reliance on philosophies of immanence risks reviving the theological and teleological senses of internal productivity that opens up to new forms of mysticism. How, then, does Merleau-Ponty locate himself in this landscape? As a short-cut, we shall try to pin down his position by means of three extracts from one of his last essays *Eye and Mind* (in Merleau-Ponty, 1964).

> Visible and mobile, my body is a thing among things; it is caught in the fabric of the world, and its cohesion is that of a thing. But because it moves itself and sees, it holds things in a circle around itself. Things are an annex or prolongation of itself; they are encrusted into its flesh, they are part of its full definition; the world is made of the same stuff as the body. (1964: 163)

This first extract shows Merleau-Ponty's affinity for what is sometimes labelled 'new materialisms' (Coole and Frost, 2010). His ontological framework weaves together subject/object as well as culture/nature. In his courses on nature in particular, he – like later Deleuze and Agamben – takes inspiration from the zoologist Jakob von Uexküll's *Umwelt* theory in developing this connectivity (Merleau-Ponty, 2003). The idea of *Umwelt* serves as an animal equivalent to Husserl's *Lebenswelt,* as an 'intermediary reality'; a section of the world that exists for the behaviour of the animal and to which it addresses itself. Merleau-Ponty's aim was to articulate a structural connection between consciousness and nature on the basis of a relational bond. He would show how the human order is founded upon, while taking up and transforming the vital order, which in turn is taking up and transforming its own foundation in the physical world (Churchill, 2008).

> The enigma is that my body simultaneously sees and is seen. That which looks at all things can also look at itself and recognize, in what it sees, the 'other side' of its power of looking. It sees itself seeing; it touches itself touching; it is visible and sensitive for itself. It is not a self through transparence, like thought, which only thinks its object by assimilating it, by constituting it, by transforming it into thought. It is a self through confusion, narcissism, through inherence of the one who sees in that which he sees, and through inherence of sensing in the sensed [...] (1964: 162–3)

What Merleau-Ponty talks about in this extract is the capacity of the body for self-perception or for auto-affection (Serban, 2010). For him, it constitutes a difference between the human body and the material world. The surrounding world still has a 'pregnancy of possibilities', but its agency is on another, less productive plane. Human bodies, together with everything else in the world, are the coherence of materiality and meaning as a universal element of a being; and it is a process of immanent generativity. But there is still a contrast between the wild being, which we share with animals, plants and things, and the immediacy of our human existence; the cohesion of the self-sentient body and the socio-cultural lifeworld.

> Further, *associated bodies* must be brought forward along with my body – the 'others', not merely as my congeners, as the zoologist says, but the others who haunt me and whom I haunt; the 'others' along *with* whom I haunt a single, present, and actual Being as no animal ever haunted those beings of his own species, locale, or habitat. (Merleau-Ponty, 1964: 161, emphasis in original)

This extract shows that Merleau-Ponty's emphasis on the lifeworld is not subjective. It is intersubjective – a vibrant field of consensus and conflict as well as an opportunity for agency. Returning to the lifeworld means rethinking subjectivity in a way that does not consider it an abstract, transcendental ego, but a subject that, immersed in existence, is both intersubjective and historical. It is also from this interworld that he approaches the political as a field of forces and struggles for co-existence. From these extracts, then, we can see how he did travel along the posthumanist lane, but in a way that, at the same time, maintained a certain distinctiveness of human existence.

The second step we want to take is to differentiate the rather generalized notion of humanism in order to consider how parts of it are still defensible and others are ripe for abandonment. For that part, it might be useful to seek help in Schatzki (2002), who offers a clarifying differentiation of the discussion by distinguishing between five forms of humanism: (1) epistemological humanism, which privileges the human subject-mind as the exclusive place of knowledge; (2) psychological humanism, which considers humans to be masters of both their psyches and the phenomena of meaning; (3) definitional humanism, which argues that the essence of humanity is such that human life differs absolutely from animality or animal life; (4) agential humanism, which considers human agency the highest form of agency and the type of greatest significance to life on earth; and (5) value humanism, which proclaims that humans – as opposed to God, being, the order of cosmos or the structure of reason – are responsible for political-ethical values. The first three of these forms have for a long time been indefensible. As regards the last two, their destiny is more ambiguous but also, as we see it, decisive to critical engagement. If ideas of creating a better world – more human, just and hospitable – are to make sense, they have to be granted existence somehow or other.

This is where we will claim that a critical phenomenology offers a good alternative to the excesses of posthumanism – not a final one, of course, nor the only one. For example, you can see the postcolonial writer Edward Said in one of his last works arguing for a new humanism. He argues that 'it is possible to be critical of humanism in the name of humanism' and that 'schooled in its abuses by the experience of Eurocentrism and empire, one could fashion a different of humanism that was cosmopolitan […] and absorbed the great lessons of the past' (Said, 2004: 10–11). What we seek, then, is an approach that anticipates elements now associated with poststructuralism and posthumanism but which maintains a more robust sense of politics, experience and agency.

Merleau-Ponty shares the critique of the abstract 'rational man' with poststructuralism and posthumanism, but he offers an alternative understanding of agency. He reformulates it into the form of *agentic capacities* that originate in the body and the intercorporeal interworld (Merleau-Ponty, 1968). It is corporeality that opens up the perceived world for a limited freedom simply because it is materially and symbolically situated in bodies that, in the first place, are exposed to negative experiences of closure. These agent-oriented capacities – for meaning, reflexivity, interrogation, improvisation and transformation – are not properties of a singular ontological subject. They are capabilities emerging contingently within an interworld of materiality and meaning. Two achievements come out of such a redefinition of agency: first, it anticipates the notion of the subject as emergent, which many has looked to more wholehearted anti-humanist approaches to find (see e.g. Wylie, 2010); and secondly, it sees the political as an intersubjective field of forces where agents emerge and styles of coexistence are negotiated within the dense texture of everyday experience.

A similar argument is forwarded by Sonia Kruks (2012), who draws on Simone de Beauvoir's *The Ethics of Ambiguity* and argues for an *ambiguous* humanism. It must, she says, take seriously the posthumanist charges against abstract humanism. Yet it should not erase, deconstruct or decentre 'the human'. 'To erase "the human" from consideration is to cut from under our feet the ground on which we may contest certain practices and situations as oppressive', she says (2012: 32). De Beauvoir's ambiguity is a fundamental ambiguity, rooted in our existence. Each of us is a peculiar amalgam of consciousness and fleshy materiality, of freedom and constraints, and of transcendence and immanence. This ambiguous ontological condition is not limited to the singular body, it is also a collective one; ambiguity will also permeate our social relations. In this understanding of the ambiguities of collective life, that is, as an always already-situated, always material, always social existence, lies the ground for a humanism avoiding both the classic rationality of an abstract 'humanity' and the posthumanist dehumanization of human life.

Other current phenomenologists discuss the fate of humanism in relation to biopolitics and to the execution of extreme violence (Dalton, 2005; Guenther, 2011; Diprose, 2017). They all at some stage relate to Agamben and his notion of 'bare life'. For example, Lisa Guenther, with reference to Robert Antelme (who is writing from his experiences as a French political prisoner in German concentration camps in 1944–5) writes:

> He argues: 'we are unable to become either animals or trees'; the executioner 'can kill a man, but he can't change him to something else'. This impossibility of becoming anything but human could form the basis of a non-anthropocentric claim to humanity, one that resists defining the human in opposition to the non-human animal, while still providing grounds for resistance against dehumanization. (2011: 19)

The point is that the body-subject reduced to 'naked life' still has a source of resistance, a relation to alterity which is the minimal form of human community that cannot be destroyed. Life is never 'bare', even when exposed to an unimaginable extremity of violence and affliction, the subject retains a relation to alterity which provides a starting point, however minimal, for resistance. What we end up with, even in the most extreme exploitation of the body's vulnerability, is not only the inhuman in the human, but also the still-human in the dehumanized. These discussions lead towards a 'new humanism' not as the old ones grounded in affirmations of the abstract human potential, but rather in a new potentialization that comprehends its historical moment and is rooted in an 'ethics of alterity' (Guenther, 2011) or 'ethics of responsibility' (Dalton, 2005). As such, it is a thinking that can be seen as a continuation of the one of Merleau-Ponty, Levinas and Arendt referred to above.

It is from this ontological-theoretical framework and from the (unfinished) discussion of critical phenomenology that the chapters to come will theoretically and empirically address embodied practices, meanings, emotions, spatial negotiations and power relations in social and cultural encounters as well as their realization in urban, national and transnational relations. An underlying understanding throughout the text is that more general forms of sociality are formed by embodied interactions and everyday social encounters, and patterns of interaction and intersubjectivity shape the norms and meanings structuring our social lifeworlds. Turning points in this exercise will be the three key notions by which we tried to pin down the ideas of critical phenomenology: embodied experiences, difference and alterity, and problems of coexistence.

NOTES

1. When using the notion of experience in the English language, we find it important to emphasize that to us it involves a dialectic between two phenomena that in German and Scandinavian languages are characterized by two different terms – '*Erlebnis/Erfahrung*' or '*oplevelse/erfaring*', respectively. *Erlebnis (oplevelse)* is a concept derived equally from social and aesthetic theory and describes the immediate impression or isolated experience connected to an incident or an event occurring in a precise point in time. The concept of *Erfahrung (erfaring)* refers to longer experience and connects to the German root '*fahren*' (to ride, to travel). It implies journeying, a temporal dimension of duration, habituation and biography. Approaching from a thinking of embodiment, '*oplevelser*' might or might not be incorporated as '*erfaring*' that influences later practices.
2. We shall return to Merleau-Ponty's phenomenology of the body in the next chapter.
3. While the contribution from these feminist and postcolonial writers as regards power and processes of differentiation significantly adds to Merleau-Ponty's thinking, it does not mean that he ignored these issues. For example in *The Primacy of Perception* he discussed racist and sexist attitudes linked to ideas of 'psychological rigidity' where internal aggression is externalized and projected onto others.

$$\boxed{2}$$

Bodies and Embodiment

Our approach to bodies and embodiment takes its starting point in Merleau-Ponty's embodied phenomenology. Now, turning to phenomenology is not a new exercise within geography. Most prominently it was done by humanistic geographers in the 1970s who were concerned with the essences of human experience of place and space and pursued it by means of phenomenological thinking. These efforts have later been criticized for essentialism, idealism and voluntarism. Independent of that, a remarkable exception was the work of Seamon (e.g. 1979), who used Merleau-Ponty's concept of body-subjects to overcome the separation of material life from thought and sought to capture the meaning of place as orchestrated through 'pre-reflexive intentionality'. What we want to do here, however, is to carry out a re-reading of Merleau-Ponty *after* the critiques from (post)structuralism and posthumanism, arguing that he anticipated many of their concerns and taking into account his political as well as his philosophical writings (see e.g. Merleau-Ponty, 1969, 1974).

Writing about the body is, according to Weiss (1999: 1), 'a paradoxical project'. The expression 'the body' in itself can easily give occasion for an idea of the body as a discrete phenomenon, a singular entity that it is possible to investigate apart from other parts of our existence. Such an understanding is problematic in two ways. First, it involves a risk to lose sight of the fact that the body is never isolated in its activity; it is always already engaged with the surrounding world. Activities and projects take their meanings not merely from an individual's intentions, but from the (temporal and spatial) situation out of which they have emerged and within which they are enacted. Secondly, writing about 'the' body might suggest that the body in itself is a neutral phenomenon. However, as indicated in Chapter 1, there is no such thing as 'the' body. Whenever we are referring to bodies, they are taking meaning as particular bodies, that is, a woman's body, an Asian body, a mother's/father's body or a daughter's/son's body, an ageing body, etc. Therefore, rather than viewing the body as a cohesive, coherent phenomenon, we should, in the words of Weiss, argue for 'a multiplicity of body images that are co-present in any given individual' (1999: 2).

Starting from phenomenology and Merleau-Ponty, then, involves a return to ontology, in the case of Merleau-Ponty in the form of an ontology of becoming; a return to the question of 'wild being', to the question of the substance of the world, the relations between mind and matter and the centrality of perception in conceptualizing their intertwining, a concern that permeated all of his work and took a new (unfinished) form in his final writings. It is an ontology where consciousness and life do not find themselves in a world but make themselves subjects at the same time as they make the world into things, objects or entities through their activity, their engagement and their labour – but always in an indeterminate way. Active becoming is emergent. This ontology furthermore means that Merleau-Ponty's work moves away from the widespread image of phenomenology as a *transcendental* phenomenology, describing a purified, intentional consciousness and its constitutive acts of giving meaning, towards a *genetic* phenomenology that studies meaning in its genesis. It situates practical, embodied consciousness in the world, that is, an interworld where meaning and materiality are inseparable. This means that materiality and ideality, matter and meaning, body and mind, must be conceived of as irreducibly interwoven and folded at every level, from the corporeal to the philosophical (Merleau-Ponty, 1962, 1968). Merleau-Ponty, then, develops a sense of a *generative* materiality that can locate his philosophy within what Coole and Frost (2010) designate as 'the new materialisms' and subsequently also within current efforts to 'rematerialize' social and cultural geography. The last-mentioned project, having its background in the earlier overemphasis on signification and representation in Anglo-American 'new cultural geography', embraces different approaches and ontologies, ranging from studies of material culture, through theories of practice to non-representational theory and 'more-than-human' geographies (see e.g. Anderson and Tolia-Kelly, 2004; Cook and Tolia-Kelly, 2010). What Merleau-Ponty can offer in this connection with his account of material existence as 'folded flesh' is an understanding of materiality that emphasizes corporeality as well as sociality and matter. This contribution relies upon the fact that the body, as stated by Morris (2008), stands in the heart of Merleau-Ponty's philosophy as both a theoretical and methodological term.

THINKING THE BODY

Merleau-Ponty saw his work in opposition to and as an attempt to destabilize the thinking in binary oppositions which dominates so much of Western thought. His understanding of corporeality is in line with that based on a non-dualist ontology of the body and its environment. The body concerned is not just an object in the world as studied by science, neither is it a mere assemblage or juxtaposition of its parts – a mere aggregate of organs and senses; it is a *phenomenal, lived body*, a dynamic unity that changes through interacting with an environment that it both responds to and actively structures. It is the conditions and context through which one is able to have a relation to objects and other body-subjects. This body is always contingent and in process – a quality also appreciated and applied by Simone de Beauvoir (2010) in her discussion of the contingency of the gendered body (see also Moi, 1999). The body emerges in its perceptual engagement with the world as an open form that reaches out to and questions its environment. It is through this engagement that significance appears and a non-cognitive way of knowing is practised. The practically oriented body continuously weaves meaning throughout the course of its existence, while its own forms and capacities materialize contingently through its interactions with others and with its environment (Coole, 2007b). It also is an expressive body – dramatic and performative – expressing its singularity as a particular style of existence. This, as stated several times at this stage, should not be mistaken for individualism. Merleau-Ponty's account of the body is radically intercorporeal and the notion of style is about coexistence, about the position of the body within the order of things and/or within the unfolding of collective life.

The body, then, is always situated in a world in reference to which it continually orients and reorients itself: 'the body not only flows over into a world whose schema it bears in itself but possesses this world at a distance rather than being possessed by it' (Merleau-Ponty 1973: 78). According to Merleau-Ponty, the primary means by which the body 'possesses' the world are through perception and bodily motility, and it is on the other hand also through perception and bodily motility that the body itself 'flows over into the world'. This reciprocal, reversible relationship between body and world whereby the body 'flows over' into a world whose 'schema it bears in itself' draws attention to the role of the moving body in his phenomenology. In an extension, or maybe rather a revision, of Husserl's central notion of intentionality, which describes the directedness or aboutness of all consciousness, he shows that intentionality is bodily and that this corporeality is connected to movement. Bodily movement is laden with meaning and intentionality. It is carrying out meaningful projects that cut across meaning-laden things and places. 'Consciousness is in the first place not a matter of "I think that" but of "I can"' (Merleau-Ponty 1962: 137). In order to understand these projects and activities Merleau-Ponty (influenced by Henry Head and Poul Schilder) develops the notion of the *body schema* as a spatiotemporally structured and structuring model of the subject, a 'schema' that mediates between its worlds and its practices. The body is able to move, to initiate and undertake actions, because the body schema is a series of possible actions, plans for action, maps of possible movements the body 'knows' how to perform. The body schema is also a field in which the subject's cohesion and identity as a subject and its intimate incarnation in and as a particular body take place. An important part of this understanding appears in the study of habit because 'habit has its abode neither in thought nor in the objective body, but in the body as mediator of a world' (1962: 145). Morris (2008) elegantly sums up how Merleau-Ponty with his notion of the body schema contributes to an understanding of the ontological openness of the body as being-in-the-world:

> [T]he body schema engenders meaning in virtue of being ontologically open to a temporality of the body (in habit and perceptual learning), to space (in movement), to language (in expression) and to others (in intersubjectivity). (2008: 118)

Let us, after this short introduction, develop a bit on four issues in this understanding that we find central to our purpose.

HABITUATION AND CORPOREAL AGENCY

Habituation is a central aspect in Merleau-Ponty's understanding of the body. It is a way of preserving patterns of perception, communication and practice that prove useful in everyday life. Its way of functioning is based in social temporality; it lends continuity to our lives, it performs its function in its own rhythms and it has its own significations that leave their traces on all aspects of our lives. The body-subject needs to draw upon *habit* to construct a familiar lifeworld. In this way, habit enables us to 'inhabit' the world; it enables an unfamiliar space to be transformed into a familiar environment. Moreover, since bodies are always bodies of the world, habit is not just about singular bodies. It is also about collective history and culture. Our being-in-the-world is cultural and historical, reflecting the historical period to which we belong. In Merleau-Ponty's understanding, this is based on the ability of the body to acquire habits through incorporation of external patterns and past experience in the form of know-how and corporeal schema:

> Although our body does not impose definite instincts upon us, as it does other animals, it does at least give our life the form of generality, and develops our personal acts into stable dispositional tendencies. In this sense our nature is not long-established custom, since custom supposes the form of passivity derived from nature. (Merleau-Ponty, 1962: 146)

This is close to (and behind) what Pierre Bourdieu talks about with his concept of *habitus* (1977, 1990). But where Merleau-Ponty emphasizes the bodily dimension of habit, Bourdieu take the social dimension of habit as his starting point. He locates his understanding in the traditional freedom/determinism dichotomy, which he aims to overcome through his notion of habitus seen as an acquired system of generative schemes internalized since early childhood and strongly connected to social class:

> This infinite yet strictly limited generative capacity is difficult to understand only so long as one remains locked in the usual antinomies – which the concept of *habitus* aims to transcend – of determinism and freedom, conditioning and creativity, consciousness and the unconscious, or the individual and society. Because the *habitus* is an infinite capacity for generating products – thoughts, perceptions, expressions and actions – whose limits are set by the historically and socially situated conditions of its production, the conditioned and conditional freedom it provides is as remote from creation of unpredictable novelty as it is from simple mechanical reproduction of the original conditioning. (Bourdieu, 1990: 55)

While these two concepts are overlapping and in some sense can be seen to be supplementary, for two reasons we would argue that the approach of Merleau-Ponty represents an advance upon the position of Bourdieu.

The first one concerns, as also noted by Crossley (2013), the relationship to material culture and artefacts. In Merleau-Ponty's theorizing of habit, material artefacts are important and they are seen as a part of our self and agency – an extension of our self. He famously discusses that by the way of the example of the blind man and his stick:

> The blind man's stick has ceased to be an object for him, and is no longer perceived for itself; its point has become an area of sensitivity, extending the scope and active radius of touch, and providing a parallel of sight. (Merleau-Ponty, 1962: 143)

He uses that discussion (and other examples) to extend his notion of habit:

> If habit is neither a form of knowledge nor an involuntary action, what then is it? It is knowledge in the hands which is forthcoming only when bodily effort is made, and cannot be formulated in detachment from that effort. (1962: 144)

This shows how he already laid the ground in *Phenomenology of Perception* for the affinity of the so-called 'new materialisms' that we hinted at in Chapter 1.[1]

The second difference concerns the ability of the concepts to grasp how radical change or spontaneous innovation can occur at the individual or collective level. Here, Bourdieu seems to be somewhat inhibited by his strong emphasis on 'class habitus'. In *The Logic of Practice*, for instance, he maintains that for members of the same class (group), the singular habitus are united in a relationship of 'homology'. It is an 'immanent law, *lex insita*, inscribed in bodies by identical histories', [...] and personal style 'is never more than a deviation of the relation to the style of a period or class' (Bourdieu, 1990: 59–60). In this way, Bourdieu ascribes an all-compassing role to the habitus in an individual's life. His statement that the common schemas are 'inscribed in bodies by identical histories'[2] renders it difficult to see what room there is left for actions or expressions of individual bodies that are not reducible to the class habitus. Agency seems to be reduced to habitus. Even though Bourdieu obviously takes inspiration from Merleau-Ponty and talks a lot about bodies and embodiment, it seems as if his determinate decision that phenomenology is subjectivist and trapped in a notion of conscious intentionality has hindered him in gaining inspiration for a more nuanced conception of corporeal agency. Merleau-Ponty's understanding of habit does open for such a strategy. In *Phenomenology of Perception* he states that '[h]abit expresses our power of dilating our being-in-the-world, or changing our existence by appropriating fresh instruments' (1962: 143). That is, habit is not only limiting human possibilities, but also expanding them. It helps to establish ontological security and openness towards the world and makes room for creativity and dynamic engagement with the world.

As already hinted at in Chapter 1, Merleau-Ponty lays a basis for an alternative understanding of agency, seeing it as *agentic capacities* originating in the body and the intercorporeal interworld. These ideas are convincingly carried on by Diana Coole (2005, 2007a) in her attempts to accentuate the political in his work. She recognizes the work done in the agency-versus-structure debates in social science whose protagonists she thinks have given important contributions to the spectrum's middle region. However, she still thinks that the tendency is that they either involuntarily remain trapped in dualistic thinking or end up leaning towards one side or the other. The reason, she argues, is that they are short of a social ontology that would be adequate to the *trans*personal domain. That is what she finds in phenomenology, and in particular in Merleau-Ponty: 'Phenomenology does not begin with an idealist model of agents then seek their facsimile in real world; rather it reads ambiguous signs of agentic expression as they emerge within a shared lifeworld' (Coole, 2005: 125). Beginning instead with the perceptual, corporeal lifeworld allows the phenomenologist to suspend any presupposition that these processes must be located in discrete, reflective selves.

Therefore, we have to set a strong connection between agency and corporeality. Coole (2005) considers it ironic that this connection has been largely invisible to political scientists, since it is the most visible register of coexistence where bodies act and suffer, where power is etched onto the body, and where communication takes place through a mute yet eloquent corporeal exchange. In continuation, she identifies some agentic qualities at this corporeal level. They are: (1) 'bodily knowing: a practical reasoning' whereby disparate elements are gathered into existential meaningful forms; (2) 'limited freedom' for the bodies when it comes to stylistic improvisation in its compositions; (3) bodies are 'intentional and motivated' in their relationship with their environment – this means, that bodies are interrogative and act in the span between habituation and extemporization; and (4) there is an 'intercorporeal communication' where meaning is conveyed via gestures and styles of comportment which carve out architectural and emotive spaces of engagement. We shall return to these different corporeal qualities in the sections to come.

ORIENTATION AND DISORIENTATION

This issue starts from the notion of *intentionality*, one of phenomenology's most basic but probably also most contested concepts.[3] According to this notion, consciousness is always directed towards something and as such reaching outwards. This relationality rules out any immanence of consciousness as a pure psychology of mental states, but the close connection with consciousness still renders the concept vulnerable to critique. Merleau-Ponty tended to eschew this trap through his emphasis on bodily experience and the subsequent displacement of the concept towards a *corporeal and operative intentionality* (Keller, 2005, 2010). Operative intentionality orients the body towards the external world but it also actively arranges that world according to practical needs and tasks by casting an 'intentional arc' around the body. It is this lived intentionality that gives the body's formative capacities their direction and meaning. Other authors fasten on Merleau-Ponty's increasing emphasis on *interrogation* (Deleuze, 1994; Coole 2007a). It shifts the emphasis to an ontological and normative 'questioning body' performing openness and engagement with the other and with the world – a critical, questioning attitude. Interrogation is an 'original manner of aiming at something, as if it direct were a *question-knowing*' (Merleau-Ponty, 1968: 129). It is both a valuable attitude and an existentially motivated process based in experience. In this way, a direct connection can be drawn from bodily experience to critical orientations of collective life.

In prolongation of that, we prefer to use the concept of *orientation* as suggested by Sara Ahmed (2006, 2010). It involves the same elements of openness towards the world as the concepts of operative intentionality and interrogation, and it also includes a distinct spatial dimension. In this way, there is close connection between orientation and perception. 'The word perception indicates a direction rather than a primitive function,' Merleau-Ponty says (1962: 12). Perception is an orientated activity – you can perceive an object only insofar as your orientation allows you to see it. Perception can however itself be twofold: you can perceive an object, but you can also have a specific perception of it (like it, admire it, hate it and so on). Ahmed starts from this twofoldness when she identifies three ways in which orientations influence our relation with objects and others. They shape

- how we inhabit the surrounding space
- how we apprehend this shared inhabitance
- 'who' and 'what' we direct our energy and attention toward.

This understanding of orientation once more refers to the spatiality of the lived. Heidegger, for example, sees orientation as a question of the familiarity of the world: 'I necessarily orient myself both in and from my being already alongside a world which is "familiar"' (1962: 144). Familiarity is connected to the given from where the body gains the capacity to orientate itself in one way or another.

The question of orientation, then, is not only about 'finding our way' but also about 'feeling at home'. Further, familiarity is neither delimited nor static; it is continuously in formation. The work of inhabiting space involves a dynamic negotiation between what is familiar and unfamiliar, such that it is still possible to incorporate new impressions dependent on which way we turn and what is within reach. These impressions shape the body as well as the 'inhabited' space, such that the body, as we can say with Lefebvre (1991a), produces itself in space and simultaneously produces that space. When bodies orientate towards objects in the world, the surroundings tend to take shape around the (material and immaterial) practices in play. Orientation starts from our body and its 'here' and reaches out towards 'something else' or 'somebody else', something different from ourselves. It can give occasion for both an extension of our reach, of what we can have and what we can do, and an opening towards the other. None of that is however given. The formation of the surroundings can happen through the way 'spaces and tools take shape by being oriented around some bodies more than other bodies' (Ahmed, 2006: 132) – that is, some bodies' formation of space creates blocks for others' possibilities and practices and for the extension of their reach.

Adopting a social view of orientation also renders obvious that it can take many forms; we orientate ourselves in time and space, but we also assume political, sexual, cultural and social orientations. Lefebvre points to the broadness of the term

> I speak of an *orientation* advisedly. We are concerned with nothing more and nothing less than that. We are concerned with what might be called a 'sense': an organ that perceives, a direction that may be conceived, and a direct lived movement progressing towards the horizon. (1991a: 423)

We can follow the lines (material and immaterial) which exist as paths created by past journeys, or we can arrive at situations opening new lines. Following a line is never neutral: it takes time, resources, energy and social investment. A lifeline also expresses our identity. We should however maintain that life is not linear. It includes crises, accidental encounters that redirect us, turning points, setbacks or possibilities of opening up new worlds.

In this sense, orientation also involves what Ahmed (2006) calls *moments of disorientation*. She refers this idea to Merleau-Ponty who, even if he is not using exactly the same concept, talks about how instability and shifts in our world '[produce] not only the intellectual experience of disorder, but the vital experience of giddiness and nausea, which is the awareness of our contingency, and the horror with which it fills us' (1962: 254). Moments of disorientation turn our world upside down. Disorientation is a bodily feeling that can shape insecurity and shatter one's sense of confidence in the ground of one's existence. It is a situation which can make bodies react defensively, as they reach out for support or search for a place to reground and re-orientate their relation to the world.

The feeling of being shattered might persist and become a crisis, or it passes if the ground returns or one returns to the ground. Moments of disorientation, then, can be seen as destabilizing and undermining, but they can also be seen as productive moments leading to new hopes and new directions. Examples of moments of disorientation can be migration, which can be described as a process of disorientation and reorientation as the bodies both 'move away' and 'arrive', or, on the other hand, if arriving bodies are perceived as 'out of place' – as disturbing the picture – and as such creating disorientation in others. But it can also be situations of failed orientations where bodies inhabit spaces that do not extend their reach, where they live with social experience of restriction, uncertainty and blockage. It is therefore clear that disorientation is unevenly distributed, that some bodies more than other bodies experience crisis in their involvement in the world. Merleau-Ponty's hopeful utterance 'I can' will in these cases be better replaced by an 'I cannot'.

INTERCORPOREALITY AND REVERSIBILITY

While bodily experience, perception and the mind/body problem occupied Merleau-Ponty throughout his work, the way he framed them, parallel with the development of the notion of intentionality, shifted. In *Phenomenology of Perception*, he defined the phenomenological world as 'the sense that is revealed while the paths of my various experiences intersect, and also where my own and other people's intersect and engage each other like gears' and in this way he very much referred it to intersubjectivity (1962: xx). In *The Visible and the Invisible* he explores the 'intertwining' of the inside and the outside, the subject and the object, one sense and another in an outline of a more general ontology of what he called *flesh*:

> The flesh is not matter, is not mind, is not substance [...] it is not a fact or sum of facts 'material' or 'spiritual' [...] To designate it, we should need the old term 'element', [...] in the sense of a *general thing*, midway between the spatio-temporal individual and the idea, a sort of incarnate principle that brings a style of being wherever there is a fragment of being. The flesh is in this sense an 'element' of being. (1968: 139)

In this connection, Merleau-Ponty claims that 'my body is made of the same flesh as the world (it is perceived), and moreover this flesh of my body is shared by the world, the world *reflects* it, encroaches upon it and it encroaches upon world' (1968: 248). At the same time, however, he maintains that flesh in general should not be understood as identical to the flesh of our body. He states that 'the flesh of the world is not *self-sensing* as is my flesh – it is sensible and not sentient – I call it flesh nonetheless [...] in order to say that it is a *pregnancy* of possibles' (1968: 250). That means that the body gains a special status as self-reflexive flesh, but always intertwining with a social and natural world. The flesh of the body becomes part of the flesh of the world, where the flesh of the world refers to the perceptibility that characterizes all worldly reality (human and non-human) that is actualized but not created by human perception.

This leads to probably the most important aspect of the flesh, that is, its *reversibility*; a 'double sensation' by which practices and perceptions of the body-subjects are connected in an interworld or 'intermundane space'. Body-subjects are visible-seers, tangible-touchers, audible-listeners etc., enacting an ongoing intertwining of the flesh of the body, the flesh of others and the flesh of the world. A significant consequence of this 'mediation through reversal' is the way in which it grounds the principle of *intercorporeality*. As 'perceiving-perceptibles' our experiences are transitive; we share sensuous experiences and even partially inhabit the feeling side of another's body. It is, however, not only the sheer sensibility of the body that institutes intercorporeality; it is as well the meaning involved in the bodily practices of the other. One does not perceive another body as a material object; rather one is affected by the meaning of its appearance. The other body is animated and its animation communicates and calls for response. Some authors also argue that Merleau-Ponty's embodied ontology provides resources for developing a corresponding embodied ethic (Weiss, 1999; Johnson, 2008; Hamington, 2008).[4] One source for this opinion is the concept of reversibility. Johnson underlines that reversibility (in the version of Merleau-Ponty) is not yet an ethical stance. Rather, it is a condition that is the very possibility of ethics, politics and justice itself.

Reversibility is not something we *do*, it is the condition for the possibility *of* the doing and of the development of ethical procedures. In that sense he also suggests that it could enable us to reconsider the larger relationship between ontology and ethics.

A crucial aspect of reversibility is its *ambiguity* (Weiss, 2008). Reversibility is never perfect – touching and being touched are two experiences that are in dynamic interplay, but which never exactly overlap. But they still unfold within one and the same body, one and the same world. Reversibility, therefore, evokes the idea of mutuality, but not of a complete and perfect mutuality. There is a slippage or non-coincidence between touching and touched, affecting and affected, the perceiving body and the body as a thing among things – a shift where 'the two leaves of my body, the inside and the outside', are articulated over one another as a productive 'difference between the identicals' (Merleau-Ponty, 1968: 263). This is where reflexivity, creativity and agency slip in, not as a result of rational subjectivity, but as capacities that emerge within an intercorporeal lifeworld. That means, as suggested by Coole (2005, 2007a), that the agency–subject bond is loosened and *emergent agentic capacities* are valued in their own right. The phenomenological task is to discern their ambiguous emergence within and across lifeworlds, acknowledging that they might achieve more or less coherence and efficacy according to situation and context, and that they can appear within corporeal, singular or transpersonal registers of existence.

BODIES AND POWER

The phenomenal body is riddled with power; it is both vehicle and victim of power. Both Husserl and Merleau-Ponty describe bodily horizons as 'sedimented histories' (Ahmed, 2006; 56). The acts of the body develop in intersubjective fields where they are learnt and disseminated as memories and habits of the flesh – sedimented and reproduced as the corporeal equivalent of ideology. This idea of bodily *sedimentation*, appearing as a social side of the above mentioned notion of habituation, provides Merleau-Ponty's theory of the body with an element of temporality, history and power. The model of history as bodily sedimentation is carried on by social theorists, most significantly by Pierre Bourdieu and Michel Foucault (both taking inspiration from Merleau-Ponty). Bourdieu includes it in his concept of *habitus,* which he describes as 'systems of durable, transposable dispositions, structured structures predisposed to function as structuring structures, that is, as principle which generates and organizes practices and representations' (Bourdieu, 1990: 53), in this way emphasizing its element of (class) power. Foucault takes a more 'outside in' approach emphasizing disciplination and the body as an inscriptive surface, for example in *The History of Sexuality Vol. 1* (1978), where he defines the disciplinary power over life as a *biopower,* a power to regulate details of daily life and behaviour in both individuals and populations.

This model of power as bodily sedimentation has also been taken up by many contemporary feminist phenomenologists, drawing on Merleau-Ponty and/or de Beauvoir. Many examples can be mentioned but one that still stands out is Iris Marion Young, whose work spans over about 15 years, from the 1990s to the collection of several essays in *On Female Body Experience* in 2005. The use of the sedimentation model underlines Merleau-Ponty's refusal to equal experience with immediacy and his view that experience is mediated but not determined by culture. As Young put it when discussing his work, 'the body as lived is always layered with social and historical meaning and is not some primitive matter prior to or underlying economic and political relations or cultural meanings' (2005: 7). She characterizes 'the feminine' as 'a set of normative disciplined expectations imposed on female-bodies by male-dominated society' (2005: 5), and she illustrated it during her work by empirical examples from a range of fields. In her earlier essay 'Throwing like a girl' (1990a), she describes the constrained comportment and motility in different female spatial practices such as throwing, walking, sitting and lifting, and throughout her work she supplemented it by addressing constraining experiences emanating from facticities of female physiology such as pregnancy, menstruation and being breasted. Other contributors have taken other directions. Toril Moi (1999) develops Simone de Beauvoir's notion of the body as a 'situation'; she views it as a situation amongst others, but fundamental in the sense that it will always be part of our lived experience and our coping with the environment. Alcoff (2006) and Ahmed (2006) both address variations in the experiences of differently embodied groups (but still within the Western societies). Alcoff employs phenomenology to grasp the construction of sexed and racialized identities, which she considers 'most definitely physical, marked on and through the body, lived as material experience' (2006: 102).[5] Ahmed, on her part, starts from the concept of 'orientation' and explores both queer and non-white experience. A key argument in the book is that the body gets directed in some ways more than others, and that the question of orientation becomes about how we 'find our way' as well as how we 'feel at home' (2006: 7). 'Straight' and 'queer', then, are not only sexual orientations; they are ways of being in the world, and to be queer in the world that is normatively straight is often to be disorientated towards it – and also to be perceived as disorientating. By this grip, she is addressing both the experiences of being 'out-of-place' or 'in-the-wrong-direction' and the phenomenological question whether bodies are able to extend their shape and movement in the surrounding world or are inhibited and restricted in their motility.

But the body's situatedness in intercorporeal fields and socio-corporeal hierarchies not only brings about incorporation and sedimentation, it also gives rise to experiences of fragility and *vulnerability*. The flesh is vulnerable to material as well as symbolic violence and pain. It is objectified, imprisoned and exploited, and it is subjected to the look, the gaze and the surveillance of the other (Coole, 2007b). Bodies are marked by others, such that the different bodies are recognized and categorized, disciplined and excluded. The relationship between power and experience draws attention to encounters with *different* bodies as also explored in phenomenological oriented feminist and postcolonial theories (see e.g. Fanon, 1967a; Young, 1990a, b; Alcoff, 1999; Ahmed, 2000). These theories render incomplete Merleau-Ponty's idea of the social body as a body opening up into the fleshy world of other bodies. For this world is not a general world of humanity, but a differentiated world, and in such a world what is meant by the social body is more often than not 'precisely the effect of being with some others over other others' (Ahmed, 2000: 49). The social body is also an imaginary body that is created through the relations of vision or touch between bodies recognizable as friendly and/or strange. Encounters with Other bodies therefore involve practices and techniques of differentiation. Familiar bodies can be incorporated through a sense of community, being with each other as like bodies, while strange bodies more likely are expelled from bodily space and moved apart as different bodies.

One author who particularly addresses this vulnerability is Emmanuel Levinas. In his *Otherwise Than Being or Beyond Essence* (1991, orig. 1974) he goes so far as to say that the 'subjectivity of the subject' qua corporeal existence 'is vulnerability, exposure to affection' (1991: 50). The encounter with the other, he says, is not just a 'break up' of the self and being, but also a 'binding'. The encounter with the other does not simply put me in question, but actively limits my free-play in the world. It binds me to the other in responsibility, and it does so through sensibility. For it is in the flesh that the self and other are in 'proximity'. It is through the living bodies that selves experience 'the painfulness of pain', the 'malignity of illness' and 'the adversity of fatigue' (Hass, 2008). In this way flesh, encounters and vulnerability achieve a central position in his 'ethic of responsibility'. On the basis of this and earlier publications of Levinas, Paul Harrison (2008) writes a challenging essay criticizing human geography, philosophy dealing with bodies and embodiment, and social science for not taking the question of vulnerability seriously. The argument is that because the human in Western theoretical traditions nearly always has been marked out in its particularity through the attribution of a positive 'capacity' or 'power' – in terms of 'being able to' – these traditions tend to inhibit the understanding of corporeal states which take place as and through passivity and, as a consequence, limit our understanding of vulnerability. On the one hand, we are sympathetic to the argument and realize that there might be an imbalance in the thinking, but on the other hand we think that Harrison undervalues Merleau-Ponty's contribution. In Merleau-Ponty's thinking the body is simultaneously active and passive. Due to its reversibility it has interiority and exteriority; it is at the same time seeing and seen, touching and touched, etc. In other words, it is at the same time creative and efficacious and susceptible and vulnerable. This two-dimensionality is significant to its agentic and political capacities, but also to its affectivity and (physical or emotional) pain.[6] In this way, it should be possible to see these two authors as supplementary, rather than oppositional.

The whole development of the thinking on bodies has an important message to send to critical theory. The point is that critical analysis has to take the messy ground of lived experience seriously, for if it neglects it, the analysis ends up in what Merleau-Ponty calls 'high-altitude' thinking.

EMBODIED IDENTITIES

All identities are embodied. We all speak from a particular place, out of a particular history, a particular culture, particular practices and experiences, etc. On the face of it, embodied identities can be seen as grown out of everyday material practices. Let us illustrate that by way of a few quotes from our case on everyday urban policing[7]:

> I can't explain how he does it. I am sitting here looking at the same cars as him. Why can he say 'no, it is this one we have to talk to'? [...] But it becomes better and better, it makes more and more sense [...] It comes with experience. You learn to look for it. It improves, that police nose. (Police officer, describing his first period on patrol when driving with an experienced officer)

> As soon as I wear the uniform, then I am at work [...] This thing about emotions, whether you are affected by the episodes you meet: No, you have to be professional and say; now I am working. I have got this education that means that I can handle it [...] The uniform means that I feel prepared.

I might need to stop short inside myself and say, 'they have called because they need help; therefore I have to be the one who has the situation under control'. Or at least emanate that you are in control. (Police officer)

These sayings reveal what police researchers talk about as the *police gaze* or the *police-body* (Finstad, 2000; Bille, 2014). These concepts are supposed to grasp the meaning of the body in a professional field where the reversible connection between body-subject and the professional environment has a decisive influence on everyday experiences. While the 'ordinary' urban inhabitant dwells in an immediate experienced everyday space, patrolling officers find meaning in a professional space – a horizon of meaning that forms a professional basis for the police-body's orientation in space and time. In a phenomenal sense they seek significant patterns in others' movements, gestures, attitudes, etc., which potentially refer to critical incidents. Police-bodies sense more than words can grasp, and this sensible approach to the world is significant for their work-life experiences. So, the forming of the police-body is about the learning or incorporation of experiences from similar, but not identical situations. Following Merleau-Ponty we can talk about the becoming of police-subjects through habituation and a gradual inclusion into a police world – a specific structure of meaning where you have to develop a particular explorative approach to the social world.

However, this incorporation does not work unmediated, it is worked out by the means of a range of artefacts. Again following Merleau-Ponty, we emphasize the coherence of materiality and meaning and how there is a meaningful corporeality of the artefacts, a style that is intertwined with our bodies. Keller (2005) talks about *styles of usability* as a means to grasp the felt practical significance of things, tools and equipment and the way in which they come into practical and meaningful intertwinement with the body (like the blind man and his stick). In the police world, then, artefacts in use in everyday practices such as uniforms, weapons and police cars take the form of practical and meaningful extensions of the police-body. In our example above, the police officer symbolically melts into the uniform. Through experiences, a form of fusion of person and uniform occurs forming the police-body and its professional identity. It (both inwards and outwards) provides the body-subject with a specific emanation of authority. Meeting the situations from the perspective of the police world brings about a form of distancing, moving the experiences from the personal to the professional field, thereby somehow protecting against potential disturbing affects of the job.

VISIBLE IDENTITIES

Such considerations of bodily practices and experiences do not of course exhaust the question of embodied identities. Another (more general) issue concerns identities marked on and through the body. As mentioned earlier, an excellent source for considerations of such 'visible identities' is Alcoff (2006). She starts with a historical/philosophical account of identity in general ending up with the statement that 'Hegel brought Western philosophy face to face with the crucial fact of our dependence on the Other for our very identity, the very quality and form of our subjectivity and affective life' (2006: 81). This emphasis on interdependency and interaction in identification is one she shares with many current theories of identity. Most theories of identity will see two interdependent processes as necessary to such identifications: the specification of *similarities*, and of *differences*. It makes no sense to talk about 'ourselves', either as individuals or groups, without relating to 'the Other' (or the stranger). Jenkins (1996, 2000) identifies two ways in which this interaction between similarity and difference works – namely what he calls 'the internal and external moments of the dialectic of identification' (2000: 7). They concern how we identify ourselves (internal self- or group identification), how others identify us (external social categorization) and the ongoing interplay of these in processes of social identification. This is of course reversible, that is, simultaneously a matter of how we identify them, how they identify themselves, and so on. Social identification, then, is a *relational* process and can be seen as an ongoing *becoming* which arises as an emergent product of these processes.

What Alcoff in her work with (in particular) sexed and racialized identities adds to this general, relational account of social identification is the emphasis on their corporeality, their visibility and their basis in lived experience. She argues that to say that they are social does not reduce them to some linguistic thing: 'They are most definitely physical, marked on and through the body, lived as a material experience, visible as surface phenomena, and determinant of economic and political status' (2006: 102). That's why she (with addition of insight from other approaches) turns to existential phenomenology, and especially to Merleau-Ponty, de Beauvoir and Fanon. Drawing from their embodied phenomenology she includes both visibility and lived experience, but still with recognition of the social character of identities:

> The most important implication of the phenomenological approach for the question of social identity is to reject the dualist approaches that would split the acting self from the ascribed identity. (2006: 111)

Identities gain their meanings always in a social (temporal and spatial) context rather than simply from intrinsic features, for how one is perceived and treated by others, how one is situated, also become constitutive of the self. This draws attention to the self–other connection, which for Merleau-Ponty is primordial, ineradicable and inscribed in our being – we are fundamentally an 'openness'. Alcoff argues (oddly enough) that we might see the body as a kind of mind, but one with a physical appearance, location and specific instantiation. We perceive, incorporate, reason and are intellectually trained in the body. That can help us to understand, she says, why race and gender are integral to the self: bodies are positioned by race and gender structures and have access to differential experiences and may also have some differences in perceptual orientations and conceptual assumptions.

RACIALIZATION AND EXPERIENCED OTHERNESS

> When I started going out with friends from high school or my workplace, it was very, very obvious. Without exaggerating I would say that 95 times out of 100 I was rejected. It was just like getting slapped in the face all the time. 'No, you can't enter'. And it was not only when I was together with 10 other coloured people. I have tried *all* combinations. Many times it was when I came together with 'Danish' girls and boys from my school class. (Hanif, 27)

> If you for example stroll in Strøget [main pedestrian street in the city of Copenhagen] midday when the shops are open. If you enter into a shop, then I feel – it's not that I will accuse people in there of anything – I just feel that that people keep an eye on me. I mean, you *are* allowed to enter a shop and have a look and leave again if you don't want to buy anything. And there I feel the difference, like people think 'he is going to steal something'. If you are in my situation, looking how I do, and enter – that's how I feel. (Neezan, 24)

> Wearing the headscarf is an active choice for me, I could just take it off [...] but I still wear it. I have realized that if I end up taking it off [...] no matter what I do, I have my brown eyes and my black hair. If I take it off, I will still look like a 'perker' [Danish invective on people of Middle East origin], so it doesn't matter what I do. So I think: 'It is fundamental in my life. I am damned well holding on to it'. So I don't care. In this case I am strong, ain't I? (Shahda, 38)

> I take the train to Malmö and back. You should see their eyes when they see somebody like me enter the train. People really stare. For example, after what happened in London. Then you think, 'shit, I'm the problem here'. If I had just said 'boom', the two persons next to me would have fainted [...] You begin to think 'I am the wrong one here. I am standing in the wrong place'. People are frightened or getting nervous. Sometimes I have experienced that they say 'now we have to look out'. Then I turn around and smile to them. (Abbas, 38)

These four extracts, all coming from in-depth interviews collected amongst Copenhagen residents with a Pakistani background in the project 'The stranger, the city and the nation', illustrate different situations in urban everyday life giving rise to *experienced Otherness*. All were connected to the visual identities of the respondents. Experienced Otherness can be described in terms of the bodily and social experiences of restrictions, uncertainty and blockage in all cases giving rise to strong and ambivalent emotions. It is connected to processes of estrangement: the respondents are *made* strange on the basis of their bodily appearance through what Sara Ahmed characterizes as techniques of reading the bodies of others and telling the differences between what is familiar and what is strange (Ahmed, 2000). The four mini-narratives describe different situations. Both Hanif's and Neezan's stories were about access to everyday commercial activities – for Hanif the urban nightlife[8] and for Neezan city shops. It is a question of letting the 'stranger' in or keeping him/her out of the place. They first experience becoming Others in the movement they make when they try to enter the place. The rejection or the surveillance produce them as *body suspects* already recognized as strangers. The examples illustrate how the *technology of racism* operates and incorporates discourses of *stranger danger* in the bodily encounter. The 'stranger' is stopped because he/she is imagined to be the origin of danger, related to trouble and violence, or imagined to steal 'our' enjoyment and ruin the party (see Žižek, 1993). The young men are not strangers in the sense that they are unknown; they are already recognized as such in the moment in which they are faced or seen. They both describe the emotional effects and feelings of being *out-of-place* in these processes of estrangement.

Shahda's story relates to the obsession with Muslim clothes that exists in Europe (including Denmark) where the 'figure of the Muslim' (Goldberg, 2009) has been a major subject of racialization (see also Rosenberg and Sauer, 2012). Shahda is aware that the headscarf makes her a 'stranger'. She is quite reflexive about her clothing and the headscarf. For her, it is a fundamental part of her subjectivity and self-identity. In relation to the negative social construction of the headscarf, she says, it is necessary to be strong. In this way there is an element of *resistance* to the social oppression of Muslim women in her wearing it. The headscarf becomes a *political symbol*, part of a fight against stereotypes and a state that tries to control the body of the Muslim woman.[9]

Abbas's story adds yet another layer to the process of racialization. He commutes every day from Malmö (in Sweden) to Copenhagen. After the terror attack in London (2005) he entered a train and suddenly he realized that people were staring at him. Abbas experienced his otherness through the *visual*. He was fixed and dissected under the eyes of the other passengers. An unfamiliar weight burdened him and suddenly he realized that he was the 'problem'. Abbas explains that he can feel how people around him are frightened and nervous. In this example, the bodily encounter becomes charged with fear of the Other. He became the figure who posed danger by his very presence. The example illustrates how the global production of fear is played out and experienced in everyday life (see Pain et al., 2008). It is a kind of *banal terrorism* (Katz, 2007) where geopolitical conflicts and the fear of terror become compressed into the intimacies of everyday life and incorporated into everyday embodied encounters.

We can summarize a common understanding of these racialization processes in three points.

The first rests on the *temporality* of race and racism in two connected scales. It is about the historical genealogy of the concept of race. Most critical race studies agree that the idea of race is a modern phenomenon, working in

Europe since early modernity and related to a knowledge regime involving ordering, mapping and classification based on essential difference (Foucault, 1970; Goldberg, 1993, 2009). The conceptualization of race relations were constituted through the colonial designation of 'Europeanness' and 'non-Europeanness' (Hesses, 2007). In the wake of the Holocaust, however, the concept of race became unmentionable in Europe. It was deadened and, in the words of Goldberg, 'Buried. But buried alive' (2009: 157). This is the context in which we shall see the actual experiences of everyday racism. Merleau-Ponty's concept of habituation is helpful here by establishing a basis for understanding how bodily and perceptual orientations become central to the racialization of identities. His idea of 'habitual perceptions' can 'explain both why racializing attributions are nearly impossible to discern and why they are resistant to alteration or erasure' (Alcoff, 2006: 188).

The second interpretative point in the understanding of the Danish–Pakistani narratives is the concept of *double consciousness,* famously introduced by W.E.G. DuBois in the early twentieth century and taken up by Frantz Fanon in his *Black Skin White Masks* (1967a). In the white world, Fanon says, the 'man of colour' under the influence of the white gaze develops a third-person consciousness: a consciousness of one's body as a body-for-others. Somehow challenging Merleau-Ponty's notion of the body schema (Mahendran, 2007), Fanon identifies an underlying 'historical-racial schema' consisting of sedimented experiences of racism, causing 'corporeal malediction' and creating an atmosphere of uncertainty around the body. He describes his feelings:

> The white man is all around me; up above the sky is tearing at its navel; the earth crunches under my feet and sings white, white. All that whiteness burns me to a cinder. (1967a: 94)

All the mini-narratives demonstrate such experiences of being *objectified* by the white gaze. They have to reconcile themselves to the 'double consciousness' experiencing one's body from inside and outside alike.

The third, and connected, point we shall emphasize concerns *inhabiting space*. Phrased in another way, Fanon's contribution is about how black bodies are limited in their inhabitancy of space. The 'white world' disorients black bodies and their possibilities of belonging:

> The 'matter' of race is very much about embodied reality; seeing oneself or being seen as white or black or mixed does affect what one 'can do', or even where one can go, which can be redescribed in terms of *what is and is not within reach*. (Ahmed, 2006: 112)

Ahmed connects this differentiation to the question of orientation and sees it as a matter of how bodies inhabit spaces through shared orientations. To be orientated or to be at home in the world is also to feel a certain comfort. That means that white bodies feel comfortable because they inhabit spaces that extend their shape. The spaces are lived as being comfortable because they allow the bodies to fit; they have taken shape according to their habits and allowed their movements. The space is 'white' by allowing the 'passing by' of some bodies more than others. But non-white bodies do also inhabit white spaces. They are however made invisible when the space appears as white, or they become hypervisible when they stand apart and appear out-of-place. The proximity of bodies that stands out can result in moments of disorientation amongst both 'staying' and 'arriving' bodies. This point renders topical yet another quality of the body.

THE TEMPORALITY AND SPATIALITY OF THE BODY

The phenomenal body is spatial and temporal. It is irremediably situated in space and time and also spatializes and temporalizes. This quality of the phenomenal body has previously been appreciated within geography – for example, by Seamon (1979), who develops the notions of body ballets, time–space routines and place ballets to join people with environmental time–space, or by Thrift (1996), who uses Merleau-Ponty's thinking on sensible bodies as a stepping-stone on his way to non-representational theory. Originally, Merleau-Ponty and Lefebvre alike developed on this quality of the lived body (see also Simonsen, 2005a).[10] Our body is not merely '*in* space' or '*in* time', it *inhabits* space and time, and 'the space and time that we inhabit are always in their different ways indeterminate horizons' (Merleau-Ponty, 1962: 139, 140); 'each living body *is* space and *has* its space: it produces itself in space and it also produces this space' (Lefebvre, 1991a: 170). The presupposition for this production of space is a *spatial body* that is

> a practical and fleshy body conceived of as totality complete with spatial qualities (symmetries, asymmetries) and energetic properties (discharges, economies, waste). (1991a: 61)

This means that active bodies, using their acquired schemes and habits as well as their gestural systems, position their world around themselves and constitute that world as 'ready-to-hand', to use Heidegger's expression (or as a 'practico-sensory realm' to use the Lefebvrian one). These are moving bodies 'measuring' space in the construction of a meaningful world. In taking up or inhabiting space, bodies move through it and are affected by the 'where' of that movement. It is through this movement that space, as well as bodies, takes shape. Inhabiting space is both about 'finding our way' and how we come to 'feel at home'. It therefore involves a continuous negotiation between what is familiar and unfamiliar, making space habitable but also receiving new impressions depending on which way we orientate and what is within reach.

Lefebvre (1991a, 1996), with his double interest in the social history of the body and the social ontology of the body, can add to this with a stronger emphasis on 'body politics' (Simonsen, 2005a). He describes a history of capitalism as a process of abstraction and decorporealization of space and time in the form of homogenization, fragmentation and hierarchization (see also Gregory, 1994). In this way, in the intersection between its history and its social ontology, he is turning the body into a critical figure – a site of resistance and active struggle.

> Thanks to its sensory organs, from the sense of smell and from sexuality to sight [...], the body tends to behave as a *differential field* [...] breaking out of the temporal and spatial shell developed in relation to labour. (Lefebvre 1991a: 384)

This means that the body, as a producer of difference (through rhythms, gestures, imaginations), calls forth a *right to difference*, formulated against forces of homogenization, fragmentation and hierarchical organized power. Inspired by Nietzsche and his 'will to power', Lefebvre emphasized two aspects of such struggles. One is the 'festival', as the site of participation and of the possibility of the 'poesis' of creating new situations from desire and enjoyment. The other is sexuality, involving struggles of relations between the sexes (a feminine revolt) as well as relations between sexuality and society. In relation to lived space it involves participation, conflict and the appropriation of space for creative, generative, bodily practices, also formulated as 'the right to the city'.

RE-SCALING IDENTITIES

In the intersection between identity and spatiality emerges the problem of spatial identities or belonging – the problem of 'finding our way' and 'feeling at home'. In the following we in a little more developed form shall discuss the *habitability of space* for a group of people of Pakistani heritage living in the city of Copenhagen, seeing it as an ongoing negotiation between identity and strangerness moving across different scales or spatial formations (body, home, neighbourhood, city, nation, globe). In this way, it is not a process about being fixed into a place, but rather about the possibility of becoming part of a space where one can expand one's body.[11]

We start from the question of *national identity*. Several participants express their uncertainty over this question. They express an emotional ambivalence connected to the discrepancy between feeling Danish and not being recognized as such by others. Hanif, for example, says:

> Actually, it is one of the biggest and best questions which I – every day, from I wake up to I go to bed, I am doubtful. Sometimes I say *of course*, sometimes *never*. Sometimes I think: *No!* I'll never be sure that I will become recognized as Danish. I feel 100 per cent Danish. But when

> I experience this discrimination, then it immediately pops up, this thing about *not* being Danish [...] Look at my album and tell what the difference is except that we have darker skin [...] We have been in Legoland with the family. We have been to the zoo. We have pictures where we are wearing clap hats, Danish flags and Danish clothes when watching an international football match; and from Legoland with feathers in our hair roasting twistbread on the fire. I mean, *what in hell do you want more?* (Hanif, 29)

Hanif was born in Denmark and in this extract he expresses the doubt and the *ambivalence* raised by the recurring question of being recognized as a full member of the Danish community. He describes how his emotions constantly alternate between 'of course' and 'never'. His words illustrate a repeated theme in the narrative material – the discrepancy between feeling Danish and not being recognized as a valid member of the nation. Although he feels 100 per cent Danish he finds himself in a constant struggle for *recognition* (see Honneth, 1995). Hanif feels that he belongs but that he is denied the recognition from the surroundings, mainly because of discrimination. Later in the interview he illustrates the problem of recognition with an example. Even if he gave up his corporeal cultural practices related to alcohol and pork, he says, it would not change the predicate of being a stranger but instead invoke astonishment: 'Do you drink, and eat pork?' The main issue here is about how boundaries are constructed through estrangement that for Hanif (and others) comes into conflict with his self-identification with the nation. In the extract he illustrates his Danishness through a 'fictive' family album that in a concentrated visual form raises questions about what is needed to be recognized as a Dane. 'What in hell do you want more?' is more than a rhetorical question. It gives voice to uncertainty and disoriented feelings about the possibility of being fully recognized. It is an affiliation with the nation that takes place between inclusion/exclusion and separation/connections. Hanif becomes a *border figure* located inside and outside at the same time.

All the stories express that ambivalent affiliation with the Danish nation. Ambivalent Danishness is also identified in other Danish studies (e.g. Mørck, 1998; Røgilds, 1998). It is however most often interpreted as the result of having 'one leg in each camp', that is, as hybrid or hyphenated identities. Our analysis showed examples of that as well, but mostly the ambivalence referred to experiences and feelings of disorientation and doubt about the possibility of becoming a full member of the imagined community.[12] The feelings can be summed up as: *I feel Danish but...* None of the respondents is able to speak about their Danishness without this 'but', which is connected to the experiences of being reproduced as the border figure of the nation. The result is a double position between inclusion/exclusion and proximity/distance, mirroring the contradictions between how the respondents identify themselves and how they are identified by others.

However, the ambivalence does not imply that the respondents disregard their Danishness. Basically, they try to shift the focus from a very burdensome debate on Danishness, in which they have experienced an extensive degree of estrangement and exclusion, to set forth new and different perspectives about what it is to be Danish. Common to them is a search for a Danishness which can be inclusive and multifarious – as for example in imaginations of a 'multicultural Danishness' or a 'Muslim Danishness'. In addition to that, they show great creativity in attempts to shift the perspective away from the issues they find burdensome and prioritize some that are not culturally laden: for example, a 'participatory Danishness' imagining a community based not on ethnic and cultural values, but on social engagement and responsibility to the community.

One way to try to escape the sensitive question of national identity appeared in *urban identifications*. They relate to processes that have made many urban theorists characterize the city as a 'world of strangers', a spatial formation populated with people who are personally unknown (or even strange) to each other, in this way making encountering 'the stranger' an inevitable condition of urban life (Simmel, 1950a [1903]; Lofland, 1973; Donald, 1999 amongst others).

> I think it is great because, in contrast to the representation in the media, you can actually feel that both Danish and non-Danish have accepted the fact that we have this mixed composition. And they think it is normal. The way we are told that it is so strange having these different cultures. I can't recognize that picture when I go about in the city. It seems to come naturally to people [...] it by now characterizes Nørrebro and Vesterbro [former working class neighbourhoods] and the inner city as well. I think, it is good that you can leave all that talk about problems and conflicts. For us ethnic minorities, who are born and bred in Denmark, it is no problem, we can handle the mixture. And for most young Danish people I don't think it is either, at least not for those who grew up together with them, in particular in Copenhagen. You live together across these boundary lines. In the streets you have a common culture, you have a common language where you integrate Arab or Asian expressions in the Danish language, and you develop common norms. I think it is good that it happens – and about time too! (Yasmeen, 26)

For Yasmeen, as for other participants, the city is definitely a world of strangers. They have grown up in the diaspora, in the ambivalence of borderland positions and hybridity, and they identify with the city exactly because they see it as a multicultural place. Yasmeen opposes this to the representations in the media and in this way addresses the inflamed public debate on minorities in Denmark. On a banal, practical level she connects what Keith (2005) calls a 'cosmopolitan hope' to the life in (parts of) the city. It is connected to what we earlier have called a *lived multiculturalism* (Simonsen, 2008b), primarily based on transcultural relations performed in everyday situations. A connection could also be made to Gilroy's concept of metropolitan 'multicultural conviviality' with its emphasis on routine everyday features of social life (Gilroy, 2006). The core of the topic is about attitudes generated in everyday contexts. They can of course take many forms, as also implicitly suggested by Yasmeen when she says that it is 'about time it happens' or connects her hope to the generation that has grown up together in the city. Yasmeen connects the attitudes to the shared adolescence in the city. We can talk about 'dialogical identity' where the 'strange other' slowly changes to a 'familiar other' and becomes part of the social environment.

Several participants identify themselves (with a Danish phrase) as *Copenhagener with a big* C, thereby expressing a strong affiliation to the city. What they concurrently say is that it is easier to become a Copenhagener than to become a Dane. In this way, the nation takes the role of the 'constitutive outside' in relation to their identity as Copenhageners. The phrase materializes a difference between the city and the nation when it comes to habitability and possibility of identification. It shows some of the complexity of the boundary work. Cultural/ethnic identity in itself involves a symbolic boundary resulting from internal group identification and/or external categorization. In this case, bridging these boundaries becomes a quality which is used to differentiate between spatial entities as more or less habitable – that is, in the construction of spatial boundaries.

Processes of identification also emerge from communities of practice that we call *aesthetic communities*:

> It has become more than a sport to us. It is a life-style, a way to be, so it is part of our identity[...] What I like about taekwondo is when you stand there in your track suit, you are neither/nor. There is nothing called national identity. When you are in a fight, it is not a Muslim or a Christian or anything else. It is just somebody training taekwondo[...] If you would compare it to the cultural, you in taekwondo have principles about respect and humanity and about accept of other people that for me are ideal. (Tariq, 37)

Some of our respondents (and their families) were practising taekwondo and saw that as defining their lives. They emphasize the 'colour blindness' of the sport: 'the only colour that matters is the colour of your belt'. In the sport neither skin colour, national identity nor religion make a difference, only your abilities within the specific community. Within the community you are neither/nor, Tariq says, in this way turning the undecideability of 'the stranger', suggested by Bauman (1991), from a negative to a positive quality – here it is not a basis for insecurity and ambivalence, it is an expression of a community where the categories lose significance.

What these young men reveal is a process of identification based on a *bodily-aesthetic community* where bodily capabilities play a crucial although not exclusive role. It is a community of practice that unites the corporeal and the spiritual, body and mind, by combining bodily activity with encouragement of values involving honour, discipline and respect for other people. Other aesthetic practices also assume such an identity-forming role. One example is music: a performer of *sufi*-music tells how he, by combining his own tradition with inspiration from his current surroundings, tries to create a room where he can feel comfortable in his specific (hyphenated) Danish-Pakistani identity. Yet another aesthetic process of identification connects to *religious communities*. However, the narratives show great variety as regards the meaning of religion. For some, it is primarily a platform for social engagement, for the performance of voluntary work within their local communities; others take a pragmatic approach and talk about religion as a 'habit' – as institutional practicalities that they perform more or less adequately; and others again place it as their basic attitude to life – e.g. expressed by 'I am a Muslim 24 hours a day', 'For me, Islam is the focal point in my life'.

The final important process of identification relates to *cosmopolitanism* – to the global aspects of life, practices and identifications crossing national borders.

> I am very comfortable in many of the modern Muslim networks, it is fascinating to meet these people and discuss politics and spiritual matters[…] Much of my international networks are about that. Then I have some networks which are about urban life, the enjoyment of cities, and when I am together with them, it's about enjoying the city and the leisure industries[…] So there are like four groups in my international networks; the fun entertainment group, the more serious Muslim group, and then two partially overlapping groups of business men and medical people standing for the professional stimulation. (Jamal, 31)

Jamal says that the question of Danishness does not occupy him much; he identifies with his networks. He travels a lot in connection to his work and he talks about affiliation to different *global networks*, some based on professional language games, some based on friendship and some on religion. The last mentioned connects to an interest in participating in the development of a modern European Islam. He later adds a European family network. He feels that this fact influences his view on his Pakistani heritage. What he in some sense distils is a *European-Pakistani identity* based on common history of immigration and parallel experiences within his own generation where they, notwithstanding national differences between the European countries, can 'be mirrored in' each other's lives due to parallel problems and experiences during their upbringing. Even if it demonstrates several layers, Jamal's story reveals a *cosmopolitan mode of life*, a mobile everyday life which is lived 'globally' but held together by specific networks making connections all over the world. As suggested by Calhoun (2003), this shows that cosmopolitanism is not necessarily an absence of belonging. When national (or other) borders are transcended, this is not disembeddedness but integration into relationships which form different spatialities. They are embedded in specific networks which are mobile and maintained over spatial distance, and as such they constitute their own forms of identification and affiliation.

Summing up, what we have seen here is double processes of estrangement and identification that lead to an *ambivalence* in the affiliation to the Danish nation. The ambivalence and the pain, which are connected to this failed identification process, draw attention to alternative spaces of identification. The result is a displacement of identification from the contested national scale towards other spatial formations. In this connection, we can, with an expression borrowed from Smith (1992), talk about *jumping scale*. For Smith, the notion describes a political strategy, that is, a practice whereby political claims and power established at one spatial scale can be expanded to another one. We will, however, use it to describe how identity problems on one scale can initiate a displacement of identification towards other scales. Problems of recognition at the national scale then give rise to a downgrading of national identity in favour of more habitable spaces at global, urban, local or bodily scales – or, in other words, a 're-scaling of identities'.

AFFECTIVITY AND EMOTIONS

Throughout this chapter it has become apparent that dealing with bodies and embodiment must also include the issue of emotions. In general, we have talked about feelings of ambiguity, disorientation, vulnerability, and physical and emotional pains involved in these feelings. In relation to experienced Otherness, we talked about how it was 'just like getting slapped in the face all the time', about feeling the weight of the gaze and of the white surroundings, about being perceived as posing a danger and creating fear, and about the feeling of deviance in the wearing of the veil. In relation to identification, we talked about feeling at home or out-of-place and about the ambivalent affiliation and feeling of disorientation around national identity. In this last section, we shall try to conceptualize this issue of emotions. By doing that, we locate ourselves in the middle of a current debate within geography dealing with the advantages of the thinking about emotion and affect, respectively, and the differences between them (see, e.g., Bondi, 2005; Anderson and Harrison, 2006, 2010; Tolia-Kelly, 2006; McCormack, 2006; Pain, 2009; Smith et al., 2009). We shall not go deeper into that debate, but rather argue that a starting point in Merleau-Ponty's non-dichotomous ontology can cut through the distinction between emotion as embodied (subjective) experiences or significations and affect as an impersonal 'set of flows moving through the bodies of human and other beings' (Thrift, 2008: 236).

Merleau-Ponty did not explicitly develop an account of emotions, but emotional phenomena appear throughout his writings and provide us with material to elaborate on a non-dualistic approach to affectivity and emotion (see also Cataldi, 1993; Cataldi, 2008). Situatedness and the collapse of the distinction between 'inner' and 'outer' are crucial aspects of Merleau-Ponty's ideas of emotion. Emotions are neither 'purely' mental nor 'purely' physical, but ways of relating to and interacting with the surrounding world. Emotions are inseparable from other aspects of subjectivity, such as perception, speech, gestures, practices and interpretations of the surrounding world, and they primordially function at the pre-reflexive level. They are, in short, ways of relating. This account gives occasion for a double conception of emotional spatiality (Simonsen, 2007, 2010).

One side of emotions are an *expressive space* of the body's movements, which might be seen as an active or performative element of emotion. Emotions are something practised and shown. Here, emotions are connected to the expressive and communicative body. The body, Merleau-Ponty argues, is comparable to an expressive work of art, but one that expresses emotions in the form of *living meaning*. Emotional meanings are 'secreted' in bodily gestures in the same way that musical/poetic meaning is 'secreted' in a phrase of a sonata or a poem. These meanings are communicated and 'blindly' apprehended through corporeal intentions and gestures that reciprocally link one body to another:

> Faced with an angry or threatening gesture, I have no need, in order to understand it, to recall the feelings which I myself experienced when I used these gestures on my own account. [...] I do not see anger or a threatening attitude as a psychic fact hidden behind the gesture, I read anger in it. The gesture *does not make me think* of anger, it is anger itself. (1962: 184)

Emotional experience is something public and 'in-between' – situated in the perceptibility of its bodily gestures. In this way, emotion as living meanings relates not only to meaning in the above-mentioned sense of something created through practice and the experience of mobile bodies, but also to meaning as it is found in artwork, expressed in poetic or musical meaning. This feature also endows them with a cultural situatedness. Biological and constructed alike, they, like speech are contextually performed: 'It is no more natural, and no less conventional, to shout in anger or to kiss in love than to call a table "a table". Feelings and passional conduct are invented like words' (1962: 189).

The other side of emotional spatiality is *affective space*, which is the space in which we are emotionally in touch – open to the world and its 'effect' on us. This means that emotions are not just actions, something that our bodies express or articulate. Another aspect of them is how we are possessed by them or swept into their grasp, as when experiencing or appreciating a work of art. It is related to the experience of the world around us, to things, rooms and architecture, but also feelings elicited, for example being gripped with fear or seized by terror, overcome by shame, filled with joy, cast into despair, and so forth. In that way, it is the felt sense of having been moved emotionally, the more passive side of emotional experience.

Together these two sides suggest an active–passive circularity (in the form of mutual implication) as a complementary relation (Cataldi, 1993). Emotions are neither 'actions' nor 'passions' (forces beyond our control that simply happen to us) – they are both at once. The active–passive complementarity can be connected to the idea of reversibility, of spaces of differentiation where active and passive, or expressive and affective, 'sides' of the flesh can be seen as crossing over each other. It suggests that there are at least two sides to affective experiences and that neither of those sides is intelligible apart from the other. They overlap and cross over into each other, but they never completely become the same. Furthermore, emotions are public and *relational*. They are formed in the intertwining of our 'own' bodily flesh with the flesh of the world and with the intercorporeal flesh of humanity. They have a sense of mutuality that should not be mistaken for harmony; they take the form of the whole register of different emotions such as, for instance, love, desire, hate or fear.

The concept of reversibility has had a central role in this chapter on bodies and embodiment, particularly in the above understanding of the expressive–affective circularity of emotions. As touched on before, Johnson (2008) argues, with reference to both Hannah Arendt and Seyla Benhabib, that reversibility of perspectives should be considered essential both to ethical considerations and transformative politics. Its element of mutuality, but an imperfect and ambiguous mutuality, means that you cannot assume a complete understanding of the other, but still an understanding of his/her sufferings can lay the foundations for our ethical (non)response. That is the point of departure for an exploration of encounters with the Other, which we shall turn to in the next chapter.

NOTES

1. This affinity is often linked with his posthumously published book *The Visible and the Invisible* (Merleau-Ponty, 1968), but there is no doubt that this interest in the relationship to material culture and artefacts permeates all his work.
2. One could also question that claim in general, for what two bodies can truly be said to possess identical histories? See also Weiss (2008).
3. We saw earlier how Bourdieu, with a basis in the concept of intentionality, had come to a view of phenomenology as, amongst other things, solipsist and subjectivist.
4. These and other attempts at developing embodied ethics are connected to the literature of feminist ethics of care, originally catalysed by the work of Carol Gilligan in *In a Different Voice: Psychological Theory and Women's Development* in 1982. We shall return to these ethical questions later in the book.
5. We shall return to this question on embodied identities in the section to come.
6. In his argument, Paul Harrison draws on a critical essay by Levinas, addressing Merleau-Ponty's understanding of intercorporeality by using his well-known example of two hands touching each other. Here, Levinas comments that for him the image of two hands touching does not indicate a conjoining or a mutual understanding, but rather a radical separation between the two hands. However, taking into account the ambiguity involved in the reversibility of sensing, this might not be a question of either/or, but rather both/and. We cannot predetermine the character of the relation between perceiving and being-perceived.
7. This case will be the subject of a more extended presentation in Chapter 3.

8. People with darker skin more often than others experience being stopped, rejected and excluded from places in the Copenhagen nightlife. This may happen as direct discrimination where on the basis of bodily appearance (skin colour or clothing) people are stopped and excluded from a place, or on the basis of quota systems for how many 'foreigners' the place will let in (Nørregaard-Nielsen and Rosenmeier, 2007).

9. This is interesting seen in relation to Fanon's text about the veil in *A Dying Colonialism* (1967b) that describes how the French colonial power meant that the best strategy to dominate Algeria was through the conquering of the Algerian women, who had a central role in the resistance. For the colonial power, the covered woman was source of frustration. She was a mystery. She could 'see' without being 'seen'. To make her take off the veil was for the colonists the key to power. What they never understood was that the women took the veil on and off as a part of the strategy of the resistance.

10. Reading Merleau-Ponty and Lefebvre together renders appropriate a note on Merleau-Ponty's relationship to Marxism. Being a part of the left, intellectual milieu in France during and after World War II, it was of course one of his concerns. While he was critical of institutionalized communism (see e.g. Merleau-Ponty, 1969) and never joined the communist party, Merleau-Ponty's attitude to theoretical Marxism was more mixed. Here he distinguished between Marxism's 'grand narrative' and its methodology. He rejected the anthropological theory of human essence of the early Marx, the identification of the proletariat as the primary subject of emancipation and the teleological account of history, but he was reluctant totally to abandon historical materialism or dialectics. He saw historical materialism as 'concrete conception of history' that bases history and ways of thinking on 'ways of existing and co-existing, that is, on human relationships'. (Merleau-Ponty, 1962: 171) Dialectic thinking, to him, consisted of an ongoing process of critical engagement in the material and symbolic reversals of collective life that he found perfectly in line with his phenomenology and a call to 'remember that his central ontological figure – the practical, perceiving body – is situated in socioeconomic and historicocultural contexts to which it responds and which transfigure it' (Coole, 2007a: 108).

11. The illustration can of course only pick out a few exemplary stories to show the main axes of identification. For a more developed presentation of the analysis see Koefoed and Simonsen (2012).

12. We are of course aware that a number of works deal with the same topic, especially in an English context, e.g. Gilroy (1991) and Raj (2003).

$$3$$

Encountering the Other

In continuation of the understanding of bodies and embodiment developed in the previous chapters, in this chapter we turn to embodied encounters as they pass off in different urban spaces. The particular focus will be cross-cultural encounters and the way in which we continuously negotiate the complexities of cultural differences in their repetitive appearances in everyday life. In the words of Michael Keith it is a situation where we 'at one moment [are] made to feel our singularity, at another to sense our otherness fragmenting in the fleeting connections of community and dependency expressed in the glance or gesture that bridges a gap, dissolves a boundary, initiates a dialogue' (2005: 101). Before going into detail on different modes of encounters, we will however present our take on the concept of encounters.

THE CONCEPT OF ENCOUNTER[1]

Encounter is about the *production and negotiation of difference,* as stated above. It makes no sense to talk about 'ourselves', either as individuals or groups, without relating to 'the Other'. Any kind of identification, whether we talk about internal self-identification, group identification or about external social/political categorization, unavoidably involves social interaction (Jenkins, 1996). The designation of an 'I' or a 'we' requires a meeting with others. In other words, the subject comes into existence precisely through encounters with others. As such, the meeting takes ontological priority over the being of the meeting parts, expressing a relational social ontology based on radical intersubjectivity. That, in accordance with our critical phenomenological approach, is characterized by opening onto otherness in a common space where our worlds overlap and intertwine.

The concept of encounter has been a point of analytical interest in the emerging literature on 'geographies of encounters' (e.g. Amin, 2002; Valentine, 2008; Matejskova and Leitner, 2011; Leitner, 2012; Wilson, 2017a, b). When we use the term 'encounter', however, it is supposed to add to this idea of meeting that goes beyond contact. The term suggests a meeting, but a meeting particularly involving two characteristics: surprise and time–space (Merleau-Ponty, 1968; Ahmed, 2000). It involves surprise and sometimes conflict because of its inevitable content of similarities and difference, processes of inclusion and exclusion or incorporation and expulsion that constitute the boundaries of bodies or communities. Encounters are unpredictable and premised with the unknown that does not allow us to control the encounter or predict its outcome. Encounters are temporal and spatial because they always involve at least two subjects approaching each other, and because, through repetition over time, they can shift the boundaries of the familiar. So encounters are not about different pre-existent 'cultures' meeting each other. On the contrary, *difference* is produced in the encounters, meaning that encounters have the ability to make and transform difference, destabilize, rework or reproduce it in unpredictable ways (Darling and Wilson, 2016: 6).

At one level, encounters refer to *face-to-face meetings* as we experience them in everyday life. It can be face-to-face meetings ('eye-to-eye') involving visual economy of recognition or 'skin-to-skin' involving an economy of touch (Ahmed, 2000). They are, however, also temporal and spatial through historical–geographical mediation. They presuppose other encounters of facing, other bodies, other spaces and other times. In this way, they reopen prior histories of encounter and geo-political imaginations of the Other and incorporate them in the encounters as traces of broader social relationships. Encounters between embodied subjects always dwell between the domain of the particular and that of the general, with the encounter framed by broader relationships of power and antagonism. In other words, encounters 'are points of unanticipated exposure to difference that are situated within personal and collective histories as well as imagined future' (Darling and Wilson, 2016: 11).

As such, this understanding of encounters adds to Merleau-Ponty's ideas of the social body as a body opening up and intertwining with the world (other bodies and materialities) by accentuating that this is not a general but rather a *differentiated world*, and in such a world, what is meant by the social body is more often than not 'precisely the effect of being with some others over other others' (Ahmed, 2000: 49).

Hence, the constitution of Others involves *spatial negotiations* over mobility and home, (imagined) communities, boundaries and bridges. 'Like bodies' and 'unlike bodies' do not precede encounters of inclusion or expulsion. Rather, likeness and unlikeness as 'characteristics' of bodies are produced through these encounters. Part of that process is the experience of being exposed to oppressive visions or emotions. Fanon (1967a) describes the phenomenology of incorporating Otherness and the development of a 'double consciousness' due to the enculturation of the body. Men and women of colour, he says, develop a third-person consciousness trying to reconcile their own experiences with the operation of a 'historical-racial schema' within which their corporeal schema is supposed to fit.

Encounters, then, are deeply charged with emotions. The 'strange encounter' (Ahmed, 2000) is played out *on* the body, and it is played out *with* emotions. It is basically a sensuous process involving an affective opening out of bodies to Other bodies. But encounters with Other bodies also involve practices and techniques of differentiation. Various familial relations involve particular forms of emotion and ways of touch, while the recognition of some-body as a stranger – a body that is 'out of place' – might involve disgust or fear of touching (see e.g. Fanon, 1967a; Douglas, 1994). In this way 'like' bodies and 'different' bodies do not just precede the bodily encounters of incorporation or exclusion; likeness and difference are directly produced through these encounters. Bodily encounters are processes where bodies come together and co-mingle in different ways, slide away from each other again and become relived or reformed in their apartness.

ENCOUNTERING THE OTHER AND ORIENTALISM

As argued by Ahmed, encounters between embodied subjects 'always hesitate between the domain of the particular – the face to face of this encounter – and the general – the framing of the encounter by broader relationship of power' (2000: 8). The face-to-face encounter cannot be isolated from broader relationship of antagonism. The encounters we have with unknown Others reopen prior histories of encounters that can potentially violate and fix Others in a regime of difference. More than anything else, the contribution from postcolonial analysis, taking off from Said's (1978) now well-known analysis of Western imaginations of the Orient, informs the strength and inertia of binary us/them distinctions in historical–geographical imaginations of Other people. As a Western means of dominating and gaining authority over the Orient, Orientalism is, in Said's words, a style of 'thought' based on an ontological and epistemological distinction between the Orient and the Occident. Said describes how this style of thought, in literature and academic studies, produced the image of the Orient, as a threatening, inferior and underdeveloped Other. This discussion on Orientalism has three important implications.

First, in his critical discussion on Orientalism Said introduced the concept of *imaginative geography* as practices and constructions that create a familiar space in our minds which is 'ours', and an unfamiliar space beyond 'ours' which is 'theirs'. Imaginative geography works by producing contradictions between East and West, between 'us' and 'them', both in terms of mentality and 'territoriality'. Inspired by Gaston Bachelard's concept of the 'poetics of space', Said argues that space is converted into meaning in a poetic process with imaginative and figurative values related to naming and emotions.

The Orient and the Other is a field of knowledge that is represented as a kind of theatrical stage to the distant European audience. This oriental stage is inhabited by people with a range of representative figures or tropes: stereotypical characters such as braggarts, misers and gluttons and a whole cultural repertoire of monsters, devils, heroes, terrors, pleasures and desires. The argument is that the staged Orient was imagined as an enclosed space representing the whole of the world of the East, and that, in a very powerful way, it shaped the perception and modes of encounter between East and West. Imaginative geography became a rigorous system of morality and a disciplined regime of truth, represented and produced through a network of corporate institutions. It was the institutionalized Western knowledge of the Orient that created the background for an almost mythical representation of the Orient, or as Said puts it, a latent Orientalism: a powerful 'fantasy' in which the Orient existed as a place isolated from European progress.

> In a way, orientalism involves the transformation of 'farness' as a spatial marker of distance into the property of peoples and places. 'They' embody what is far away. [...] In other words, while 'the other side of the world' is associated with 'racial otherness', racial others become associated with the other side of the world. They become to embody distance. (Ahmed, 2006: 114, 121)

In this way, imaginative geography works by *dramatizing geographical distance* and difference between what is close and what is far away. Orientalism works through spatialization, turning distance into difference, and producing two spaces by drawing a line between two continents with real and very visible material consequences. As argued by Derek Gregory (2004), Orientalism produces the effect that it names. In this case the Other comes to embody the distance (what is far away). The artificial lines between East and West, between 'us' and 'them', are symbolic, and oppositionally fabricated through the reproduction of a double discourse system. The 'Other' is imagined negatively as primitive, barbaric and wild in contrast to the European self, which is imagined as civilized, advanced, rational and modern. Islam and Muslims in particular have always represented a trauma in the Western imagination as something that is religious, hysterical, strange and dangerous.

Secondly, Orientalism is not an airy fantasy or innocent idea but a *power relation* – it is a Western system of dominance and authority in the unequal relationship between the Orient and the Occident. It can be understood as a regime of knowledge – a disciplined system of power – that not only describes, teaches and rules, but also 'produces' the Other. The argument is that the complex of ideas, images, representations and academic writings about the Orient actually 'creates', rather than describes, the Other or, as Said suggested, the Orient was *Orientalized*; it was 'made' Oriental. The important point is that Orientalism is not a false knowledge construction, but a *power relationship* with political implications.

Thirdly, much analysis following Said (1978, 1997) has tended to focus on Orientalism mostly as an institutional 'regime of knowledge', thereby placing the analytical perspective on the workings of institutions, discourse and texts. It has been argued that acts of representation are not innocent. The degree to which Orientalism is (re)produced and negotiated in banal, bodily and sensuous practices, has, on the contrary, been less prominent in the discussion. Therefore we, in addition to Said's textualist perspective, introduce the notion *practical orientalism* (Haldrup et al., 2006). It can grasp how hegemonic ideas translate into everyday practices and infiltrate the 'banal' spaces of ordinary life, including everyday sociality and sensual experience. Small things such as the sight of an Other outfit, the hearing of Other languages/sounds and the taste of Other food can provoke emotional reactions which come to permeate cross-cultural encounters.

POLITICS OF THE ENCOUNTER

> The urban, we might say, is the place of the drama resultant from the encounter and the site where we encounter the drama of the encounter itself. (Merrifield, 2013: 69)

Political dramas come out of particular moments and conjunctions and have no teleological master plans. They are collectives of comings together, of sheer co-presences held together by common feelings of indignation. The encounter, Merrifield (2013) argues, is like a twinkling, radiant cosmic constellation, an expression of a plurality of participants.

Encounters, then, are inherent in politics. They are about the making and unmaking of borders, and they can produce anxiety, fear and resentment, as well as curiosity, fascination and conviviality. Much work has been done on how encounters are still marked by (post)colonial imaginations, for instance by being mediated through enduring but 'unspeakable' taxonomies of race (Goldberg, 2009), or by being imbued with security logics and anticipation of terror (Gregory, 2011; Anderson, 2014). Others, on another level, try to identify how encounters can involve transformative potentials. For example, Merrifield (2013), through the work in Althusser's *The Undercurrent of the Materialism of the Encounter* and Lefebvre's *The Urban Revolution*, explores the potentiality of urban encounters. He emphasizes the basic contingency of encounters, and by way of examples such as the Occupy and Indignados movements, he illustrates the transformative potentials of urban encounters. The city brings together multiple diverse struggles and, at the same time, pushes for a new order. The urban, argues Merrifield,

> is loaded with weeds as well as wealth, with undergrowth as well as overgrowth; it's a vast space where the fight for the transformation of the world will now take place. Yet the urban isn't a point fixed in absolute space. It's no longer a fixation on a center, no longer really any point at all, but a space of and for encounters: a space of and for a citizenship that might intervene in the current, rather dubious, neoliberal hegemony. (2013: 34)

The politics of the encounter is not only about people meeting each other in public spaces. It is radically about how it enables the collective power experiment with reality as also discussed by Lefebvre through the concept of *the right to the city*. As Harvey writes:

> The right to the city is far more than the individual liberty to access urban resources: it is a right to change ourselves by changing the city. It is, moreover, a common rather than an individual right since this transformation inevitably depends upon the exercise of a collective power to reshape the processes of urbanization. The freedom to make and remake our cities and ourselves is, I want to argue, one of the most precious yet most neglected of our human rights. (2008: 23)

For Lefebvre, the right to the city is not an individual right but more radically the urban seen as a possible world where we change ourselves – a new beginning or urgent utopia turned towards the possible. The right to the city is not a passive but active demand and participation characterized by meaningful common engagement and social connections. It is collective power where citizens are reclaiming space in the city. As formulated by Lefebvre, the right to the city:

> should modify, concretize and make more practical the rights of the citizen as an urban dweller (*citadin*) and user of multiple services. It would affirm, on the one hand, the right of users to make known their ideas on the space and time of their activities in the urban area; it would also cover the right to the use of the centre, a privileged place, instead of being dispersed and stuck into ghettos (for workers, immigrants, the 'marginal' and even for the 'privileged'). (Lefebvre, 1996a: 34)

The city has for a long time been viewed as a space for being and becoming political in which different groups and publics constitute their identity and lay claim to political visibility. Encounters can introduce a different way of conceiving the politics of urbanization and the conflictual interrelation between the lived and the world history (Merrifield, 2013).

DIFFERENT MODES OF ENCOUNTER

As indicated, we see encounters as meetings between two or more body-subjects, but meetings that involve surprise; that shift the boundaries of the familiar. Such encounters can be manifold and differentiated. The following analysis is based on a wider project titled *Paradoxical Spaces: Encountering the Other in Public Space* that explores how the complexity of cultural difference is experienced and practised in different public spaces in Copenhagen. Through a number of different cases, the aim is to understand *how* the Other is encountered and *what* such encounters can tell us about possibilities and limitations for cultural exchange and coexistence in the city. The focus is concrete encounters in different settings and the reactions and meanings arising from them. In the following we will distinguish between three different but interrelated *modes of encounter*. First, *collective, planned encounters* such as festivals or other events in the city involving cross-cultural interaction. Secondly, *encounters with authorities* such as the police, social street workers or public transport employees. And finally, *everyday encounters* taking the form of accidental meetings in the city's streets, parks or on public transport. An important point here is the mutuality and reversibility of the encounters. How encounters are bodily and verbally negotiated and what reactions they generate, we consider an open empirical question that should be explored from both (or more) sides.

In the following we will use empirical examples to illustrate different forms of embodied encounters based on 'thick' analyses of different kinds of meetings. Here, we are in accordance with our critical phenomenological approach, emphasizing experiences, raising empirical questions like how the complexity of cultural difference is negotiated in public space. How do we make sense of meetings in public space? Which emotions do they generate? How are encounters marked by security efforts from different actors and authorities? What are the cultural schemes and broader social relationships embedded in the meetings? Theoretically and empirically, we will present encounters in public spaces as both conflicting and dialogical spatial practices. The aim is to gain an understanding of how the Other is encountered and what these different meetings can tell us about possibilities/limitations for cultural exchange and coexistence.

COLLECTIVE, PLANNED ENCOUNTERS

Planned and organized encounters have become a widespread strategy to address intercultural conflicts and challenges related to cultural differences in the city (Christiansen et al., 2017). Some research studies across the social sciences underline that, under the right conditions, 'being together' can create familiarity, inspire social and political changes, and play a role in developing trust and respect. This research highlights the character of encounters and their opportunity to produce 'meaningful contact'. The 'contact hypothesis' was first proposed by Allport (1954). He suggested that positive effects of contact occur in situations characterized by four key conditions: equal status, intergroup cooperation, common goals, and support by social and institutional authorities. A review of recent advances in intergroup contact theory concluded that intergroup contact can produce positive outcomes, such as greater trust and forgiveness. These contact effects occur not only for ethnic groups but also for other groups (Pettigrew et al., 2011).

In this sense, planned encounters are often organized as a solution to potential intercultural conflict or as a celebration of living together in the cosmopolitan city. According to Christiansen et al. (2017), organized cultural encounters can be more or less *scripted events*: time, place, roles and interactions are regulated in advance of the encounter. Planned and organized encounters take place within more or less already established institutional contexts and are thus shaped in important ways by the existing norms, discourses, roles and hierarchies. An important element of cultural encounter scripts is bringing people together in close bodily proximity in order for them to experience the Other as a real physical presence. However, as argued by Wilson (2017b), planned encounters are inherently risky, since their potentiality is tied in with unpredictability – they are social spaces that are located in a here-and-now event of a coming together of embodied subjects. As pointed out, the risk is also differentially distributed, and this is tied to the unpredictable nature of encounters and the generally unequal positions of their participants. The shocks and ruptures as well as the creativity of encounters may leave some participants in more vulnerable positions than others.

Collective planned encounters are manifold. They can be art projects with the aim of bringing people together (Whyte, 2017), workshops, planned meetings or activities aiming at intercultural dialogues (Bessone, 2017; Lapina, 2017; Marselis, 2017; Riis, 2017); micro-publics like sports centres and public meeting places (Amin, 2002) that are designed to foster tolerance and develop conviviality. Here we will focus on the role of 'multicultural' festivals in the city (see Koefoed et al., forthcoming). We find 'multicultural' festivals useful events through which to explore collective planned encounters that can create social and cultural transformations of urban spaces. They are mainly about participating in the creation of community identity forged by food, music, dance, arts, sports and/or other aesthetic practices. They become sites for on-going negotiations within urban space where participating individuals and groups attempt to construct meaningful concepts of identity as well as notions of inclusion/exclusion. The planned encounters explored through 'multicultural' festivals do, however, take a specific form; they are mediated through processes and activities on different levels.

First, they are, as already indicated, mediated through historical–geographical processes and imaginations. This is about how the embodied encounters at festivals are embedded in broader social discourses and power relations, more or less coloured by colonial heritages and geographical imaginations of Others.

Secondly, encounters are mediated through the specific event constituted by the festival. Ryan and Wollan summarize as follows:

> The encounters are instant and synaesthetic: they engage several senses and are created, performed, and experienced in a limited time and place. Festivals are comparable with theatre, and belong to a playing culture. Even if the landscape is part of something strictly choreographed, we argue that such performances are never completely choreographed because of the playful and liminal aspects of the event. (2013: 110)

The pivotal point is time–space. Festivals are associated with spontaneity, and with a sense of being carried away by the momentum of the event. They have a special intensity that comes with a collapsing of time and space and an apparent blurring of the distinctions among participants. This makes some authors characterize the festival as 'time out of time' (Falassi, 1987). However, such an inattention to the social embeddedness of the festival seems exaggerated. We should rather view it as an activity that simultaneously breaks with and has a web of connections to people's everyday life. When it comes to space, it is about the festival site: the location, the design and the (urban) landscape of the festival. Encounters are mediated through the position of the festival, the arrangement of the activities and the utilization of the material environment in the activity.

Finally, encounters are mediated through the different practices and activities taking place at the festivals. Whether they are performances, participatory bodily activities, (religious) rituals or political expositions, they all function as social and/or material mediators in cross-cultural meetings. It is particularly these different mediations and their effects that interest us in the analysis of multicultural festivals.

EATING THE OTHER

> The overriding fear is that cultural, ethnic, and racial differences will be continually commodified and offered up as new dishes to enhance the white palate – that the Other will be eaten, consumed, and forgotten. (hooks, 2006: 380)

In the following we will use empirical examples from Kulturhavn, an annually recurring cultural event and festival that has about 80,000–100,000 visitors, taking place alongside Copenhagen harbour and lasting for three days (Simonsen et al., 2017). The empirical fieldwork was conducted through participant observation, on-the-spot interviews, photography and audio recording (2014–16). The experiences and activities at the festival cover a broad range of cultural activities and performances such as dance, music, theatre, children's activities, water sports, etc. The festival has two general aims. One is to support and recruit to the cultural and sports associations, the other one to support cross-cultural integration.

In accordance with our critical phenomenology approach, we have analysed the festival as a 'polyrhythmic ensemble' of social and bodily interrelations, each with their own rhythms – from general flows of visitors and activities, to encounters among visitors and performers. The festival offers sensuous experiences of views, sounds, smells and of being jostled by co-visitors. It momentarily creates an atmosphere where the pulse and corporeal intensity make you rub shoulders with and 'somehow matter to each other' as formulated by a participant. Cross-cultural encounters, however, mostly relate to the organized activities to which the visitors assume roles as *spectators* and momentary participants. They provide sensuous experiences of difference through the aesthetic and communicative practices of the performing bodies, creating a duality of *expressive* and *affective* space extending out from the performance sites.

Initial observations during the festivals show openness in the encounter with Others resonating with the aim of celebrating difference in the city. Our analysis further showed that consuming difference added to the visitors' identity as cosmopolitan, urban citizens. Openness to Other's products or performances becomes part of what Nava (2002) has analysed as an aesthetic or *affective cosmopolitanism*. The visitors' performance of openness, for example, resembled a kind of *culinary tourism*, where food is a means of learning about other cultures. During our observation, we noticed how eating at the many different food stalls from around the world 'without knowing what you're going to end up eating', as one person says, is not about understanding the particular culture of a chosen cuisine. Rather, as Molz (2007) points out, it is about consuming cultural difference *per se*. Culinary tourism is 'not necessarily about knowing or experiencing another culture, but rather about using food to perform a sense of adventure, curiosity, adaptability, and openness to *any* other culture' (Molz, 2007: 79). In this sense, eating at the food court during the festival demonstrates how urban food consumerism, through its taste for diversity, is able to produce a sense of worldliness and cosmopolitanism (Cook and Crang, 1996; Duruz, 2005; hooks, 2006; Molz, 2007; Cook et al., 2008).

However, these encounters at the festival often take the form of what, we call, sharing hooks' (2006) critical perception, 'eating the Other'. Whatever we say about cultural activities like food, dance or sport, this issue of consuming the Other is prominent. It connects closely to the critical analysis of Orientalism where the exoticization and romanticization of the Other are theorized as a powerful component of Western hegemony. Different observations during the festivals support this.

First, the significance of the issues of consumption and identity connects to the ethnic composition of the participants. While the performers of the activities were of an ethnically mixed composition, the dominant make-up of the visitors was of white, Danish ethnicity. It made the negotiations of identity complex and paradoxical. The emotional attitudes of the visitors were curiosity, openness and enjoyment, but the *consumer position* tended to instantiate distance and to underline differences rather than transcend them. The performance of identity within a 'multicultural' framework can, as argued by Duffy, turn into images of difference of the exotic, especially the exotic East (2005: 684). What she revealed from her study of performance of music and dance at multicultural festivals was that a significant part of the identities performed in the cross-cultural context were situations where the performers were constructed as non-white Australian identities performing for a white Australian audience.

In this case, the multicultural festival becomes a site of the commodification of Otherness. Here, freedom becomes choreographed and limited by the *gaze* and the festival becomes more a site for cultural consumption (see e.g. Jamieson,

2004). The construction of the exotic East becomes a product to consume, and ultimately a process of commodification. The festival becomes a place for consuming the Other:

> The commodification of Otherness has been so successful because it is offered as a new delight, more intense, more satisfying than normal ways of doing and feeling. Within commodity culture, ethnicity becomes spice, seasoning that can liven up the dull dish that is mainstream white culture. (hooks, 2006: 366)

Here, pleasure and enjoyment of encounters with difference comes as a *desire* for the primitive or fantasies about the Other where members of the dominating group and race reaffirm their power over the exotic Other. The Other becomes a product, a caricature that serves as a resource for pleasure – as hooks formulated it: 'The overriding fear is that cultural, ethnic, and racial differences will be continually commodified and offered up as new dishes to enhance the white palate – that the Other will be eaten, consumed, and forgotten' (hooks, 2006: 380).

Secondly, anxiety about *authenticity* in dance performances signals to us a wish to maintain distinct identities expressed through ethnic practices. The festival has four different stages for dance performances and these were generally very well attended. We observed several dance performances, including flamenco, tribal dance, oriental dance and hip-hop dance for children. The performances all finished their show by inviting interested members of the audience to come to the stage and join in. The dance performances and the accompanying music were successful in affecting the audiences. To visitors just passing by, the rhythms would typically draw them into the dance pavilion, quite often occasioning a fairly intense atmosphere with the entanglement of music, dancers and spectators. The observation was that the dance creates what we call an *expressive space*, a lived space performed by body-subjects communicating simultaneously the symbolic, the sensual and the emotional. The bodily movements of the dancers become an extension of their body space and the rhythms cross and re-cross, superimposing themselves upon each other bound to space. This includes the relations among musicians, dancers and spectators, also involving participation on stage. In the rhythmic dance relations, the expressive space merges into an *affective space*, the more passive side of emotional spatiality. Mobile bodies, music and rhythms together create affective space. The material practice of music has the power to draw people into the dance marquee and hold them by the intense atmosphere of the entanglement among music, dancers and spectators. The performances, then, create encounters of shared *emotional experiences*. These are encounters where sensing, feeling and tacit understanding are more prevalent than articulation and representation.

However, it was generally the case that dance associations represented members of different ethnicities, while visitors were predominantly of Danish ethnicity. Visitors were welcoming and appreciative of the wide range of different cultures, but at the same time consuming it as an exotic product of cultural difference. The enthusiasm was particularly prominent when dancers were performing what seemingly were their own 'native' dances. Here, the performers are cast as 'mythical bodies' with certain predisposed abilities to dance (Hensley, 2011) and/or the performance is perceived as being more authentic following the imagination of an authentic Other (Duffy, 2005). What is at stake are typical examples of Orientalism (Said, 1978). Orientalism not only occurred in the encounters between performers and audience, but also within performances. An extreme example was the association performing what they called 'tribal dance'. This particular style, they said, originated in San Francisco as a mix of styles borrowed from belly dance, flamenco, hip-hop and gypsy folk dance. The result is what we can call an 'American Orientalism', with hybrid fantasies and imaginations of the Other, now finding its way to a Danish cultural context as the product of the global cultural politics of Orientalism.

CROSS-CULTURAL COMMUNITY

One of the sport activities that attracted a lot of attention at the Kulturhavn festival was the taekwondo performances. Taekwondo is a bodily practice that unites body and mind and consists of different crushing and fighting techniques originating from various forms of ancient Korean martial arts. Compared to other combat sports like boxing (Wacquant, 2004) and mixed martial arts (Spencer, 2009; Green, 2011), taekwondo is more codified and has a concern for details, analysis and philosophical knowledge where the instructor guides and demonstrates and where progress is clearly marked by visible signs like the colour of the belt.

Most of the performers in the show and the viewers were 'ethnically' mixed, creating a transcultural *space of encounter*. First we observed a small performance including fighting, various crushing techniques and defensive martial arts. The most spectacular part of the show was a specific bodily technique where pieces of wood were crushed into two pieces with the foot, accompanied by a high-pitched battle cry. The show was guided by the instructor and was followed by exercises with different fighting techniques. After the show, people were invited to participate in a workshop trying basic martial art techniques. What had looked fascinating, easy, elegant and controlled turned out to be quite difficult and challenging.

A first observation is that the taekwondo performance creates a *bodily expressive space*. It is a sensuous experience and practice of embodied competencies existing below language and consciousness. The show is performed rhythmically. The actions flow into each other in a dynamic way. All techniques, however, are clearly marked. Martial arts like taekwondo include control over breath, balance, power, coordination, agility and stamina. The show is at one moment infused with silence and concentration – a female spectator watching the show raised her hand to her mouth just as the high sound of the fighting cry *kihap* helped the performer to break a piece of wood. *Kihap* creates the necessary bodily energy and strength, the instructor explains. It consists of 'ki' – life energy, and 'hap' – concentration. In taekwondo, bodily capability plays a crucial role in intimate relation to other bodies.

But taekwondo is more than bodies in motion. It is also about values that have spiritual and *existential* dimensions. As one of the spectators, the mother of a 12-year-old girl who, in her own words, loves taekwondo, explains:

> Taekwondo is both martial arts and a lot of different values like discipline and respect. And you learn to focus on things that are important in life – troubled kids learn to focus, and shy and introverted kids to be more outgoing. It works fine with mixed cultural backgrounds. In taekwondo they are all equal – when they stand there in their tracksuits, the only thing that separates them is the belt. (Female, Danish ethnicity, 35–40 years old)

Taekwondo is more than a sport, the taekwondo teacher explains; it is also a lifestyle, a form of spiritual discipline, group attachment and respect for others. It is a community of practice that unites the corporeal and the spiritual, body and mind, by combining bodily activity with the encouragement of honourable values. The teacher from one of the clubs explains that the members are very mixed, with backgrounds from Korea, the Philippines, Indonesia, Pakistan, Afghanistan and Denmark. It is also a *social community,* he explains, where friendship and values such as respect for difference, are important. Even though Western representations of martial arts are powerfully associated with specifically Asian traditions and the Asian body, the experience was that the taekwondo performance and the participants created a cross-cultural encounter with a focus on sport and community more than on ethnicity and orientalist fantasies about the Other. In the on-the-spot interviews, many of the respondents emphasize the symbolic 'colour blindness' of the sport. Like we saw in Chapter 2 in relation to 're-scaling identities', the colour of the belt was emphasized as a dominant marker of difference as opposed to skin colour, national identity and ethnicity.

GEOPOLITICS AND SECURITIZATION

Arriving at a smaller festival (Taste the World) in Copenhagen, we were taken by surprise. The festival was staged as a celebration of cultural diversity in Copenhagen, with approximately 50,000 visitors and organized with street food, performances such as dance, theatre and music, as well as minority associations and organizations. The initial observation was the *securitization* of the food festival. On arrival, we observed armed police strategically positioned at the entrances and at different important spots at the festival. It was, as Merrifield (2013) puts it, a place of drama. We soon discovered that the reason for the securitization was the controversial Danish Zionists' Association, which had its stand decorated with Israeli flags. Next to the Danish Zionists, the Danish-Moroccan Friendship Association, as a silent demonstration, had a Palestinian flag hanging. The previous year, a similar presence by the Zionists had turned into open conflict followed by demonstrations. The provocation gave rise to happenings at the festival by Palestinian activists, who argued that the Zionists were breaking the principal aim of the festival of cultural diversity and the possibility for the Palestinian people to live in freedom without suppression in the occupied territory. This year, people passing the stand reacted by shaking their heads or making brief critical comments directed towards the presence of the Zionists, but no stronger reactions occurred. In front of the stand, the press was interviewing the Israeli ambassador. He said, amongst other things, that 'I'm being threatened daily. On Facebook. When I'm in Nørrebro. I become threatened. The Jewish school has been attacked, so it had to be evacuated. It has been soiled with graffiti. I worry and fear attack.' In this way, he was trying to draw the conflict into the festival.

This is an example of how geopolitics, war and repression, and the violent conflict between Israel and the Palestinians become incorporated into the encounter and the space of the festival. The festival space becomes mediated and marked by security logics, fear and anticipation of terror. This is an example of what we, with Gregory (2011), call *the everywhere war*, where everything becomes a strategic site of 'permanent' war and where it is not clear where the battle space begins and ends (see also Graham, 2008 and Elden, 2009). This causes the food festival to become more than just performances of world food. The political and ideological aspect becomes visible and dominating in the landscape of the festival – in the way the hegemonic power performs security.

TRANSFORMATIVE SPACES

> As opposed to the official feast, one might say that carnival celebrated temporary liberation from the prevailing truth and from the established order; it marked the suspension of all hierarchical rank, privileges, norms, and prohibitions. Carnival was the true feast of time, the feast of becoming, change, and renewal. It was hostile to all that was immortalized and completed. (Bakhtin, 1984: 10)

Festivals are paradoxical. They can function as socially integrative and simultaneously be the vehicle of protest, opposition and resistance to hegemonic power, exclusion and alienation. This ambiguity within the cultural form of festivals is also what creates the festival's political significance. As an aesthetic force, we suggest that a multicultural festival is positioned between *liberation* and *domination*. Bakhtin, for example, says in the opening chapter of his book on carnivals that he must stress that a striking peculiarity of carnival laughter is 'its indissoluble and essential relation to freedom' (1984: 89). Bakhtin's account of the 'carnivalesque' emphasizes the empowered body that spontaneously dances and breaks down social distance and how that move suspends everyday life's order of power, thus providing space for redefining meaning and social order. The liberating force of festivals relates to the elimination of hierarchical barriers among people, replacing them with more equal relations and feelings of lived community. In a similar way, Lefebvre argues that festivals have transformative potentials:

> Certainly, right from the start, festivals contrasted violently with everyday life, but they were not separate from it. They were like everyday life, but more intense; and the moments of that life – the practical community. (Lefebvre, 1991b: 207)

As an intense, temporary event, a festival creates a space that is in opposition to everyday life, at the same time mirroring it. It can be characterized as a 'heterotopia' (Berg, 2011). For Lefebvre, the festival is an exceptional *moment* in everyday life, attempting to achieve the total realization of a possibility. Like art, says Lefebvre, a festival is related to political action. With the notion of *revolution-as-festival*, the idea is that festival marks both a break in everyday life and a rehabilitation of the everyday. In this way, Lefebvre highlights the role of the aesthetic in social change.

It was noted that the 'Taste the World' festival also offered transformative potentials and liberating forces. Many of the activities at the festival were organized dialogically in the way the different performances actively involved participants. In a 'tent of faith', four religions were present: Christianity, Judaism, Islam and Buddhism. The atmosphere in the tent was bustling with activities. The four representatives were each standing by a high café table inviting people to ask questions on religious issues, thus engaging in a direct religious dialogue with visitors. People were invited to participate in a religion quiz. By being present together in the tent, they created a feeling of interreligious communities. This is an example of a religious encounter that works with the elimination of barriers among people created by different forms of stereotypes and hierarchies, replacing them with more equal and respectful relations. The atmosphere in the tent signalled an attempt to define meaningful concepts of religious identity and belonging, more than violent confrontation and condemnation.

Next to the tent, the Danish Border Association was performing a show and a quiz on immigration and being an ethnic minority in Denmark. People were invited to ask questions of representatives from two different minority groups in Denmark. One representative belonged to the German minority in Denmark and had moved to Copenhagen six months earlier. The other representative was from Somalia and had emigrated to Denmark when he was five years old. The headline of the quiz was: Is it possible to be more than one thing? This addressed the question of transnational and hybrid identity formation. The performance invited spectators to question their prejudices through questions like: 'Who do you think has been in Denmark for the longest time?' or 'Who do you think speaks Danish at home?', thus challenging routine ways of thinking, categories or prejudice based on skin colour. In this way, the performance used real-life examples and personal narratives that could challenge politically produced stereotypes. Many of these prejudices are related to Danish nationalism and fear of the Other that arises in the discussion on national identity and discussions on who should be included and excluded from the imagined community.

ENCOUNTERS WITH AUTHORITIES

The second mode of encounter, encountering authorities, takes a specific form. As encounters between ethnic minorities and authorities, they take an *asymmetrical form* (power relation). Authorities like the police force not only possess legal authority but also coercive power, and citizens are well aware of that fact. As Holmberg (2000) argued, police work and policing can involve three different forms of power: the power of *definition,* that is, the power to define a specific person or act as suspicious and therefore relevant for preliminary control or as something that should pass without further investigation; the power of *procedure,* which is the power to formalize the definition and establish a legal action; and lastly, decisions to resort to the legal use of *force* in order to prevent resistance to either of the other two forms of power. The police mediate between legal rights embedded in abstract, universal citizenship and lived everyday practices. Through their practices of control, urban policing develops a systematic differential economy of legally behaved and outlaw citizens on the basis of visible signs. They constitute what Lipsky (1980) called a 'street-level bureaucracy'.

Fassin (2013) compares law enforcement with a drama – in two ways. First, for individuals undergoing police investigation, it takes the form of a spectacle holding a powerful emotional charge, at the same time as arousing a sense of the seriousness of what is at stake. Secondly, as a methodological point, when they write about it, researchers attempt to reconstitute something of the emotion felt and the seriousness perceived.

On the basis of empirical examples from the everyday urban encounter with the police in Denmark, and encounters between passengers and bus drivers in the city of Copenhagen, we will explore different experiences of encountering authorities (Koefoed et al., 2017). The empirical material referred to here is almost exclusively the result of semi-structured, in-depth interviews about experiences and feelings in concrete encounters: with bus drivers and passengers, police officers from different generations and different divisions of the police, with street workers employed by the municipality and/or clubs to help young people to 'keep out of trouble', and finally with some young people (age 20–23 years) gathered in a focus group in Copenhagen.

PROFILING, STOP-AND-SEARCH

> When I lived in Sweden I was stopped in my car by the police several times. It was really as if they followed me for a long time. And then they asked: 'Where do you live?' and things like that. 'Can you describe your home? And do you sleep in your own bed?' Then I said, 'I'm going home.' 'Well,' the police responded, 'have you forgotten the way to Sweden? It is not the road you are on now.' Then I said, 'Yes, sorry, what's the problem?' 'Is it illegal to drive in Denmark or what?' 'Well,' so they checked and searched. And then after this 20-minute harassment – I would call it so – they said: 'Well, have a nice trip home.' And then on the next corner there's a new police car after me, and they stop: 'Yes?' 'Where are you going? Can we see some ID?' (Hanif, 27)

> 'Why is it always me you stop?' they say. Sometimes they also play the racism card. There are many people with other ethnic backgrounds, who think that we stop them only because they have dark skin. We patrol a lot in Nørrebro and observe a lot of gang crime. Ninety-eight per cent of gang members in Nørrebro have a non-Western ethnic background. But in their defence, they *are* also stopped three, four, five times a day in their cars. Even if they have nothing to do with gangs. But it is difficult to see the difference sometimes. (Police officer, male)

For some, the car is something that extends mobility and it is related to the feeling of freedom, flow and the possibility of moving anytime you want. For others it is turned into something suspicious. In the first extract Hanif explains how he found himself blocked in his mobility several times while driving. With residence in Sweden, Danish citizenship and a Pakistani background he is made a *suspicious body* that has to be held up in order to be checked. In the encounter with the authorities, he is policed and under a kind of surveillance. He is followed and suspected of being 'out of place', in the wrong direction and in the wrong place.

The second extract illustrates that stop-and-search is an everyday technology that, from a police perspective, has to do with *profiling*, meaning that the police pay special attention to specific car models that are usually stopped more than others. The car becomes the symbol of criminality (Sollund, 2006). Car models that are associated with gang members are stopped more frequently than others, especially if the driver has a stereotyped profile (non-Western background). As the respondent explains, 'in their defence, they *are* also stopped three, four, five times a day in their cars. Even if they have nothing to do with gangs.' Another police respondent explains: 'they all call themselves brothers' and 'it is sometimes difficult to distinguish for us' and 'they sometimes look the same'. Thirdly, there is a general awareness among the police respondents that people with immigrant background are overrepresented when it comes to being stopped and searched.

We can summarize the understanding of stop-and-search in three points. First, it is about *bodily appearance*. The 'core client', the hyper-visible group of minorities in the urban landscape, consisting of young men with immigrant backgrounds, is encountered by authorities as a potential 'risk group' and is therefore more often a target for control, even if there are no indicators of criminality (Sollund, 2006).

Secondly, the blocking is part of an *uneven political economy of stopping*. People with immigrant backgrounds are regularly produced as 'body suspects' that have to be checked by being questioned. 'Stop-and-search' is part of a political economy that renders them strangers. The 'stranger' is stopped because he/she is imagined to be the origin of danger, related to trouble and violence. The young men are not strangers in the sense that they are unknown; they are already recognized as such in the moment in which they are faced or seen.

Thirdly, a powerful tool to grasp this is suggested by Sara Ahmed (2006) with her concept of *the phenomenology of being stopped*. Each question, she says, 'is a kind of *stopping device*: you are stopped by being asked the question, just as asking the question requires you to be stopped' (2006: 139). Questions like 'Where do you live?', 'Where are you going?' 'Who are you?' (ID) become a kind of stopping device that slows them down. To stop can have many meanings; e.g. to cease, to cut off, to arrest, to check, to prevent, to close, etc. To be stopped is not only a simple delay; in encounters with authorities, policing involves a differential economy of stopping – some bodies more than others are 'stopped' by being the object of police attention.

ON VIOLENCE

In encounters with authorities, the use of physical violence is legitimated by the state, which has delegated its monopoly on the legitimate use of physical violence to the police and other authorities. What distinguishes the police from other professional groups in society is the legal possibility of using *force* to solve a given problem if they consider it necessary in the given situation. As previously mentioned, 'brown' youngsters have had several experiences of stop-and-search while driving or walking in the city. They explain that physical violence is part of their everyday life and their encounters with the police. A street social worker talks about similar experiences with the police. Once, he was repairing a car together with one of the young boys and suddenly, he tells us, 'there's just a bunch of police officers in there, and they yell and scream, and this little boy that I'm helping, he wants to be a mechanic. He was simply chased out of this car and the police were throwing him up against the wall. They were just standing there and yelling: "Off, off, off." He had a knee up in the back. He's no bigger than this, this little boy here [showing his height with his hand].' From the perspective of the youth, the use of physical violence is experienced as a humiliating act with no rational legitimacy. To be thrown up against the wall and chased out of the car is perceived as unnecessary brutality. It is experienced as unjustified and degrading and considered to go hand in hand with prejudice from the police. As the youth asked: 'What is it that makes the police see me as dangerous?'

Cross-cultural encounters between ethnic minorities and authorities are located between what we call soft and hard encounters. *Soft encounters* with authorities are, in our case, characterized by social policing and its direct contact with people living in vulnerable residential areas. It can be preventive policing that works in close cooperation with social street workers, schools and social services. In a similar way, bus drivers describe how being the person of authority is related to what happens inside the bus. All drivers emphasize the interrelational practice with human difference. As a driver you meet all kinds of people. As a point of reference, the driver also deals with the socially marginalized, urban outcasts, the homeless and the mentally ill. Some drivers describe how they sometimes face extraordinary situations, of conflicts, violence and accidents where they have to act immediately; including driving a man to the hospital, solving violent conflicts, talking to mentally ill individuals. A soft encounter with authorities is characterized by empathy, proximity and dialogue.

Hard encounters, in contrast, relate to the exercise of force and violence. As one police officer explains to us in an interview, 'we are the "clenched fist"'. A hard encounter with authorities is connected to the asymmetric relationship between the police and their clients. It can take the form of *physical violence* that is experienced by young people living in vulnerable neighbourhoods as unnecessary and unjustified brutality. The hard encounter goes hand in hand with a growing *militarization* of equipment and their appearance. Securitization of urban spaces gives priority to special forces in the city and the performance of security through heavy armament. The result is affective power of the police equipment and also of the police themselves. But it also affects the surroundings with a growing production and circulation of fear. This goes hand in hand with systemic violence, which is characterized by violence inherent in the system, legitimated by the state, which has delegated its monopoly on the legitimate use of physical violence to the police. It is related to the political climate and can take the form of institutional racism such as racial profiling, characterized by the use of racial criteria in the decision to perform a stop-and-search.

Thinking about violence, there is a tendency to fixate on what Žižek (2008) calls 'subjective' physical violence – the directly visible form of violence performed by a clearly identifiable agent. We will argue that a differentiated understanding of violence is necessary. This includes *symbolic violence* that works through humiliation and affects dignity, sense of worth and value, and integrity. As formulated by Scheper-Hughes and Bourgois: 'Violence can never be understood solely in terms of its physicality – force, assault, or the infliction of pain – alone. Violence also includes assaults on the personhood, dignity, sense of worth or value of the victim. The social and cultural dimensions of violence are what gives violence its power and meaning' (2004: 1).

> Often a lot of children board the bus, children of foreign origin, and they just walk in without buying a ticket. Then three stops later, a little Dane of eight or nine years gets on and raises his hand to buy a ticket. And it is this that annoys me so much, right? That it is like that. (Dejan, driver)

> In the street, when I meet those of another ethnic origin (it is awful that you don't know what to call them, isn't it?) but people who are different from us [...] What I am fed up with is that they keep on whacking me with their Koran and say 'our Islam'. Because one is supposed to wear a scarf, another one is not [...] And then I'll not call it religion; I'll call it culture. I think that we in Denmark are too afraid of being called racists. It is not that we won't give them their rights. But we shall not just say, 'well, since you are allowed to come and live here, then we will of course also adjust our society to you'. That won't do – it can't be right that we in our primary schools just say 'of course we rebuild the showers because there are two children who are not allowed to shower'. Then they damned well must refrain from showering [...] And the same about their halal meat, it is ridiculous. What about the Danish children? Are they then supposed to eat halal meat? (Police officer, female)

Symbolic violence is embodied in language and its form. It is related to and participates in systemic violence, but it refers more specifically to the violence of language. Language practices are violent insofar as they presuppose and reify relations of domination. For example, the politics of fear and fear of the over-proximity of the Other is handled through a symbolic protective wall that keeps the Other at a proper distance. On a deeper level, language creates a symbolic field of meaning that is external to the things it names. Verbal violence is not the second distortion, but the ultimate human violence that is related to the way we use language to create images, stereotypes, figures and essence that moves us in a particular way. Violence exists in the 'essencing' ability of language. The world is given a partial twist, like a partial colour giving the tone of the whole. It is through Heidegger that Žižek reads this essential violence as something that grounds – or at least opens up the space for – the explosion of physical violence (Žižek, 2008: 60).

Symbolic violence works through the way the Other is encountered – in this case, by *Orientalist* discourse: an imagination of cultural diversity building upon a binary dichotomy between 'us' and 'them'. In the first extract, the driver creates a distinction between the passengers in 'us' and 'them'. The honest Danish child stands in contrast to the cheating and aggressive Other. But it is not an unfamiliar stranger. As Sara Ahmed argues, the stranger is not simply anybody whom we do not know. The stranger is '*some-body* whom we have *already recognised* in the very moment in which they are "seen" or "faced" as a stranger' (2000: 21). The figure of the stranger is 'painfully familiar' in its very strange(r)ness. It has already come too close and been recognized as a body out of place. In the narrative of the police, we meet it most distinctly in the phrase telling that we are dealing with 'people that are different from us'. This is exactly what Billig (1995) is talking about when he draws our attention to 'the banality' of the everyday construction of national identity through a routinized use of *deictic* markers – that is, small unnoticed words gaining their meaning through the context in which they are used; for example, 'we', 'us', 'here' and 'this'. These 'trivial' words help to naturalize our affiliation to the national space and consequently to alienate the 'others'.

Orientalism also operates through stereotyping the Others and imagining them as fixed in their 'original' culture – 'then I'll not call it religion; I'll call it culture'. At the same time, however, it requires assimilation to 'Danish' culture. Minorities are supposed to drop inappropriate norms and values and conform to 'Danish' culture. It would be unreasonable to expect 'us' to try to understand, let alone accommodate, 'their' habits. An interesting point is to see how much examples displayed difference and 'strangeness' are by way of everyday, banal and bodily phenomena such as dress ('one is supposed to wear a scarf, another one is not supposed to wear a scarf'), showers ('Of course we rebuild the showers because there are two children who are not allowed to shower') and food ('What about the Danish children? Are they then supposed to eat halal meat?'). Therefore, it might be a good idea, as we have argued, in addition to Said's textualist perspective, to talk about a practical orientalism (see also Simonsen, 2005b; Haldrup et al., 2006). It can capture how hegemonic ideas translate into everyday practices and infiltrate the 'banal' spaces of ordinary life, including everyday sociality and sensual experience.

> We always know when we meet some of these narrow-minded cops. I experienced it during the gang war, where my friend and I were pulled aside because they thought we had thrown away a firearm. We were placed on a bench and his dog was next to me. Then, just to provoke me, he said 'sit Allah' to the dog. When they didn't find anything on us, they said that we could go. We said, 'Can you move the dog', and they just responded, 'Does it scare you?' (Young people)

In this extract, the respondents explain how symbolic violence works through humiliation and stereotypes. First, by *naming* the dog Allah, the police affect the dignity, sense of worth and value, and integrity of the young people. The processes of naming and the creation of images are violent here because they are related to domination and control. Secondly, it exemplifies the feeling of *powerlessness*. Confronted with a dog called Allah, they are unable to move. Thirdly, symbolic violence is experienced in this case as *cruelty,* which adds another dimension to our understanding of violence.

But it also applies the other way around. The police officers report that they increasingly feel in danger or under threat of the use of physical violence, especially during gang wars. And we do also see discrimination directed towards the authorities, when the authority is a person whose body is marked as different by the surroundings, as one police officer explains:

> Actually, I have tried it both ways. One was a 'Danish-Dane' we stopped, who would not talk to me because of the wrong colour of my skin. He said that he wouldn't talk to me because he didn't like foreigners. He would only talk to my colleague. Reversed, the other one was something ethnic other than Danish. It was some gang-related thing, where I arrested one of them. He told me that I was a traitor and that he wouldn't talk to me. (Police officer)

The second case is different. Here a traitor perspectives appears supposing that 'we foreigners' should stick together as a group. The respondent explains that he does not dwell on it much. But the stories came up as the most challenging encounters experienced while practising his job. A bus driver of immigrant background recounts:

> There was this situation. It was two elderly, retired people – the man was in the front and he refused to give me the ticket. I asked him to see the ticket but he replied that he would not show his card to foreigners. Despite the fact that I was working, and the work I do is legal. I am not mad. You drive people around the city – you drive them to work, shopping and home again. It is good, but sometimes there can also be bad experiences. (Nasib, driver)

For the driver, the problem is related to being categorized as a stranger and met as a person that is 'out-of-place' and not at home. The driver tells us that is a bad experience and that he is sometimes called 'Paki'; this makes him the Other and reproduces estranging geographical imaginations.

TERRITORIAL STIGMATIZATION

A common issue is related to discrimination based on territory. Authorities often speak in terms of specific areas or territories:

> Sometimes when my friends call me and ask me what I am doing I say: 'I am right here, Fallujah, Kirkuk or Islamabad'. Do you understand? It is a difficult area, it really is. (Dejan, driver)

> All the problems start at Hulgårds Plads. I am not a racist but they are many and they behave badly. The problem with foreigners is that they don't smile […] We have a lot of problems with passengers who wear a burqa. We can't inspect them and they create a lot of trouble. (Susanne, driver)

Especially in these 'ghettos'. They just know each other, then it just becomes part of living in [housing estate], then you are a criminal. Because that is almost what everybody else is. (Police officer, male)

In the first two extracts, the drivers represent the multicultural neighbourhood Nørrebro as a strange place outside the borders of civilization – it is an 'imaginative geography' that connects geo-political imaginations of the Other to specific parts of Copenhagen. In the eyes of Susanne, the area is characterized and dominated by strangers who do not smile, behave badly and are impossible to control. The experience takes the form of 'strange encounters', and of things that threaten them as a person of authority.

These areas – the 'ghettos' that the police officer speaks of – are the same ones that the state continuously records on a so-called 'ghetto list' of problematic residential areas, based on a range of statistical measures – including ethnicity (see also Chapter 4). This is best understood through what Waquant (2008), combining Bourdieu's concept of symbolic power with Goffman's stigma, calls *territorial stigmatization,* illustrating how derogatory representation attaches to both places and residents.

EVERYDAY ENCOUNTERS

The third mode of encounter, everyday encounters, can take the form of accidental meetings in the city's streets, parks or public transport. By way of empirical examples, we here use bus 5A, which forms a central part of the urban mobility in Copenhagen (Koefoed et al., 2017). It is the busiest route in the Nordic countries both loved and hated among bus drivers, who have named it 'the suicidal' route. The bus transports all kinds of people and connects many different places in the city. The empirical work combines observations, participation and interviews. We conducted the ethnographic fieldwork and observations between 2014 and 2015, spending around 80 hours on the bus at different times of day and night. We held on-the-spot interviews and informal conversations with passengers either on the move or waiting for the bus and talks with drivers taking a break. Finally, we complemented the observations with qualitative in-depth interviews with selected bus drivers and passengers.

As a specific icon of public space, the bus is composite, contradictory and heterogeneous, involving multiple practices that are performed bodily and are emotionally charged. In this case, it makes sense of the meetings that take place in the socio-material site of the bus. This centres the question of the bus as *public* space. Public space is a disputed concept (see, for example, Fyfe, 1998; Mitchell, 2003; Staeheli and Mitchell, 2007). A broad definition could be that 'public space is that space where "the public" is formed and thus social and cultural rules governing public behaviour predominate' (Mitchell and Staeheli, 2009: 511). Seen from this angle, the bus as public space is a particular space.

Not only is it a mobile space, but it is also simultaneously a 'public' space and a highly controlled space. It is controlled by the formal authority of bus drivers, and practices on the bus are regulated through both formal and informal rules of conduct. The materiality of the bus's interior and seating regulates the opportunities of spatial practice.

We consider the urban bus as an important site of everyday intercultural encounter in the city (O.B. Jensen, 2009; Wilson, 2011). To travel by bus is not simply transport from one place to another. Public transport is part of everyday life in the city and, for many, a necessary banal aspect of everyday routine. While travelling, we become part of a mobile collective. Mobility *with* others therefore involves relational practices – in bus travel, intense embodied encounters with others are often unavoidable.

An evolving theme in mobility research is the relational practice of being mobile with others (Sheller, 2004; Laurier et al., 2008; Löfgren, 2008; Adey and Bissell, 2010; Bissell, 2010; Swanton, 2010; Adey et al., 2012; Jensen, 2012). In a world where international migration flows are increasingly intertwined with the flows of urban everyday commuting, everyday spaces such as the bus to work can become a meeting place for global difference. This makes public transport particularly interesting as a mediator of subjects meeting with ethnic diversity and imagined Others. Journeys by public transport create spaces in which strangers interact in much tighter spaces than can be found elsewhere (O.B. Jensen, 2009, 2010; Wilson, 2010). Using public transport requires a number of practical skills. From mastering route planning and timetables (O.B. Jensen, 2006), to making travel time effective by transforming the train into a mobile office (Löfgren, 2008), to mastering sleep techniques on the move (O.B. Jensen, 2006; H.L. Jensen, 2012). Navigating in the dense, shared space of public transport puts the passenger in a situation of constant choice. Here we argue for the usefulness of the notion of *negotiation in motion* to capture the social interaction made in a mobile space of norms, values and power. Some of these ways of encountering our 'mobile other' may be linked to an already existing repertoire of actions, mobile negotiation techniques and mobile interaction tactics (O.B. Jensen, 2010: 13). The dense spatial economy of a bus ride makes one aware of one's body and the intensity of corporeal relation. This makes the mobile negotiation an embodied and situated practice. Even though verbal communication is limited, communication is still occurring, through gazes and the spatial organization of bodies (Bissell, 2010: 271).

Mobile encounters show certain characteristics. First, the mobile space of the bus can be seen as an extreme case of the intensity of meetings that characterizes urban life. Travelling by bus involves a particular 'throwntogetherness' (Massey, 2005), and encounters with others are often very intense. There is a certain proximity with others, bodies touch bodies and become exposed to others, and there is an intensification of experiences and an over-stimulation of several senses. Therefore, travelling by bus involves specific embodied skills

related to what we can call *tactics of placement*. There is an ongoing negotiation over space that takes place with bodily signals and through either
avoidance or tolerance. Seats are often selected according to sameness of
gender, age and ethnicity (safe seat). As one of the respondents observes, there
is a certain sort of grouping and social order in the bus. Often negotiation
of space is unproblematic without spoken communication, but sometimes
it develops into conflicts, when, for example, the essential grammar of the
situation is challenged.

Secondly, encounters that occur on the bus are extraordinarily ephemeral.
There is a constant stream and flow of passengers that makes encounters transi-
tory, but that also gives occasion for 'temporary congregations' (O.B. Jensen,
2010) exchanging experiences within the urban environment.

Thirdly, and related to the first two characteristics, encounters are charged
with emotions, where bodies in movement create an expressive space of emotional performance. Finding a proper seat and meeting the Other face to face and
body to body involve emotional experiences that also affect others. Discomfort,
irritation and occasionally anger or aggression pop up.

BETWEEN 'THE LITTLE RACISM' AND 'HABITUAL MULTICULTURALISM'

As a cross-cultural meeting place, bus 5A appears as a public space stretched out
in the intersection between what we call *habitual multiculturalism* and different
modes of racialization.

The bus connects very different parts of Copenhagen. It is the experience of
this fact that makes many passengers tell us that they are used to diversity:

> I don't think much about it [...] I believe that in this part of the city you
> are more or less merged, there is not so much – nobody frowns at anybody,
> or anything at all. (Lis, passenger)

> Maybe it is because it is the Nørrebro bus. You know that the spectrum is
> broad and that you have to be more open-minded. I believe that because
> Nørrebro has this diversity, you are prepared when you board the bus. You
> are prepared to meet somebody that you are not exactly ready to meet.
> (Michael, passenger)

> There are quite a lot of young guys, and they are really mixed when it
> comes to ethnicity. It is a meeting place for them. They meet, share some
> info and then they part again. It is really *a rolling marketplace* sometimes.
> (Michael, passenger)

For these people, living with diversity has become a routine. They expect the
unexpected. They do not celebrate difference; it is just a fact of life. The notion
of habitual multiculturalism is used to understand this mode of coexistence in
which living with diversity has become a fact, giving rise to neither positive nor

negative reactions. Several passengers connected this feeling to the specific route 5A running through one of the most multicultural parts of Copenhagen. Diversity is expected and passengers are prepared for the unexpected. The encounter with strangers on the bus is more or less taken for granted – one passenger in this connection characterizes the bus as a 'rolling marketplace'. The bus becomes a mobile place formed by moments of encounter between many different ethnicities. These passengers are close to performing what Tonkiss (2003: 300) calls an 'ethics of indifference' where 'differences go unremarked because unremarkable, where otherness is ordinary, where a logic of anonymity displaces one of visibility'. They accept a mutual strangeness that makes the strange Other a familiar Other. That is why we prefer the concept of habitual multiculturalism here. We can follow Goffman (1963) and Simmel (1950a, [1903]) – and many current writers on mobility – by arguing that these attitudes of *civil inattention* and *indifference* are, in fact, a basic form of urban sociality that allows people to coexist with all the largely unknown others. Indifference is one way in which difference can be *lived* in everyday social spaces. Also, the intensity of contact in the space of the bus opens up pre-personal emotional registers spanning from the performative to the passive end.

It can be characterized as an urban cosmopolitan competence, involving an ability to manoeuvre in an urban 'globalized' landscape – a 'lived multiculturalism', coupled with transcultural relations performed in everyday life situations (Simonsen, 2008b; Koefoed and Simonsen, 2011). Some of the bus drivers even indicate that this is the pleasure of driving bus 5A. Its diversity and cosmopolitan character render the tour an experience felt as driving through continents 'just like a garden with different flowers having all kinds of colours'.

But encounters on the bus also involve specific *techniques of differentiation*. Likeness and difference are directly produced through embodied encounters on the bus. They involve particular forms of recognition of some bodies as strangers or bodies out of place and also emotions like disgust and fear. Everyday cultural racism takes the form of processes of racialization producing unknown Others as strangers. These processes occur both between passengers and in the meeting between passengers and drivers. Between passengers, it often takes the form of what we have called *the little racism*. It primarily takes place in the form of bodily gestures: the specific gaze, the avoiding touch, moves of avoidance expressing distancing, gripping your bag tighter, etc. These are all gestures that generate the feeling of being an Other, producing what Fanon (1967) describes as a third-person consciousness. But it also takes more outspoken forms, as we saw in relation to the question of language or through outspoken reactions to visual racialized markers like the headscarf.

> Even if you don't wear burqa, you get such a look from time to time […] There was this elderly man; he didn't approve of Muslims and scarves and such. He had a whole lot to say. I overheard the discussion, and then I left the bus. (Sufia, passenger)

> I can see that I actually do it a bit myself. When a group of young immigrants gets on the bus, then I strengthen my hold on my backpack or my bag. (Charlotte, passenger)

While such incidents are not uncommon, the dominant picture of the bus more often involves what we could call 'the little racism'. A Pakistani immigrant describes this to us with a strong use of body language. He looks askance and moves away a bit from an imagined person next to him, wrinkles up his nose and says, 'Ashh', in this way performing distanciation. Another respondent confirms this impression by telling us: 'You can feel it on the Danes, in particular when it is crowded.' She has difficulties finding words but talks about discomfort and anger.

A much-disputed racialized marker is the headscarf. In the public debate in Denmark – as all over Europe – there has been an obsession with Muslim dress. The hijab, niqab and burqa have been some of the most controversial issues in relation to religious pluralism. The most common framing of the debate is the victimization frame in which Muslim women are represented as oppressed by their community and in need of liberation (Andreassen and Lettinga, 2012). In these encounters, Sufia has been exposed to two different techniques of estrangement, one visual and one verbal. Both are charged with emotions and both mark out boundaries and redefine her body as a body 'out-of-place'. Sufia tries to act untouched, but ends up leaving the bus.

Sometimes it pops up in rather undisguised forms – for instance, with regard to language. A typical example refers to an episode where two women of Pakistani origin were speaking Urdu together. A woman seated close by became very angry and yelled at them: 'You are in Denmark; you must speak Danish together,' in this way performing a cultural hegemony.

What is at stake here is a sensing of an affective space, the more passive side of emotional experience, where emotions such as fear, discomfort, anger and disgust are circulating in the intense atmosphere of the crowded bus. This affective space is also at work in the background when young boys, asked about visions for the future, elaborate a utopia of a bus without racism (Bladt, 2013).

In this sense, the urban bus is a place for coexistence and potential intercultural dialogue, but at the same time still haunted by racialization, stigmatization and intolerance.

Therefore we find a double perspective on encounters absolutely necessary. On the one hand, some urban scholars speak of a cosmopolitan hope in which encounters are believed to give rise to hybrid cultures and dialogue with creative potential (Sandercock, 2003; Binnie et al., 2006). On the other hand, postcolonial thinking emphasizes the powerful production of otherness, cultural racism and stigmatization of 'foreigners' (e.g. Ahmed, 2000). It is in the interspace of this metropolitan paradox between 'cosmopolitan hope' and 'postcolonial melancholia' (Gilroy, 2006) that we locate the different modes of encounter, seeing encounters in public space as possible sites of both intercultural dialogue and racist intolerance.

NOTE

1. The chapter is based on the research project 'Paradoxical spaces: Cross-cultural encounters in public space'. This project focuses on concrete encounters in public spaces and how they are performed. In the study we explores how the complexity of cultural difference is experienced and practised in different public spaces in Copenhagen. Through different cases we focused on three different modes of encounters (collective planned encounters, encounters with authorities and everyday encounters). The aim was to understand both how 'the stranger' is encountered and what these meetings can tell us about possibilities for and limitations on coexistence in the city.

$$\left(\begin{array}{c}4\end{array}\right)$$

Urban Perspectives

The *urban* cannot be defined either as attached to a material morphology (on the ground, in the practico-material), or as being able to detach itself from it. It is not an intemporal essence, nor a system among other systems or above other systems. It is a mental and social form, that of simultaneity, of gathering, of convergence, of encounter (or rather encounters). It is a *quality* born from quantities (spaces, objects, products). It is a *difference*, or rather, an ensemble of differences. (Lefebvre, 1996a: 131)

THE FLESH OF THE URBAN

Our starting point for revisiting the urban is Merleau-Ponty's concept of flesh, as developed in his unfinished work *The Visible and the Invisible* (1968). As we saw in Chapter 2, Merleau-Ponty saw the flesh as an element of all being, human as well as non-human. The ambiguity, indeterminacy and chiasmatic reversibility described with the concept can meaningfully be conveyed to the dynamic and turbulent materiality of urban existence. As we emphasized earlier, 'the flesh' should not be understood as identical to the flesh of our body. It is a broader concept within which the human body is only one part. Merleau-Ponty turned to the notion of 'element' when describing it, referring to 'a *general thing*, midway between the spatio-temporal individual and the idea, a sort of incarnate principle that brings a style of being wherever there is a fragment of being' (1968: 139). On the one hand, the flesh stylizes, by conditioning an ongoing differentiation of styles of life – thus implying difference in many forms (class, race, gender, sexuality etc.). On the other hand, the flesh also unifies; it weaves together bodies, meanings, movements, materialities and situations into a dynamic texture which is continually being reworked, made and unmade. The city itself is an excellent example of such a texture, combining visible materiality and invisible conditioning and imagination. The urban is, as Lefebvre wrote, *an ensemble of differences*, of differences among cities resulting from history or division of labour, and of differences among ways of inhabiting the city, that is, of plurality, coexistence and simultaneity in urban patterns, of styles of living urban life.

In order to come to terms with this differentiation of urban life we need to overcome a whole range of 'violent binaries' (Weiss, 2008; see also Williams, 1975). The root of them all is the classic Cartesian mind/body dualism, the transcendence of which was the very starting point for Merleau-Ponty's whole project. Even if this dualism has been challenged from many sides, it has been influential by being translated into other binaries. Exposed by critical analyses by feminist theories and critical race theories, it has had both gendered and racialized connotations and has been (and still is) used in sexist and racist political agendas. Furthermore, the distinction is reflected in those of nature/culture, pure/polluting and rural/urban as romantic invocations of purity and peacefulness of nature versus the pollution and violence of urban existence. It is about how 'the violence of the city, conceived of as a wholly human creation, has often been contrasted with the peacefulness of the natural, that is, non-human world' (Weiss, 2008: 130). While this distinction still exists in public 'common sense' and is heavily politicized, although with variations of the content of the two sides, it has been strongly challenged in academia. A range of critical urbanists argue that old distinctions such as the one between city and countryside are redundant conceptions that require an upgrade and a rethink (Lefebvre, 2003; Merrifield, 2013, 2014; Brenner and Schmid, 2015). A significant example is Amin and Thrift (2002) who, from a posthumanist ontology engage with the urban question, not as a grounded materiality, but as a conjunction of multiple pathways along which the complex materialities of the urban might be assembled. From the point of view of our critical phenomenology, however, the posthumanist levelling of the human and the non-human will be replaced by an urban flesh as a 'unity composed of difference':

> The flesh hold seers and the visible together (they are of the same flesh), while still respecting their difference and keeping them apart (as, respectively, the flesh of the body and the flesh of the world). (Evans, 2008: 191)

From that perspective, the urban should be approached through the body's chiasmatic, interdependent relationship to its environment. One widely cited source introducing this discussion is Elisabeth Grosz's essay 'Bodies-Cities', in which she (inspired by Gilles Deleuze) explores the dynamic interfaces that link bodies with the places they inhabit – in this case, the city.

On the one hand, her main argument is that '[t]he city in its particular geographical, architectural, and municipal arrangements is one particular ingredient in the social constitution of the body. [...] the form, structure, and norms of the city seep into and affect all the other elements that go into the constitution of corporeality' (Grosz, 1995: 108), and she supports this view with a range of different examples. She considers how the material form of the city affects how the subject sees others as well as its understanding of and affiliation to space. This is done with reference to different forms of lived spatiality (understood in a material way) including factors of a very general kind such as the verticality of the city as opposed to the horizontality of the landscape, down to specific factors such as domestic architecture and their effects on our lived space and our corporeal alignments, comportment and orientations. She also considers more biological effects by discussing how the terrain of the city through everyday activities affects the body's corporeal exertion, its muscular structure and its nutritional context and generally provides elementary support and sustenance of the body. Finally, she considers how the city becomes the site for the body's cultural consumption, a place where the body is inscribed by, formed, transformed, contested and reformed by images, representational systems, the mass media and the arts. On the other hand, she states, that 'the body (as cultural product) transforms, reinscribes the urban landscape according to its changing (demographic) needs, extending the limits of the city ever towards the countryside that borders it' (Grosz, 1995: 108).

Even if Grosz, in this essay, talks about the constitutive and mutually defining relations between corporeality and the metropolis and about a two-way linkage defined as an interface, her emphasis on the power of the city to shape our corporeality is the stronger one and tends to give precedence to this side of the body/city pair. She seems to moderate this tendency in a later publication, *Architecture from the Outside,* where she presents the relation as both more complex and more open and indeterminate. It depends on the types of bodies (racial, ethnic, class, gendered) and the types of cities, and it is 'immensely complicated through various relations of intrication, specification, interpolation, and inscription that produce "identities" for both cities in their particularity and populations in their heterogeneity' (2001: 50). This indeterminacy, she claims, also opens up a space of the 'in-between' – a space of possibility that can be used creatively to promote a new and different future.

In order to amend the problem that we saw in Grosz, it is worth going back to the phenomenological roots. Both Heidegger and Merleau-Ponty encourage us to rethink the body's creative relationship to its immediate environment. Heidegger, in his classic essay 'Building, dwelling, thinking', maintains that when inhabiting the world we 'attain to dwelling only by means of building. The latter, building, has the former, dwelling, as its goal' (1997: 100). To Merleau-Ponty, the corporeal body, as indicated earlier, is in itself a lived spatiality that actively spatializes through its movements, activities and gestures – thus participating in the 'flesh of the world' and reconfiguring its immediate environment. Drawing on both of them, Edward Casey discusses how the body opens out onto a 'place-world'.[1] He endorses the chiasmatic relationship between alterations in the built environment and self-alteration by stating: 'In creating built places, we transform not only the local landscape but ourselves as subjects: body-subjects become fabricating agents' (1993: 111) – in this way paraphrasing both Merleau-Ponty and Lefebvre. In a more detailed discussion of the relationship, he concludes that built places are an extension of the bodies: 'places built for residing are rather an enlargement of our already existing embodiment into *an entire life-world of dwelling*' (1993: 120). This understanding should, however, be supplemented by what we (with Sara Ahmed) wrote in Chapter 2 about the differentiation and racialization of the habitability of space. Spaces take shape by being oriented around some bodies more than others. Bodies extend themselves into the world through the way in which they are oriented towards objects and others. But the extension of some bodies can work as constraints or inhibitions to others, restrict their reach into the world and make them feel out-of-place. This leaves us with an understanding of the flesh of the urban as an 'ensemble of differences', gathering human and non-human elements, multiple encounters between bodies that are contingent upon each other, and different spatialities and temporalities circulating in concordance or in conflict.

An additive perspective here is Henri Lefebvre's outline of what he saw as a new mode of social analysis: *rhythmanalysis* (Lefebvre, 2004; see also Simonsen, 2005a; Meyer, 2008; Edensor, 2010). It can be described as a kind of phenomenological-hermeneutic analysis of the relationships among the body, its rhythms and its surrounding space. Briefly, two qualities of rhythmanalysis should be highlighted. First, it accentuates the centrality of the body to social understanding. It is the point of collision between the cyclical, rhythmic nature of the lived body and the linear, repetitive time of the technical and the social world, and it accentuates the flows and networks of moving bodies without presupposing singular models of temporality and spatiality. Secondly, rhythmanalysis underlines the inseparability of space and time. Rhythms can be defined as movements and differences in repetition, as the interweaving of concrete times but always also implying a relation of time to space and place. Lefebvre talks about localized time or temporalized place to underline the spatio-temporal reality of rhythms and their participation in the production of space. Rhythmanalysis is an unfinished project from Lefebvre's hand, but enables the development of alternative methodologies in order to grasp the more opaque sides of social life (see Edensor, 2010).

Lefebvre himself, in a couple of essays, explores the rhythms of the city – from flows of bodies, spectacles and sounds to political centrality, and struggles between homogeneity and diversity (parts of them are translated in Lefebvre, 1996b). The essay titled 'Seen from the window' is both a very personal and an epistemological exposition. In a phenomenological vision Lefebvre invites the reader to follow him looking out of the windows of his apartment in the centre of Paris – a position not only enabling sights but also leading to insights. He observes people passing by in variations of a daily cycle, in a flood of noise and sounds, exposed at the same time to the stop–start rhythms of traffic and their own bodily rhythms. In the other one, 'Rhythmanalysis of Mediterranean cities'

(Lefebvre and Regulier, 1996) they explore the particularity of the rhythms of Mediterranean cities, from the relationship to the movements of the sea and the climate, the intensity of urban life, differences between private and public spheres, rituals (religious, festive, political) punctuating daily life, resistance emanating from the everyday lived rhythms, to more generally the conflict between homogeneity and diversity – that is, conflicts between rhythms imposed by political and economic centrality and the polyrhythms of different cultures, languages and sexualities. In this way, the original elements of repetition and the cyclical/linear opposition are overlaid by circulations in different (temporal and spatial) scales.

However, it is important to maintain, as touched on above, that cities are not only material, they are imaginary as well; it is the chiasmatic intertwining of the material and the imaginative, the visible and the invisible, that helps to construct both limits and possibilities of urban experience. Merleau-Ponty considered 'operative language', not understood as systems of relations between signs and meanings but as a language of life and action, a central articulation of being (Merleau-Ponty, 1968). Imageries in this sense are not simply constructions of mental images; they are a proliferation of generating axes and schemes for visibility emerging from carnal experiences. Another interesting contribution emphasizing this duality comes from Collins (2010), who pursues his understanding of the city by combining the thinking of Merleau-Ponty with that of Chantal Mouffe on discourse and agonistic pluralism. However the take on language in our understanding, is less on discourse, and more on spoken language as a practice. A fruitful way to concretize the concurrence is the one suggested by de Certeau (1998) when considering two 'networks' of decisive elements in people's active construction of the city: *gestures* and *narratives*. Both can be characterized as chains of *operations* done on and with the environment. In two distinct modes, one practical and the other linguistic, gestures and narratives manipulate objects, displace them and modify both their distribution and their uses. In the following, we will try to establish a framework for approaching the everyday construction of the urban by considering, in turn, what we call 'the embodied city' and 'the narrative city' (see also Simonsen, 2005b).

THE EMBODIED CITY/IES

The display of the embodied city should be seen in continuation of the understanding of bodies and embodiment as it is developed in Chapter 2, in particular regarding the spatiality and temporality of the body. Primarily with the help of Merleau-Ponty and Lefebvre, an indispensable relationship between bodily practice and time–space is suggested. The connection of 'body-subjects' with space can never be one of simple location: it is an active engagement with the surrounding world involving a production of meaning. The social body can then be seen as 'the geography closest in' – as a constitutive social spatiality reaching out towards other socio-spatial scales from local, urban and regional configurations to national and supra-national/global connections. In order to specify this connection on the urban scale, we can again turn to de Certeau (1984), this time to his account of the constructiveness of moving bodies through the metaphor of 'walking in the city'.

What de Certeau is talking about here are urban practitioners following urban pathways, but at the same time producing their own stories, shaped out of fragments of trajectories and alterations of space. It is a process in which walking in the streets mobilizes other subtle, stubborn, embodied and even resistant meanings. With reference to Merleau-Ponty he writes:

> These practices of space refer to a specific form of *operations* ('ways of operating'), to 'another spatiality' (an 'anthropological', poetic and mythic experience of space), and to an *opaque and blind* mobility characteristic of the bustling city. A *migrational*, or metaphorical, city thus slips into the clear text of the planned and readable city. (de Certeau, 1984: 93)

Walking in the city, then, is one of those everyday practices or 'ways of operating' that make up the game of ordinary people, of 'the others', when they move along in a creative and tactical way in a network of already established forces and representations. It is a spatial practice using and performing the urban texture in a way that secretly influences the determining conditions of urban life. It is a *lived space* – a space of disquieting familiarity with the city. Here, the affinity with both Merleau-Ponty and Lefebvre becomes suggestive.

With inspiration from theories of ordinary language use, walking in the city is dealt with as a speech act. The act of walking, de Certeau argues, is to the urban system what the speech act is to language or to the statements uttered. Walking is a space of 'enunciation', in this sense having a triple function: it is a process of *appropriation* of the urban topographical system; it is a spatial *realization* or acting-out of place; and it implies *relations* among differentiated positions, that is, among pragmatic 'contracts' in the form of movements (or moves in relation to someone).

Altogether, this means that walking practices cannot be seen only as simple movements; rather, they spatialize. Their intertwined parts give their shape to spaces. They weave places together, thus creating a diversity of subsystems whose existence in some sense makes up the city. Different characteristics of use are at work in this process. While a pre-given spatial order can organize an ensemble of possibilities and prohibitions, the walkers actualizes some of these possibilities. They make them exist as well as emerge. But they also move them about and invent others, since the improvisation of walking privileges transforms or abandons spatial elements. Thus, the walkers creates discreteness, whether by making choices among the signifiers of the spatial 'language' or by displacing them through the use of them. In this realization and appropriation of space, the walkers also constitute a here and a there; they constitute a location and in relation to that location of an 'other', thus establishing a conjunctive and disjunctive articulation of places. The whole 'rhetoric of walking' has a phatic aspect; through contacts in meetings, followings, networks etc., it creates a fluid and mobile organicity in the city.

Even if de Certeau in this way produces an understanding of urban life from 'closest in', his contribution is not a voluntarist micro-sociology (see also Crang, 2000). His moving bodies are set against a monolithic vision of power – against imaginary totalizations produced by the eye. One of these is the panoptic and strategic discourse in planning and social theory which rationalizes the city and organizes it by speculative and classificatory operations. Another is the imaginary discourse of media and commerce (de Certeau, 1997). They create cities that are 'imaginary museums' and, as such, form counterpoints to cities at work. These imaginary entities are characterized by a growing eroticization, by a celebration of the body and the senses. But it is a fragmented body, categorized by virtue of an analytical dissection, cut into successive sites of eroticization. In this context, de Certeau even talks about speech and signification as 'denaturing' acts.

Similar arguments appear from other authors. For example, in Lefebvre (1991a) when he is linking the history of the body with the history of space and puts forward an understanding of the development of modernity and the modern city as a *decorporealization* of space, to use Gregory's (1994) term. This process is based on a logic of visualization and of metaphorization; living bodies, the bodies of 'users' are caught up, not only in the toils of parcellized space, but also in the work of images, signs and symbols. These bodies are transferred and emptied out via the eyes – a process that is both abstract and visual. It is embodied in a 'will' to power and, metaphorically, an abstract space symbolizing distance, private property and violence. Another example comes from Richard Sennett, who, in the book *Flesh and Stone,* wrote what he calls 'a history of the city told through people's bodily experience' (1994: 15). With reference to German critical theory represented by Theodor Adorno and Herbert Marcuse, he argues that, through the dominance of vision and the experience of travelling at speed, modern societies have enforced a sense of disconnection from space eroding the body-subject's sensitivity to other human beings.

As we have seen, however, the moving body can serve as a critical figure as well. It is not possible totally to reduce the body or the practico-sensory realm to abstract space. The body takes its revenge – or at least calls for revenge – for example, in leisure space. It seeks to make itself known, to gain recognition as 'generative', thus appropriating or shaping urban space through everyday life, struggle (Lefebvre) or tactics (de Certeau). One problem in these formulations is the flavour of authenticity they tend to ascribe to the body and everyday life. However, by using the conception of the social body put forward above, we do believe that it is possible to avoid romanticizing the body and to understand the role of moving bodies in the constitution of and conflict over urban space as a dynamic, open-ended process.

The above considerations actualize the question of the more *sensuous* body–matter relation – or, more precisely, the sensuous and emotional relationship between the body-subject and its (built) environment. For us, an obvious place to start to explore this issue is from the theory of emotion developed in Chapter 2 and its concepts of 'expressive space' and 'affective space'. However, throughout the 2000s and 2010s a (cross-disciplinary) discussion introducing a specific concept for this relation has emerged; that of the concept of *atmosphere* (McCormack, 2006; Anderson, 2009, 2014; Thibaud, 2011; Edensor, 2012; Ingold, 2012; Griffero, 2014; Hasse 2014, 2016; Bille, 2015; Bille and Sørensen, 2016). As a starting point, this literature put the strongest emphasis on the affective space, that is, the quality of atmospheres as affective interfaces of people and things, rooms, cities, landscapes, etc. The common inspiration for most proponents of the concept is the German philosopher Gernot Böhme, who has worked for quite a while with architecture. Like Merleau-Ponty, Böhme emphasizes perception, and he offers this compelling description of the concept:

> [A]tmospheres are neither something objective, that is, qualities possessed by things, and yet they are something thing-like, belonging to the thing in that things articulate their presence through qualities – conceived as ecstasies. Nor are atmospheres something subjective, for example determinations of a psychic state. And yet they are subjectlike, belong to subjects in that they are sensed in bodily presence by human beings and this sensing is at the same time a bodily state of being of subjects in space. (Böhme, 1993: 122)

Atmosphere, then, has an ontological status as a concept of *in-betweenness* of subject and object in which sensory experience and emotion are central. Atmospheres are the perceived quality of situations, made up by the constellation of people and things. They are 'spheres of the presence of something, their reality of space' (Böhme, 1993, 121–2). Working on atmospheres, then, means 'addressing not simply "experience", but rather the co-existence of embodied experience and the material environment' (Bille et al., 2015: 36).[2] Most authors dealing with the concept of atmosphere characterize it with terms such as 'vagueness', 'indeterminacy', 'haziness' or 'fuzziness'. This has not, however, been a hindrance to empirical studies on atmospheres, not least in urban environments. Some examples are: Kazig (2008) on what he calls different typical urban squares; Edensor (2012) on illuminated atmospheres in Blackpool; Hasse (2016) on the atmosphere of places normally considered aesthetically unremarkable such as streets, bridges, tunnels and petrol stations; and Thibaud (2015) more generally on different 'ambiance operating modes'[3] within urban design serving to transform a world of built forms into a world of sensory atmospheres.

The last example draws attention to a more active side of the notion of atmosphere – with the formulation from our theory of emotion; we can talk about expressive space. There is a reversibility at stake here between atmosphere as an active and a passive force. Atmosphere is not only something people *feel*, but simultaneously positions the felt space as something people *do* (Bille et al., 2015; Thibaud, 2015; Bille and Simonsen, 2019). You can participate in the construction of atmospheres through your mere presence in a specific place and a specific (temporal) situation – or through your practices whenever they are performed at specific events or in banal, everyday situations. This in itself underlines the quality of atmosphere as a collective phenomenon. However, you can also actively try to shape experiences and moods of others by organizing objects, bodies and places – Bille et al. (2015) talk about 'staging atmospheres' in this connection. The most obvious example is architectural design. McCann (2008), for example, by way of Merleau-Ponty, evolves how architecture entangles its designer and its inhabitants with the larger world, blurring subjective boundaries and intertwining vision and visibility, sensing and sensuousness, movement and materiality – in this way underlining both architects and residents as active shapers of atmosphere as well as the intersubjective character of the process. Other examples of more deliberate orchestration of atmospheres and manipulation of moods and emotions with aesthetical, commercial or political motives can also be found.

THE NARRATIVE CITY/IES

As argued above, an understanding of the urban based on experience will involve an intertwinement of the material and the imaginative, the visible and the invisible – that is, both bodily practices and narratives. Basically, such an account can seek support in the classic text of Ricoeur (1984) in which, with reference to Aristotle's *Poetics*, he analyses narrative through the conceptual pair *'muthos-mimesis'*. These two refer to the constitutive act of 'emplotment' – the organization of events into some kind of 'whole' – and the practice of 'representation', respectively. And, as strongly emphasized by Ricoeur, the approach through the 'poetic' lends a sense of construction and dynamism to this pair of terms, which subsequently have to be taken, not as structures, but as *operations*. He is thus underlining a performative character of narratives. Let us elaborate a little on that with a few additional properties of narratives, selectively drawn from Bruner (1991) and Finnegan (1998). The first one is their *particularity*. Narratives take as their ostensive reference particular social happenings and/or environments. But these are embedded in more general scripts – there is something universal in the particular. Secondly, in their organization, narratives have some element of explanation or *coherence* – that is what emplotment is generally about. Thirdly, we want to bring up the *context sensitivity* and negotiability of narratives. This is a quality that relates to both the telling and the interpretation of narratives, and relies basically on accounts of narrative orientation and background knowledge. Finally, one feature turns up in nearly all accounts of narratives – one of utmost importance to the narrative construction of the city – namely their *temporality*.

One way of approaching the relationship between time and narrative is through the lens of the phenomenology of time. Time is here considered constitutive of human being-in-the-world and, more importantly in the present context, it is seen as a structural connection of future, past and present (Heidegger, 1962; Ricoeur, 1984). This connection takes the form of a 'threefold' present (the present of the future, the present of the past and the present of the present) indicating that a person's present disposition and actions only make sense in relation to a future and a past. Furthermore, these three dimensions are moments of mental action – as acts of *expectation*, *memory* and *attention*, respectively – each considered not in isolation but in interaction with one another (Ricoeur, 1984).

Already the introduction of these terms – 'expectation', 'memory' and 'attention' – suggests a connection between time and narrative, but Ricoeur takes us further. He adds what is perhaps too far-reaching a thesis on a correlation between the activity of narrating a story and the temporal character of human experience, seeing it as not merely accidental but presenting a transcultural form of necessity, and he does so by considering three stages of the telling of a story. The first stage is about 'refiguration' or the way in which stories are grounded in a preunderstanding of the world of action. Any narrative understanding is in some way connected to practical understanding – in other words, narratives inevitably draw from an explicit or implicit phenomenology of 'doing something'. This practical field in return opens itself to narration, because symbolic resources such as signs, rules and norms always already articulate it, and because it is organized in temporal structures that call for narration. For the sake of the last point, Heidegger's thinking on the temporality of Being is drawn on to argue for a pre-narrative quality of experience, an understanding of life as '(as yet) untold' stories (Ricoeur, 1984: 74) – that is, episodic events and repressed stories waiting to be collected and retold as life stories and personal identities. The second mode of representation concerns the creative operation of 'configuration' or emplotment. Plot, in this process, exercises a mediating function: by drawing a meaningful story from a diversity of events or incidents and by temporal ordering of episodes into 'series', 'successions' and 'endings' – altogether constituting the productive imagination of narrative. Finally, representation also involves rhetoric and 'reading', that is, the intersection of the world of the text and that of the listener or the reader. This stage is about a dialogical process that can most precisely be described by Gadamer's notion of the 'fusion of horizons' (1995). By this threefold conception of representation, Ricoeur on the one hand retains a connection between narrative and the world of practice and experience, while on the other he recognizes indefiniteness in this connection, one that is approached (but never remedied) through emplotment or the poetics of narrative.

It is such multiple temporalities that are at stake when we consider the narrative construction of the city. Memories and expectations on the part of different urban agents constitute performative speech acts in the production of urban imaginaries – from autobiographical remembering to artistic description, planning and urban marketing. Nostalgia and the imaginary city of the past are fused in public discourses, for example in images of the community or heritage industries, just as futuristic visions of speed and cyborg-capitalism are part of the urban imaginary. In accordance with the insight gained from the phenomenology of time, however, the temporality of narrative is not a question of a past of memory, a present of description, and a future of imagination and planning:

> The past exists as the projection backwards of present concerns. The desire for a good city in the future already exists in the imagination of the past. The future tense of urbanist discourse turns out to be less predictive than optative, although expressed in the present tense of the architectural drawing. (Donald, 1997: 184)

Urban narratives, then – whenever told by city dwellers, artists, planners, urban theorists or others – should be seen in the light of this fusion of past, future and present. Having said that, however, it is obvious that such narratives are structured by different temporalities and different temporal orderings – from the narratives of city dwellers structured by everyday lives and life cycles (including remarkable events and turning points) to 'grand' narratives of urban theorists, ordered by more or less evolutionary historical periodization (Simonsen, 1993; Finnegan, 1998).

While the bulk of literature on narrative and narrative inquiry emphasizes the temporality of narratives, questions on the *spatiality* of narrative call upon other sources, some of which have been widely discussed in geography. For our purpose, an expedient starting point is the contribution from Michel de Certeau (1984), who emphasizes the relationship between practices and narratives as well as the spatiality of both. To him, stories are spatial trajectories:

> Every story is a travel story – a spatial practice. For this reason, spatial practices concern everyday tactics, are part of them, from the alphabet of spatial indication ('it's to the right', 'take a left'), the beginning of a story the rest of which is written by footsteps, to the daily 'news', television news reports, legends, and stories that are told (memories and fiction of foreign lands or more or less distant times in the past). These narrated adventures, simultaneously producing geographies of actions and drifting into the commonplaces of an order, do not merely constitute a 'supplement' to pedestrian enunciation and rhetorics. They are not satisfied with displacing the latter and transposing them into the field of language. In reality, they organize walks. They make the journey, before or during the time the feet perform it. (1984: 115–16)

What de Certeau is arguing in this comment is that narrative is conditioning a map – a 'cognitive map' – one that is less inclined to produce an overall vision than to represent everyday life. It is composed by a range of active narrative operations and always related to spatial practices. Let us in the following briefly consider the function of such spatializing narrative actions.

Spaces and *places*. Stories carry out the work of transforming 'places into spaces and spaces into places' (de Certeau, 1984: 118). As spatial trajectories, every day they traverse and organize places; they select them and link them together; they make sentences and itineraries out of them. De Certeau identifies two poles of description or narrative figures in this process: the 'tour' and the 'map'. In systemic discourse, these two have been dissociated into literary and scientific representations of space. In everyday narratives, however, they coexist and interlace; narratives combine the experience of moving (spatializing actions) and seeing (the knowledges of an order of places). In this way, stories organize changing relationships between spaces and places, but also in a pre-established geography they tell us what we can do in it and make out of it. Stories not only traverse and organize places, however, they also make them habitable. As is well known from any notions of sense of place, memories, legends and other signifying practices can saturate places with meaning and emotions, even though these refer to lack as often as presence; fragmentation as often as coherence.

Boundaries and *bridges*. Stories also play an important role in the delimitation of places. This is most evident and explicit in juridical discourse, but the role of stories is a much more general one. De Certeau describes the primary function of stories as one of authorizing the establishment, displacement and transcendence of limits. This means that, in the field of discourse, it sets in opposition two movements that intersect – setting and transgressing limits – and constitutes a dynamic partitioning of space by way of the two narrative figures 'boundaries' and 'bridges'. The point is that the associated speech acts – dividing, conjoining, encircling – do not set limits *in* space, but rather they produce space.

Boundaries and bridges are, however, ambiguous narrative categories which constitute a complex relationship of contradiction and connectivity:

> In the story, the frontier functions as a third element. [...] A middle place, composed of interactions and inter-views, the frontier is a sort of void, a narrative sym-bol of exchanges and encounters. (de Certeau, 1984: 127)

The boundary establishes a space 'in-between' to see through, just like the bridge alternately welds together and opposes insularities. The two of them presuppose each other and in complex ways both distinguish and connect. Any narrative of delimitation and enclosure in some sense presupposes a relation to an alien exteriority; it is as if delimitation itself were the bridge that opens the inside to its other.

Territoriality, Othering and *naming*. The ambiguity and the emotions involved in the construction of boundaries and bridges become even more important when it comes to the widespread discussion of power in narrative spatialization. The importance of narrative in the construction of territory has been widely acknowledged since Anderson (1993) argued that nation states and national identities are 'imagined communities', constructed through a range of media and connected to the upsurge of print capitalism. Spatialized Othering is however not confined to the narrative construction of territory. Rather, this should be seen as a special case of the more extensive process of constructing imaginative geographies – seen from outside as well as inside. The understanding of that owes more to postcolonial thinking than to anything else, in particular to Said's *Orientalism* (1978), which so convincingly put the violence of representation on the agenda. At the urban scale, Marc Auger's ethnography of the Paris Metro (2002) is an eloquent example. So is Loic Waquant's (2008) concept of 'territorial stigmatiza-tion', describing how derogative categorization of socially vulnerable residential areas stigmatizes both places and residents. Naming, also, is an element in such power strategies. Colonial practices of naming were a way of bringing the land-scape into textual presence, of bringing it within the compass of a European rationality that made it at once familiar to its colonizers and alien to its native inhabitants (Gregory, 1994). At the same time, however, naming is a contested and ambiguous exercise. In spaces brutally lit by an alien reason, de Certeau argues, proper names can carve out pockets of hidden and familiar meaning. They 'make sense', construct alternative places and passages, and as such ascribe mean-ing to practices of evasion, undermining and resistance (see also Pred, 1990).

Narrative is not the whole life. But it is no small part of our social existence that we create storied pathways to live by, including performance conventions, plots, order, myths, etc. Exploring such narrative resources for creating and experiencing our surroundings, therefore, can lead to an understanding of the city as a collection of stories. De Certeau preliminarily describes the relation between spatial and sig-nifying practices by way of the three symbolic mechanisms of legend, memory and dream. They make places habitable and believable, they recall or suggest phantoms and they organize the invisible meanings of the city. The temporality and spatiality of narrative, as it is discussed above, can elaborate this relationship. They establish how memories and expectations intersect in present dispositions for action and the constitution of urban imageries; how the poetic act of emplotment involves tem-poral and spatial 'ordering' of events; how narrative figures such as tours, maps, boundaries and bridges are integral parts of the construction of social life and, in particular, the organization of spaces and places; and finally how narrative power strategies, involved in processes of territoriality and Othering, constitute hierar-chies of places at different scales – including the urban one.

TIME–SPACE FIGURATIONS OF THE URBAN

In this section, by way of empirical material from the project on 'the multiple faces of the city', we will try to illustrate some of the points made above. It is about how practices and narratives together construct the cities of individuals and collectives and about the variation of the 'urban figurations' resulting from this process. The approach to narratives we work from is close to an anthropological understanding, including an emphasis on story-*telling* and the question of context, tradition and active participants (Finnegan, 1998). In this way, there is a close connection between the narrative and the embodied city, between stories and practices. In the following we will show different figurations of the city emerging from the analysis. These figurations are not representations of the city 'as such'. They are about events and practices 'taking place'. They *produce* space through the stories and this 'taking place'. The stories are performative speech acts related to 'doing' rather than 'knowing'. However, people's stories also draw on a historical and cultural repertoire – on the existing myths and narratives of the city. Such images of the city inscribe themselves in Western culture in many ways (see Williams, 1975) from being the place embodying emancipating social relations that transcends disciplining forces in villages and small towns to being a symbol of disintegration and decay in recurrent myths of Babylon. These imaginations are based in binary oppositions such as cities/countryside or order/chaos, and they are often mediated through narratives in novels, films and/or TV serials. In this way, they enter into the personal narratives of our respondents as sediments that in a creative poetic process merge with the story of their more or less habitual practices into a construction of 'their' city. In our interpretation of these stories we identified four dominant time–space figurations of the city, of which the first two obviously relate to dominant imageries of the city in both common sense and theoretical discussions.

The first figure constructs *the city as a collage of places*. Different symbolic and social activities served as the basis for identification of the places, but they all in one way or another relied on ideas of particularity of or difference between places. A recurrent one included narratives of growing up in the city – told by people from different social groups and different generations. It describes the city from the perspective of the native Copenhagener; the story of the familiar re-viewed or reconstructed through the horizon of the child, such as:

> Sometimes you feel safer when you are at Nørrebro – that is, where you live. Because it is the place where you have lived since you were a little boy, and you know all the street corners and all the shortcuts and things like that. (Neezan, 24)

> The residents, they were sticking together. For example, at my confirmation – we lived on the third floor, but we had the dinner by those on the first floor; when Mrs Olsen's husband died, we had the coffee at our place, and things like that. Our neighbour was the first one to have a TV, so you turned up every night with your folding chair and your vacuum jug, and you were taking turns baking. (Lisbeth, 61)

The stories are different, but they do have common traits. They all have a double focus on social cohesion and public space. Public space and material surroundings are important elements in their construction of place. Descriptions of green spots, the streets, the small shops, as well as the yards at the blocks of flats and the activities they afforded (gatherings, play etc.) were included in many stories. The figure in play here is one of *local communities*, constructed through memories and emotions, but also drawing on a common figure in the cultural repertoire seeing urban neighbourhoods as 'villages within the city'. Other stories create the figure through construction of boundaries between 'insiders' and 'outsiders' or 'us' and 'them', as in the statement: 'in our block there is no-one of an Other ethnic heritage, here there are only Danish people'. Or it comes in as a lack: here, the tellers regretfully realize they do not have 'enough interaction' with their neighbours, in this way seeing it both as lack, a loss and an ideal to strive for, at the same time referring to past, present and future. And in connection to neighbourhoods under 'gentrification', the construction of place takes its starting point in historical, cultural and architectonic knowledge. The appropriation of the neighbourhoods is connected to an 'imagination' and a 'takeover' of existing place identities in which one can settle and develop new urban lifestyles.

Other place constructions are based on experiences, emotions and symbolic significations. One woman talks about a local churchyard as a favourite place of hers, saying that it 'is a very exciting place [...] it is not just a churchyard, but a whole culture. It is enormous how much it holds of people and fates and what it has been used for.' What she feels for this historic churchyard in which many authors and other historic personalities rest leans on Tuan's (1974) concept of 'public symbols', which is meant precisely to describe places that, through their content of events and collective memories, gain particular significance in the landscape. Another woman, who moved to the city from a Danish island 30 years ago, relates that her favourite place is 'where the boat from Bornholm [her birth place] lands'. This place for her becomes a personal symbol of the maintenance of her original identity. It symbolizes something absent in time and space, her past and her 'home place'. A third woman (an immigrant from Morocco) constructs places by sensing the difference among parts of the city:

> All of them are special – for example Vesterbro has a special *ambiance*, at Nørrebro it is another one. There are many special places. Nørrebro is special; there are not many Danish people. It is a different atmosphere; do you understand what I mean? At Østerbro there is yet another atmosphere, I don't know how to explain [...] All the places have an atmosphere. Different atmospheres. (Nadja, 40)

She has an emotional and a multi-sensual experience when she is walking in the city. She finds it difficult to explain in words; it is primarily experienced at a bodily and sensuous level. And in the beginning she turns to her mother tongue (French) to express herself. The story directly affiliates to the concept of *atmosphere*, in this case in particular sensed as collective moods connected to social activity and cultural difference between the different neighbourhoods. The figure of 'the city as a collage of places', thus, can take many forms, and therefore it does not support an understanding of places as enclosed units but rather as localized articulations of social practices, relations and processes, as well as experiences, emotions and symbolic meanings amongst their users (Massey, 1994; Simonsen, 2008a).

The second dominant figure is about *the city as mobility and speed*, often connected to experiences around a move to the city; it is the experiences of people coming from the provinces and their encounter with the city – for good or for bad. It is expressed in phrases such as 'almost everybody feels estranged in a big city', 'sometimes days can pass where I don't meet somebody I know', 'and then people's indifference to each other!', 'they can live there for years without saying hello to each other, without taking care of each other', and 'everybody is so busy. I don't know what they want to achieve, they bustle about, almost nobody walks at a normal pace.' Implicit in these expressions are classic imaginations of the city as a place of *alienation*, one that is simultaneously fascinating and frightening. It is a figuration that permeates our culture and can be found in academic writings since Simmel's iconic essay on *Metropolis and Mental Life* (1950a [1903]), in 100 years' thinking on urban reforms and in popular narratives. The city is characterized as hurried and superficial, with blasé manners and the individual's absorption into the crowd. It is a critical figure addressing both the city and modernity, a narrative in which the liberation from the inquisitive surveillance of provincial existence only becomes freedom to live in the conditions of anonymity.

This figuration is accompanied by two (spatial) binary oppositions. The first one is the 'city/countryside' opposition. Even if, as mentioned above, it is turned down by many urban thinkers, it is alive and living within popular cultural repertoires. In some stories it is expressed as nature vs. artificiality, 'down-to-earth' values vs. materialism, and peace and silence vs. tempo and noise. But it is also often connected to a feeling of ambivalence, expressing the pros and cons of urban vs. rural life. The other opposition at stake concerns the 'global/local' relationship. It is about how 'glocalization' processes (Swyngedouw, 1997) find expression in urban life – that is, the degree to which transnational relations affect everyday life and the structures of meaning of the inhabitants. This issue is exactly the one that permeates the empirical parts of this book (in Chapter 2 and 3, and the second part of this chapter). We will therefore restrict ourselves here to saying how the respondents' construction of and feeling about Copenhagen as a 'multicultural' city take place in a co-production between the narrative city and the embodied city, between available public discourses and their own bodily practices and experiences. The stories are stretched between an orientalist 'us/them' narrative and a 'humanist' one involving openness to Other cultures.

The third figure is what we call *the city as the 'facticity' of everyday life*. It comes out of phrasings such as:

What happens is: I wake up, and then I go to work , and then home again and straight to bed, and then wake up and talk to the children, eat with the children, sit down and listen to some music or the news, and then a cup of tea, a cup of coffee, then sleep again. Seven days a week, you know! Therefore, I don't know how it is […] (Orhan, 45)

I think, it is on equal terms with everywhere else […] I don't speak with anybody at my staircase, but I think it is fairly characteristic in such a big city. I mean, I think it is the same in other places in the city. For sure – you have, in some sense, enough with yourself. You say hello to people on the street, but whether they live in no. 11, 13 or 15, I don't really know. (Bettina, 24)

The lives of these people are characterized by what Lefebvre (1984) calls 'the everyday' or Merleau-Ponty (1968) 'the habitual'. It is the banal and insignificant that is so difficult to describe. When we act in the everyday, we are doing 'nothing'. We exist on a level of practice where activities are seldom consciously reflected or spoken of. When the everyday as a perspective is projected out to the city, it provides it with a touch of 'facticity'. People do not ascribe any significance to their neighbourhood. They are satisfied with it; it is practical and contains what they need. But they do not feel any attachment to it, neither do they feel more 'at home' or 'safe' here than in other places in the city. Similarly to 'the figure of alienation', they talk about lacking contact with their neighbours, but it is without regret or feeling of loss. It is a facticity. The city becomes a functional arena for routinized everyday life.

Finally, we identified a figure of *the city as a space of opportunities*. It is here that 'things happen'. It is again a figure that relates to 'classic' imaginations of the city, and we meet it with reference to different fields of life. On many occasions it connects to 'going out', that is, to the city as a space for social and cultural activities (associations, sports, performances, shopping, etc.), but also to conditions in which you can do that. Besides appreciating the wide choices of activities, some respondents emphasize the possibilities of casual and anonymous use of the city. Another field of opportunities is the job market. People from different occupational sectors point out that it is here where the most specialized and exciting jobs are to be found. It is particularly newcomers to the city who highlight these opportunities. It might not be surprising since job opportunities are probably an important element in their decision to move to the city. Finally, the figure of 'the city as a space of opportunities' is connected to the 'emancipatory potential' of the city:

It was also difficult because I am a woman. I love my *indépendance*. I also love to work and fend for myself. Independence. Travelling and meeting people, and not becoming a small woman. I want to be a big woman – ok, I do not have a high social level, but I am a clever woman. I have many qualifications. Now I work in cleaning to fend for myself, and then go to school to learn Danish. (Nadja, 40)

Nadja is a special case: a Moroccan woman who has been through two arranged marriages, one in Morocco and one in Denmark. Now she is working her way up, through economic independence and education and through building up a cross-cultural women's network in Copenhagen as well as internationally through former contacts. Her ambitions are to get a 'proper job' and work internationally with children's life chances. She is thus an obvious example of a person searching for the emancipatory opportunities offered by the city.

WORLDING THE URBAN FLESH

Due to our theoretical/empirical starting point in lived experience, we have so far mostly looked at the urban flesh on the scale of everyday life. However, in accordance with the broad conception of the flesh of the world and the disconnection of the question of the 'urban' from specific spatial forms, it is worth considering 'up-scaling' the urban flesh. Already the above reference to rhythm-analysis implies such an extension. Another example comes from Mendieta (2001), who presents what he calls 'a phenomenology of globalization from below' by describing 'experiences that human beings, in varying degrees, are undergoing as a result of new socio-economic-cultural and political processes' (2001: 11–12). However, one of the most ambitious recently introduced attempts to develop a coherent conception of 'the urban' is the one proposed by Brenner and Schmid (2011, 2015) on *planetary urbanization* drawing on Lefebvre's (2003 [1970]) ideas of the urban as a process of 'urbanization of society' and 'not a universal form, settlement type or bounded unit' (2015: 165). They argue against 'empiricist', 'universal', 'homogenizing' and 'totalizing' concepts and for a 'new epistemology' and 'meta-theoretical' approach to the urban process. This process is basically described through the interplay of three mutually constitutive moments: (1) concentrated urbanization, (2) extended urbanization and (3) differential urbanization, which they in concrete, historical analysis suggest crossed with Lefebvre's three dimensions of production of space, here concretized as spatial practices, territorial regulations and everyday life. This schematic model is heavily contested and criticized for evacuation of agency, subjectivity and forms of difference as well as Eurocentrism and the marginalization of gender, put forward in particular by representatives of postcolonial and feminist urbanism (e.g. Roy, 2015; Peake, 2016). Others from related camps assume a more appreciative tone in their discussion of the model, seeing it as a significant opening for building urban theorizing that takes account of the world of cities (Robinson, 2014; Goonewardena, 2018). This difference in valuation might be due to the fact that Brenner and Schmid (2015), when presenting their theses, work in two levels of abstraction and those involved in the discussion emphasize one or the other of them. The general model including the three moments of urbanization can be seen as a kind of urban ontology and allows for many interpretations;

while the more concrete processes they use to display the model lean strongly towards pure political-economic analysis, with the limitations that might involve. Thus, as we see it, they do not take into account the full richness of their original model, the work of Henri Lefebvre. From our point of view, the most important point is the way in which the moment of 'differential urbanization' is displayed and how the content of that moment can be more broadly conceptualized than through the ideas of creative destruction put forward by Brenner and Schmid. It is in this context that we talk about 'worlding the urban flesh' – or 'being-in-an-urban-world'.[4]

As a first step we can return to Chapter 1, where we argued that Fanon's critical dialogue with Merleau-Ponty led to a radical *phenomenology of difference*, grounded in an understanding of the body. Put briefly, this can be illustrated by the way in which Fanon (1967a), in order to understand 'the lived experience of the black man', below Merleau-Ponty's 'corporeal schema' that is formed through our cultural-historical existence and the basis for our agency, creates a 'historical-racial schema' that is formed in the interracial encounter of black bodies in the West, generating an existential unfreedom and a 'double consciousness' of the black body. The third term, 'the racial–epidermal schema', refers to a further step of alienation and disorientation where this historical ascription of identity becomes 'naturalized' as a condition of the skin – 'a facticity of the flesh' (Weate, 2001). In spite of this dystopic analysis, Fanon (as well as Merleau-Ponty) also sees hope and a possibility of escaping the weight of the past. Everything that reveals itself in the world is liable to multiple readings across embodied difference (of race, class, gender, sexuality, etc.). In what Bernasconi (1996) calls Fanon's 'new humanism', grounded in injustice and the body-in-pain of the Other, we move towards each other through a common sentience and a shared capacity to suffer. Similar ideas can be found in Sennett (1994), in the way he ends his work on the fleshy history of the Western city. He situates the question of pain in the moral difficulty in multi-cultural cities of arousing recognition and sympathy for those who are Other. For him, such empathies can only arise by opening a space of acknowledgement of communal bodily pain in which its transcendental possibilities become visible. Such a recognition of pain, he argues, has a trajectory in human experience. The pain 'disorients and makes incomplete the self, defeats the desire for coherence; the body accepting pain is ready to become a civic body, sensible to the pain of another person, pains present together on the street' (1994: 376).

To lift the conception of difference out from the body, identity and feelings, we once more turn to Lefebvre. Two concepts are important here. The first one is his take on the concept of difference. In *Le manifeste différentialiste* (1970) he insists upon 'the right to difference', a parallel to what he in other contexts refers to 'the right to the city'. Difference in this context raises the question of possibility for revolt against an urban world of segregated and homogenized spaces confined by private property and the commodity form, bureaucratic management, and differentiation according to class, race, gender and sexuality. The other concept is the one of *colonization*. In several places Lefebvre talks about 'colonization of everyday life', thus connecting global neo-imperial realities to analyses of the spatial relations in metropolitan areas, or macro-political economies to the experiences of everyday life (see also Gregory, 1994; Kipfer and Goonewardena, 2007). At the time he was writing, this connection concerned colonial segregation and the Algerian war on the one hand and planning in the Parisian *banlieue* on the other, in this way also establishing a link with the contemporary Fanon (Kipfer, 2007). In the twenty-first century, we can see it in military planning exercises in Iraq, Lebanon and Palestine, and the contradictory urban policies in many Western cities of segregation of poor people and people of colour in public housing neighbourhoods, to subsequently tear down their homes in order to 'dilute' their concentration.

In this way the flesh of the urban is basically about difference – or in Lefebvre's words, 'an ensemble of differences'; different histories, different spatio-temporal rhythms, different styles of urban life and different types of bodies. Together they constitute an ontology of being-in-an-urban-world.

THE URBAN AS A WORLD OF STRANGERS

THE FIGURE OF THE STRANGER

In Chapter 3, when discussing 'encountering the Other', we touched on the figure of the stranger, which we will now develop and relate to the city. In the most general sense, phenomenology recounts the meaning of the strange or the stranger. It basically understands consciousness as consciousness *of* something, of something *other* than itself, whether we talk about human or non-human objects. However, the appearance and the role of this 'other' take different forms throughout the history of the tradition. Without going into details, we will follow Kearney and Semonovitch (2011a) when they conclude: 'Simply put, where the Stranger appeared in the seminal Fifth Meditation as "alter ego", Husserl overemphasized the ego, while Derrida and Levinas overemphasized the "alter"' (2011a: 17). In contrast, they argue, as we also want to do here, that Merleau-Ponty and Ricoeur shift the focus to the hyphen between these two positions. These two authors seek a middle space between an absolute alterity or the 'no-place' of the absolute Other, isolated by Levinas and Derrida, and the 'immanent place' of the idealist and transcendental ego suggested by Husserl.[5] This 'middle space' is a space of incarnation and the intertwining or double movement of active and passive synthesis in our encounter with others. It is in this in-betweenness we shall explore the way in which we sense, shape and interpret the Other (or the stranger) in our midst. In this connection, we (with Kearney and Semonovitch) suggest that Merleau-Ponty and Ricoeur together offer a phenomenology of carnal and metaphorical beings, of hosts and strangers in all their corporeal and linguistic richness.

In Merleau-Ponty's ontology of becoming, he includes the figure of the stranger in the condition of incarnation. He fully acknowledges our multiple modes of situatedness – temporal, spatial, political, social – but underlying all these sites of hospitality/hostility, he locates the 'wild being' of the living body. His phenomenology of embodiment portrays the richly ambiguous intertwining of nature and culture, body and world, in this way rendering the physical and the cultural inseparable. Further, in the phenomenology of the flesh, the body becomes an organ of the 'for-other'. Encountering the stranger mobilizes this organ and, in this process, identifies others with similar/dissimilar schemas. We work out relation to other corporeal schemas and find that amongst the objects of our perception there are living 'similars'. It is identification, not of identical beings, but *similar* beings to which we can relate in spite of an infinite multiplicity of variation in corporeal form and of conduct across time and space. These living 'similars', mentioned by both Merleau-Ponty and Ricoeur, are beings *like* ourselves, but they are also unlike our self.

As we saw above with gestures and narratives, Ricoeur adds to the corporeal by a linguistic communication or *translation* that serves as a bridge between similar and dissimilar, same and other. For him, the similar is the paradox of the stranger: the one who is recognizable enough to appear but who nonetheless retains a distance. Kearney and Semonovitch (2011: 14) refer to this thinking as an 'ontological paradigm' of translation. They also connect it to the question of hospitality, seeing 'genuine hospitality' as an aspect of human being that crosses languages, traditions, borders and bodies. Crossing over all these differences does not imply an effacing of otherness, they say. Hospitality can only occur in a plurality of unique beings; it would be unnecessary if we were all the same (2011: 22). It is across all the differences that we find the similar in dissimilarity, the dissimilar in similarity. This is the chiasm of the stranger, to use one of Merleau-Ponty's favourite tropes.

Also within social theory, the figure of the stranger has been a classic topic, illuminatingly introduced in a short essay by Georg Simmel more than 100 years ago (Simmel, 1950b [1908]). Simmel's stranger was, not surprisingly considering the time the essay was written, a man. Simmel starts by contrasting him to the wanderer, who is known to be the one who comes today and goes tomorrow. The stranger, Simmel states, is a person 'who comes today and stays tomorrow'. He might be a potential wanderer – although he has not moved on, he still exists within a symbolic realm of coming and going. He resides within a group defining itself by way of a set of (spatial) boundaries, but his position in the group is determined by the fact that he has not belonged to it from the beginning, and that he imports qualities into the territory of the group which do not stem from the group itself.

In this way, Simmel introduces the stranger as a figure living within what we will call a spatial ambivalence of *proximity* and *distance*. He writes: 'In relationship to him, distance means that he, who is close by, is far, and strangeness means that he, who also is far, is actually near' (1950b: 402). Thus the relationship of the stranger to the place of residence is simultaneously one of attachment and detachment (or we could add of inclusion and exclusion). He/she is inside and outside at the same time. This is an important contribution rendering the stranger a *relational* figure; Simmel expresses that by seeing the stranger as 'a specific form of interaction'. He argues that the inhabitants of Sirius are not really strangers to us, at least not in any socially relevant sense. They do not exist for us at all; they are beyond far and near. The stranger, in contrast, is an element or a participant of the group in which he/she resides. The group membership might be antagonistic and contested, but it is a relationship that produces patterns of coexistence and consistent interaction.

For Simmel, the classical example of the stranger is to be found in the history of European Jews. They were, he argues, traditionally traders and therefore not 'owners of soil' – the expression referring, not only to physical goods but also figuratively to any life-substances and imaginations that are fixed in the social–spatial environment: 'Although in more intimate relations, he may develop all kinds of charm and significance, as long as he is considered a stranger in the eyes of the other, he is not an "owner of soil"' (1950b: 403). The group's occupation with intermediary trade, and often with pure finance, Simmel argues, gave it a specific character of mobility. Importantly, he implies that if the idea of mobility becomes attributed to a specific group, the group ends up embodying exactly that synthesis of proximity and distance which constitutes the position of the stranger. In this way, Simmel includes issues of disembeddedness, ambivalence, imaginary mobility, relationality and embodiment in his understanding of the construction of the stranger.

These issues are exactly the ones taken up by a whole range of authors dealing with the figure of the stranger during the past century, only a few of whom we can deal with here. The question of *ambivalence* is most thoroughly taken up by Zygmunt Bauman and associate authors (see, for example, Bauman, 1991; Diken, 1998). Here, the stranger is seen as the prototypical example of ambivalence, where ambivalence is 'the possibility of assigning an object or an event to more than one category' (Bauman, 1991: 1). Belonging to more than one category means ambivalence, contingency and indeterminacy, as long as the search for definitions based on either/or is the norm. Bauman relates to the friend/enemy opposition which, among other things, sets apart truth from falsehood, good from evil and right from wrong. The stranger rebels against these 'cosy' antagonisms. He/she belongs to the family of *undecidables*, those baffling unities that are neither/nor. If we press upon the stranger the friend/enemy opposition, he/she will come out simultaneously under- and over-determined – in this way exposing the failure of the opposition itself. The stranger is therefore a constant threat to the order of the world.

The specific form of *relationality* is taken up and even strengthened by Sara Ahmed in her own development of the notion (Ahmed, 2000). In line with

Simmel's formulation, she wants to challenge the assumption that the stranger is simply anybody whom we do not know, but she goes further than that. As we have already touched on in our analysis of everyday encounters on the bus (Chapter 3), her main point is that nobody *is* a stranger, you *become* a stranger in the moment of encounter. It is a moment of estrangement involving an incorporation of earlier meetings or handed-down historical–geographical imaginations. The stranger becomes a relational figure, somebody who, through differential techniques is already recognized as a body out-of-place:

> The stranger then is not simply the one that we have not yet encountered, but the one whom we have already encountered, or already faced. The stranger comes to be faced as a form of recognition: we recognise somebody *as a stranger*, rather than simply failing to recognise them. (Ahmed, 2000: 21)

The point is that the stranger is recognized as well as produced through embodied encounters. The boundaries between strange and familiar are continuously constituted and redefined. Every time we meet the 'undecidable', we seek to re-establish ways of recognition, not only by reading the body of this particular stranger, but also to by trying to tell the difference between him/her and other strangers.

Just as Simmel in his time saw the European Jew as the prototype of the stranger, we in contemporary Europe must give that trope to the Muslim. Goldberg (2009) talks about 'the figure of the Muslim', saying that 'Islam is taken in the dominant European imagery to represent a collection of lacks: of freedom; of a disposition of scientific inquiry; of civility and manners; of love of life; of human worth; of equal respect for women and gay people' (2009: 165). In this way, the figure of the Muslim has come to stand for the fear of violent death, for the paranoia of Europe's cultural demise, and for fanaticism, fundamentalism and (female) suppression.

THE STRANGER AND THE CITY

One side of the relationship of the stranger and the city in contemporary Europe is about segregation and concentration of estranged ethnic minorities in large-scale public housing districts, which are, eventually, designated as sites of pathology populated by deviant youth, non-assimilated immigrant populations and, more recently, Islamic fundamentalists (Kipfer, 2007). All over Europe you find such housing estates as a result of resegregation of urban space along combined lines of class and ethnicity. In his book *Urban Outcasts* (2008) – as well as several other publications, for example Wacquant et al. (2014) – Loïc Wacquant developed the concepts of 'advanced marginality' and 'territorial stigmatization' to grasp aspects of this process. He did so with a combination of Goffman's ideas of experiences of stigma and Bourdieu's theory of symbolic power and violence, socially, symbolically and politically produced. Andy Merrifield (2014) talks about the situation as a 'new urban question' that turns the housing estates into a microcosm of a new process of divide and rule, a global process that he calls 'neo-Hausmannization'. He sees estates as parts of a bigger urban tissuing, a patchwork quilt of socio-spatial and racial apartheid that goes for 'Paris as for Palestine, for London as for Rio, for Johannesburg as for New York'. Rather than talking about an urban–suburban or North–South divide, he wants to talk about 'two worlds' created through processes of spatial apartheid to be found everywhere. Differences are differences of degree rather than substance.

These different and overlapping theorizations are both conducted with a starting point in the *banlieues* of Paris, and the context of course has to be taken into account. However, the processes they expound are recognizable to different degrees. As regards the Danish case, interesting comparative studies have addressed Wacquant's contribution through analyses of its usability in the French and the Danish case, and except for the influence of the difference in operation of the housing market and housing politics in the two cases, T.S. Larsen found it both relevant and productive in the Danish case (Larsen and Delica, 2017; Larsen, 2018). Against that background, let us look at the Danish segregated public housing estates, starting from the emotions expressed in an interview with a resident from our project 'The stranger, the city and the nation' (Koefoed and Simonsen, 2010, 2011):

> As I said, we live 38 different nationalities here. Really! Personally I find it very difficult to understand when some politicians call Mjølnerparken [the housing estate] a ghetto, with 38 different nationalities and countries and backgrounds and differences! They label us, don't they? And then our social minister tried to tell us that it is a positive word! (Mansoor, 42)

What Mansoor expresses is his anger and frustration over the territorial stigmatization that he, his fellow residents and the whole neighbourhood are exposed to by the politicians (and, through them, the media). He refers to the practice of several successive Danish governments of drawing up a so-called 'ghetto-list' including residential areas to which special measures are to be employed. To be included on the list, the areas should be public housing estates that, besides social criteria such as unemployment, education, income and criminality, have to contain a certain amount of inhabitants who are 'immigrants or successors of immigrants from "non-western countries"' – thus racializing the whole procedure. The interview is from 2009, and the lists have been revised several times both with regard to criteria and political measures. One from 2018 is politically radicalized and transcends the boundaries of a constitutional state as to equal rights for the law by including legal measures to be employed only in the so-called 'ghetto-areas'. The measures include mandatory day nursery for children from the age of one (with the purpose of learning Danish traditions and 'values'), double punishment for crimes committed in the areas, and a range of measures dealing with built environment, housing and residents including privatization, rules of eviction and of residence, and demolitions up to the definitive possibility of totally dismantling areas. This political development tends towards what Merrifield (2014) calls 'neo-Hausmannization' or 'the war of the *banlieue*' or what Kipfer and Goonewardena (2007) characterize as 'urbicide', saying:

> One may apply the concept not only to the military planning exercises in Iraq, Lebanon and Palestine but also to the more confined and selective cases of destroying, gentrifying and privatizing ghettoized spaces (public housing districts, racialized social spaces) in metropolitan urban centres (2007: 24).

There is, however, another side of the stranger and the city:

> I think it is great because, in contrast to the representation in the media, you can actually feel that both Danes and non-Danes have accepted the fact that we have this mixed composition. And they think it is normal. The way we are told that it is so strange having these different cultures. I can't recognize that picture when I go about in the city. It seems to come naturally to people [...] by now it characterizes Nørrebro and Vesterbro [former working class neighbourhoods] and the inner city as well. I think it is good that you can leave all that talk about problems and conflicts. For us ethnic minorities, who are born and bred in Denmark, it is no problem, we can handle the mixture. And for most young Danish people I don't think it is either, at least not for those who grew up together with them, in particular in Copenhagen. You live together across these boundary lines. In the streets you have a common culture, you have a common language where you integrate Arab or Asian expressions in the Danish language, and you develop common norms. I think it is good that it happens – and about time too! (Yasmeen, 26)

> For me, Copenhagen is *life*. It is opportunities for development and self-realization – both for me, my family and my children. And Copenhagen is for me a lot of good friends, friends of different nationalities and origins. And Copenhagen is for me a very active and dynamic city, a dynamic capital. (Mansoor, 42)

> If, instead of posing the question: 'But are you Danish?', if instead you could strengthen people's Copenhagen mentality, if they could proudly say: 'But *I am a Copenhagener*', which after all is much easier because you can be a Copenhagener in all sorts of ways. Nobody can take away from you that you are a Copenhagener, but to say proudly 'I am Danish'! I obviously have problems if I shall say proudly 'I am Danish' because Pia Kjærsgaard [leader of the right wing populist party] is also Danishness, and I am not Danish in *that* way. (Ikram, 31)

To these extracts we can add the ones in Chapter 3 from two young (ethnic Danish) bus passengers talking about part of the city they are passing through as merged and open-minded and the bus as 'a rolling marketplace'. They all, in different ways, talk about the city as a 'world of strangers' where Otherness becomes ordinary – in the case of Ikram, even with the idea of national identity as the constitutive outside of his identity and as a Copenhagener. The affinity for the city is based on growing up or working together; through the possibilities that they feel the city offers; or through indifference as an anonymous form of coexistence (Simmel, 1950a) or as a kind of ethical relation (Tonkiss, 2003). We have earlier introduced the concept of *habitual multiculturalism* to describe this relation, in this way playing on Merleau-Ponty's concepts of habit and habituation. It is a form of lived multiculturalism based on the banalization of cross-cultural encounters in the city. Gilroy's (2006) related concept of 'conviviality' is also worth considering in this regard. It refers to processes of cohabitation and interaction that have made multiculture an ordinary feature of social life in urban areas. It does not necessarily mean the absence of racism or the existence of a civic virtue of recognition, but rather a habit of negotiating multiplicity and the company of 'strange' Others as a kind of bodily training (see also Blunt, 2007; Amin, 2012, 2013; Sennett 2012). These experiences and feelings support more positive views of the possibilities for coexistence in cities of difference. For example, those of the planning theorist Leonie Sandercock (1998, 2003), who argues for an urban utopia – *Cosmopolis* – as 'a city/region in which there is a genuine connection with, and respect and space for, the cultural Other' (1998, 164).[6] She acknowledges the challenges facing planning in the conditions of (cultural) difference, in particular addressing the question of fear of the Other, but suggests what she calls a 'therapeutic approach' to planning; a dialogical approach in which planning is supposed to work as a negotiating or mediating agency between antagonistic parties.

Thinking on 'the stranger and the city', then, shows the same duality between postcolonial melancholia and multicultural conviviality (to use Gilroy's terms) as we saw in Chapter 3. In this connection, and in particular in the European context, many refer to a movement from an 'old' biological racism to a 'new', supposedly more benign cultural and differential one. This 'new' cultural racism is strongly associated with religion, including a conspicuous Islamophobia connected to the increasing mobility of refugees and immigrants. Global immigration and the religious diversity it brings about is, together with 9/11, the war on terror and subsequent terrorist events in Europe, part of the background for a group of urban theorists' ideas of *postsecular cities* (Molendijk et al., 2010; Beaumont and Baker, 2011; Cloke and Beaumont, 2012). Amongst other sources, they find the background for the postsecularity thesis in Jürgen Habermas (2006, 2008), who discusses the presuppositions for secular and faith-based 'rapprochement' in the public sphere and the possibility of a learning process 'forcing the tradition of Enlightenment as well as religious doctrines to reflect on their respective limits' (2006: 28). The concept of the postsecular is contested, in particular in relation to ideas of 'post' and novelty. For example, Ley (2011) wonders whether what has changed in the postsecular city is only our attention to it. Nevertheless, the term can become useful as a tool to grasp shifting relations between religion, the nation state and citizenship – or, in Knott's formulation a new understanding of 'a dialectic field of religious and secular knowledge-power relations' (2010: 20). This 'entanglement' involves experiences in the cities of more religious diversity as well as conflicts related to coexistence of secular/religious or religious/religious practices. Many of these conflicts are played out around the building of places of worship by religious minorities and their visibility in urban space. In the rest of this chapter, we shall illustrate that by way of a case study of the opening of a big mosque in Copenhagen.

FROM INVISIBILITY TO VISIBILITY: OPENING OF A PURPOSE-BUILT MOSQUE IN COPENHAGEN

On Thursday 19 June 2014 the first big purpose-built mosque with a community centre, the *Khayr El-Barriya Mosque* and *Hamad Bin Khalifa Civilisation Centre,* opened in Copenhagen. The event attracted much attention from both written and visual media. In Denmark, like in many other European countries, the building of purpose-built mosques – moving Islam from the private to the public sphere and rendering it visible in urban space – is a controversial issue. Many previous attempts have failed. The opening was a three-day event including a reception, inauguration ceremony, opening the mosque, exhibition in the cultural centre, Friday prayer, guided public tours, talks and a bazaar.

This event was analysed as a case of cross-cultural encounters in the city. It was part of our project 'Paradoxical Spaces: Encountering the Other in Public Space', which explores how the complexity of cultural difference is experienced and practised in different public spaces in Copenhagen.[7] We considered the opening event a good case for our general purpose because it constitutes a transformative moment that can push the question of cross-cultural encounters to extremes. However, the encounters explored in this case take a specific form: they are mediated through the materiality, the architecture and the symbolic signs attached to the mosque. Such encounters, following Merleau-Ponty, involve social bodies sensing and intertwining with the world (and its materialities) in a way that belongs neither to subject nor to object but produces attunements and emotions in their interspace. As material and symbolic forms, the mosques become interfaces among citizens of different confessions or secularities. It is about the affective power of these religious buildings and their capacity to inspire feelings ranging from emotional security and sanctuary among congregations, to insecurity, anxiety or hostility among opponents. Analyses from other European countries have shown how such feelings can be connected to the location of the mosque – whether it is located in the centre of the city or the outskirts, in residential areas or abandoned manufacturing areas (de Galambert, 2005; Gale, 2005; Göle, 2011). De Galambert asserts that one of the preconditions for enhanced visibility of Islam is spatial marginalization. Another contested issue is the architectural style of the buildings, often seen as exotic elements in the urban profile, in particular when it comes to religious design elements of domes and minarets (Gale and Naylor, 2002; Naylor and Ryan, 2002; Gale, 2005; Hatziprokopiou and Evergeti, 2014). An iconic example is the Swiss referendum on minarets in 2009 (Göle, 2011).

IN/VISIBILITY

These conflicts draw attention to the question of the *visibility* of Islam in urban space. The notion of visibility has been employed in a variety of ways in studies of migrants and ethnic minorities. Brighenti (2007) nominates recognition and control, by definition, as the two most important social outcomes of visibility. At the same time, she underlines their oppositional character, referring to the ambivalences of visibility and its effects. Here, we will emphasize the aspect of recognition, basically following Honneth (1995) in his suggestion that inter-subjective recognition is a necessary condition for intact identity formation. In this way, we can see the move from an arrangement of mosques in unrecognizable buildings to the appearance of purpose-built mosques as a question of recognition.

The ambivalence of visibility has successfully been explored in discussions of *whiteness* (e.g. Dyer, 1997; Ahmed, 2004, 2006; Shaw, 2007; and in the Nordic context, Loftsdottir and Toivanen, 2012) that emphasize how the notion is not just a characteristic of bodies; it is an ordering device that gets its power by becoming habitual. Whiteness is invisible and unmarked, as an absent centre against which other groups appear only as deviants. We do not see white bodies as *white* bodies, just as bodies. This normalization renders it possible to talk about 'white spaces', in the sense that spaces are orientated around whiteness through the repetition of acts, allowing the passing of some bodies and not others (Ahmed, 2006). And yet, non-white bodies do inhabit white spaces. However, such bodies are often *made invisible* when spaces are seen as white. At the same time non-white people can become *hypervisible* when they are not capable of passing: they 'stand out' and are seen as 'out-of-place'. In practice, however, the social relations of (in)visibility are more complex. (Leinonen and Toivanen, 2014). Brighenti (2007) characterizes visibility as a double-edged sword – it can be empowering as well as disempowering. There is a built-in *ambivalence* in the notion of (in)visibility, in particular when it refers to issues of identity and recognition. The term hypervisibility, for example, represents visibility as an undesirable condition imposing cultural and racial stereotypes on minority groups. But it can also be part of a 'politics of identity' claiming recognition in public space through visible manifestations of difference. Similarly, invisibility can relate to the powerlessness of the overlooked as well as to the possibility of passing or even the strategic performance of successful integration (Juul, 2014).

Such ambivalences are also involved when it comes to the physical and symbolic *materiality* of the mosques. This is what our analysis of the opening event explores: a transition mediated through materialization in architectural form that transforms Copenhagen Muslims from invisible migrant workers into visible Muslim citizens.

> The 'visibility' of Islam in public is […] a form of agency, a manifestation of religious difference that cannot be thought independent of the materiality of culture, namely aesthetic forms, dress codes, or architectural genres. (Göle, 2011: 383)

Such material transformations have happened all over Europe, much later in Denmark than many other European countries. Until the opening event in question, mosques have mostly been discreet and indistinguishable. In this sense, strategies of invisibility, as much as visibility, have been working among Muslims. Nevertheless, architectural form is important. Purpose-built mosques with domes and minarets represent the imprint of Islamic cultural heritage. The dome and the minaret have become a 'structural metonym' of Muslim identity. It is, however, these very visible elements that have also generated conflicts in many places (*Journal of Ethnic and Migration Studies, 2005*), in particular if the audibility of the Call to Prayer from the minarets is added to the situation (Gale, 2005; Göle, 2011).

The relationship between the visibility represented by the mosques and the formation of identities emerges clearly from interviews with different participants at the opening event. In the joy expressed by the participants, the interviews included remarks such as 'this is historical and a very special experience for me'; 'it is really great to come to a place where you feel at home'; and 'now, I can better feel at home and call myself a Danish Muslim'. It is obvious from these remarks that this is not only about identity and subjectivity but also about politics, thus in this way making topical an Arendthian politics of in/visibility (Arendt, 1958; Borren, 2008). Arendt defines the political world as the *space of appearances*, 'the space where I appear to others as others appear to me' (1958: 198–9) thus closely relating it to visibility. From her reflections on the condition of the stateless, she distinguishes between two conceptual pairs: the first pair is 'public visibility' and 'natural invisibility', which she considers capable of constituting the criteria of sound political action and citizenship; the other is 'public invisibility' and 'natural visibility', which is politically harmful and disabling since the individuals here are reduced to pure organic life, to the naked naturalness of being-nothing-but-human. Natural visibility, then, comes close to Fanon's thinking on visual exposure and the 'historical–racial schema'.

ENCOUNTERING LOCAL AUTHORITIES

The first encounters to take place are negotiations with the municipality during the planning and building process. This process shows how the organization behind the mosque negotiates its visibility through the material and symbolic form of the mosque. Such planning processes have been explored in many other European countries (e.g. Naylor and Ryan, 2002; *Journal of Ethnic and Migration Studies,* 2005). They have given rise to a number of social, religious and political conflicts as well as legislative, architectural and planning regulations. In Copenhagen, several former projects have failed because of such conflicts. Seen in this context, the planning process for the Khayr El-Barriya Mosque has been relatively unproblematic.

Through our interviews with key figures, we can identify three possible explanations for this relative smoothness. First of all, the development of the community centre was enabled by the existing building regulations of the area (the local plan), which avoided the need for a public hearing. The developers deliberately pursued a moderate architecture, materializing the ambivalence between visibility and invisibility (for a similar strategy, see Naylor and Ryan, 2002). Their idea was that the architecture should reflect the combination of Islamic and Nordic cultures. As it stands, the community centre has modest, white facades signalling familiarity with Nordic minimalism. In contrast, the interior of the mosque has ornamentation and coloured walls, carpets and furniture that are associated with Islamic traditions. The second reason was that the municipality has had a positive attitude towards the project. The left wing and social democratic political majority was interested in promoting possibilities for purpose-built mosques in Copenhagen, and the planning authorities entered the process with a helpful attitude. This partially happened in tension with national politicians and authorities, unearthing complex relationships and conflicts between the local and the national level. The centre's spokeswoman expressed frustration over the number of permissions required during the building process. However, and thirdly, that was partly counteracted by the fact that an experienced architectural firm played a key role in the negotiations between the developer and the municipality. Problems did arise, however, when it came to the minaret. It deviated from the existing local plan regarding height (about 8 metres) and its potential function of calling the congregation to prayer. The public hearing gave rise to a great number of objections from all over the country. As seen elsewhere (see, for instance, Gale, 2005; Göle, 2011) the potential audibility of the minaret's speakers calling the congregation to prayer was a central point of objection. The hearing resulted in a compromise that the minaret would be built, but remain silent.

ENCOUNTERING POLITICS AND MEDIA

The main headline circulating in the media the day before the opening event was 'The official Denmark opts out', highlighting the absence of the Royal Family, the Government and party leaders, who all refused an invitation to participate in the event. The reasons varied, but all excuses were linked to what we earlier called 'the figure of the Muslim' and the perception of Islam as a threat. The most dominant objections came in reaction to a sponsorship deal with the mosque (from Qatari Emirates) and a newspaper interview where a mosque spokesman described homosexuality as '*haram*' ('forbidden') and as an illness. In addition, the Minister of Integration could not find room in his diary, and a left-wing party leader would not attend because she was 'not religious'. The Chief Burgomeister of Copenhagen also referred to a busy diary, but he compromised by sending the Mayor for Social Affairs, who is also a Social Democrat. A few politicians – interestingly, from parties of different political orientation – attended, arguing that if you want dialogue with Danish Muslims, you have to turn up and engage. Interestingly, a woman from the Socialist People's Party simultaneously made her opinions clear by wearing an LGBT rainbow badge during the event. From the municipality only three out of eight mayors turned up. So, the political elite were sparsely represented. In this sense, the dominant secular power regime in Danish society managed to put its mark on the event from the outset.

The opening was followed closely by leading Danish newspapers, TV and radio broadcasts, and was met with heated debate around this new visibility of Islam. The debate was characterized by three main perspectives: the symbolic, of security and fear, and of gender and sexuality:

The *symbolic* debate concerned what is acceptable in public space. The mosque here serves as a religious symbol for something else. The appearance of the mosque is interpreted as a symbol of 'our' values: 'freedom of religion, democracy and openness'. The logic is that a moderate secular state such as Denmark should accept the visible presence of Islamic religious symbols in public space (Lægaard 2010). But it is a special kind of acceptance, not signalling respect or recognition but rather *tolerance,* describing an acceptance of something that you generally feel uncomfortable about. The debate was characterized by reservations, anxiety and uncertainty and dominated by statements like: 'Is there something hidden inside the Mosque?'. The mosque symbolizes 'them', who, in contrast to 'us', lack 'our' values such as freedom, tolerance and openness. The symbolic framing of the discussion slides into stereotypical us–them binaries that essentialize the difference between 'Danishness' and Islam:

> Mosques are unavoidable in a democratic society but dangerous. It has to be closely monitored 'that nothing is taught or done that is against good morals or public order', as the Danish constitution prescribes. Because Danish culture is incompatible with Islam and Islam is incompatible with Danish culture. (Hvorslev, 2014)

While the symbolic debate is preoccupied with discussions on secularism, values and culture, the *security* issue concerns the mosque as a place for radicalization and potential terrorism. It construes the mosque as a dangerous place, outside the boundaries of civilization and a threat to Danish society. An editorial in the conservative newspaper *Jyllands-Posten* linked the mosque to the war in Syria and Islamic fundamentalism, thereby relating it to the geopolitical logic of what Gregory (2011) calls the 'everywhere war'. Thus, the mosque not only brings Islam into the cityscape but also the 'war on terror'.

The third issue in the public debate was about *gender and sexuality*. The issue of gender was mostly discussed in relation to the physical separation of men and women in the mosque. The mosque and its material and architectural design were taken to stand for female oppression and traditional views on gender that are impossible to 'modernize'. In this way, gender equality was represented as something *we* have and *they* don't, 'they' being Muslim believers deeply embedded in their 'backward' culture. Sexuality also became a central issue in the debate when the mosque's former spokesman (he was replaced soon after) described homosexuality as '*haram*' (forbidden). The interview immediately created reactions and a dominating media representation of Islamic homophobia as a special case, proving there is something suspicious about 'them'.

Generally, the public debate showed how Islamophobia has a strong hold on public consciousness in Denmark. In the national context, it intersects with, and is strengthened by Danish 'welfare nationalism' (see Chapter 5).

ENCOUNTERING OTHER RELIGIONS

Within the ecclesiastical establishment the mosque was received differently, leaving the impression that religious communities recognize and welcome each other's existence. At the opening event, the Bishop of Copenhagen was represented, and the local vicars were there to congratulate their Muslim brethren. The leader of the Catholic Church was there, as were the leaders of the Shia Muslim community. In this sense, the mosque's ambition of dialogue among different religious communities was successfully realized – at least on this festive day. During the opening event, an important speech was given by the Bishop of Copenhagen. He expressed his delight with the new mosque and its appearance in the urban landscape, saying, 'It is obviously inspired by Nordic architecture and gives it new beautiful expression. It unites the Nordic with the traditional Islamic.' In this way, he touched on the question of visibility and showed his appreciation of the ambition expressed through its architectural form.

ENCOUNTERING THE NEIGHBOURHOOD

Through on-the-spot interviews with visitors and neighbours about the opening event, yet another kind of reaction appeared. Certainly, the reactions were varied – ranging from positive and optimistic to ambivalent and negative – but the majority of them had a positive attitude.

Joy and excitement about getting a *proper* mosque were the general reaction among Muslims we met in the neighbourhood. As one of them said, he was now able to 'just cross the street' to worship, instead of driving to a different neighbourhood. Many non-Muslims also expressed joy and appreciation; they were happy on behalf of 'their Muslim neighbours' because the new mosque 'finally provides a proper place' for them to practise their religion – 'we have our churches all over', one said – and they expressed hope that the community centre would serve as a symbol of recognition and social acceptance. Other reactions emphasized that the community centre brings more life to the area and potentially keeps groups of youngsters off the streets. At the opening ceremony, we also found positive curiosity among people who had travelled from other parts of Copenhagen in order to 'get a sense of it all'. Their reactions were often connected to a frustration over the public debate in Denmark and the wide-ranging Islamophobia: 'What kind of place has Denmark become?' was one of the questions posed.

Another frequent expression was *'they don't bother me'*, accompanied by a shrug of the shoulders and no visible signs of engagement. In this way they expressed *indifference* and a lack of interest. However, this indifferent reaction also seems to involve some unspoken reservations or ambivalent feelings about the centre. Their answer was often developed further with statements such as 'as long as they behave, it's all right with me'.

The general positivity in most local reactions might reflect the local context of the centre in Nørrebro, which has the most multi-ethnic population in Copenhagen. In much of the public debate, Nørrebro has become the epitome of multiculturalism in Denmark. Diversity, whether based on migrant status or social class, has always been a part of Nørrebro's identity. Political activism is also a part of the narrative of the neighbourhood (Schmidt, 2011). Accordingly, most inhabitants have become skilled practitioners of diversity and conflict, in this way forming a promising local context for the opening event and expectations of the future role of the community centre.

Generally, then, a range of paradoxes arise in connection with the reception of the mosque. Questions of participation or non-participation already reveal contradictions in the will to engage in dialogue, between the political and the clerical establishment, between national and urban politics and within political parties. In particular, the difference in attitudes of the political and the clerical establishment to participating in the opening ceremony is conspicuous. While the majority of politicians, both left- and right-wing, excused themselves, the various religious communities were present to welcome the 'newcomer'. Another paradox contrasts the dominant attitude in the public debate with that in the local neighbourhood. While the debate in the media was dominated by stereotypes of 'the Muslim' – again expressed by commentators on both sides of the political spectrum, local residents mostly expressed either indifference or joy that their neighbours could practise their religion in a worthy place. The event thus highlights the complexity of the formation of cross-cultural public space. Controversies over the visibility of Islam push stereotypes and Islamophobic feelings to the extremes. They do, however, also bring different groups together in unprecedented ways and create new constellations of political, religious and cultural boundaries.

NOTES

1. We refer to Edward Casey here because we find his understanding of the relationship between body and built environment useful, but without buying the ontologization of place which also is a part of his thinking.
2. It seems that most of the literature on atmosphere has concentrated on the man-made environment. However Olwig (2011)and Ingold (2012, 2016) argue for the importance of dealing with elements such as air, light and sound as well as more solid elements of the environment. This input is heavily criticized by Hasse (2016), who points out that, in this argument, Ingold has only acknowledged the English literature on the subject. The German philosophy of atmosphere in which the development of the concept is rooted includes several examples of discussions of air and weather. Hasse definitely has a point here. However, it might be that the most interesting element in Ingold's contribution is not so much his argument concerning exclusion as the way he seeks to develop a double understanding of the elements of air and light: the meteorological/physical one and the aesthetic/affective/phenomenal one.
3. Thibault works with the concept of ambiance rather than atmosphere. He argues that he considers it very close to that of atmosphere but prefers to use ambiance because it has a long history in French research. One of its main origins is in the field of architecture, as well as the tradition of situationist thought, particularly that of Guy Debord.
4. We are aware of how the term 'worlding' has been used in different ways within postcolonial urban theory as a strategic concept for 'worlding' the South (Radhakrishnan, 2005; Roy, 2014). We are sympathetic to this purpose, but use the concept with another meaning in our context.
5. This position also relates to our discussion of Merleau-Ponty and Levinas in Chapter 1.
6. She is thus writing herself into a long tradition of formulating urban utopias. For a historical discussion, see Pinder (2005).
7. Our work with purpose-built mosques in Copenhagen can be found in more developed form in earlier publications (Neergaard et al., 2017; Simonsen, et al., 2019).

Political Perspectives

Action, the only activity that goes on directly between men without the intermediary of things or matter, corresponds to the human condition of plurality, to the fact that men, not Man, live on the earth and inhabit the world. While all aspects of the human condition are somehow related to politics, this plurality is specifically *the* condition – not only the *conditio sine qua non,* but the *conditio per quam* – of all political life. (Arendt, 1958: 7)

Only when we come to feel ourselves part and parcel of a world in which we, like everybody else, are engaged in a struggle against great and sometimes overwhelming odds, and yet with a chance of victory, however small, and with allies, however few – only when we recognize the human background against which recent events have taken place, knowing that what was done was done by men and therefore can and must be prevented by men – only then will we be able to rid the world of its nightmarish quality. (Arendt, 2007: 384–5)

EVERYDAY POLITICS

As mentioned in Chapter 1, Merleau-Ponty contributes to political thinking, maybe not so much by developing genuine political theory, but through use of his thinking in critical analyses of the concrete political issues of his age.[1] Important issues were on the one hand problems in both the development of the liberal capitalist democracies and that of the Soviet Union and Eastern Europe under Stalinism, and on the other, the relationship between the West and its Others throughout decolonization. His grasp of politics was rooted in existence and coexistence, that is, it was based on everyday practices and experiences and the way in which collective life and structures of coexistence were formed systemically between power and communication in different social formations.

However, in seeking support in developing an extended phenomenological reconceptualization of the political, we turn to Hannah Arendt, who basically argues that politics centres on the spaces in which humans interact and take responsibility for the shared world. 'Action, as distinguished from fabrication, is never possible in isolation; to be isolated is to be deprived of the capacity to act' (Arendt, 1958: 188). Politics is not instrumental governance but the human capacity to act, engage and struggle together and thereby make new beginnings. Taking this as a starting point, *everyday politics* transcends the institutional level and implements a much broader understanding of the 'political'. Everyday politics is what we experience and live through and our shared capacity to act. It is about forms of perceiving the world and relating to it – how we make sense of the world. As formulated by Topolski, 'the political is the disclosure of the world that lies between us; it exists intersubjectively' (2015: 45). Everyday politics is centred in the lived world, drawing attention to the way we experience it from within. That includes the experiences of those who are living in and suffering from situations of oppression.

In her phenomenology of active life, Arendt distinguishes among labour, work and action. While labour and work sustain organic life and provide a stable world of artefacts, action relies on human plurality and the sharing of words and deeds. The starting point for her thinking is European totalitarianism in the 1930s and 1940s, a context she herself had experienced and lived through. In her analysis of the rise of totalitarianism and the destruction of the Jewish people, she offers a phenomenological account of the experiences of dehumanization and the loss of the human world (Arendt, 1973). First, under totalitarianism, ideology replaces the law by denying the difference between ideology and reality. Secondly, the exploitation of fear leads to the destruction of the shared bond between people and the sense of solidarity. And finally, the destruction of individuality, the experiences and existential feeling of not belonging to the world, lead to the ultimate destruction of people and their dehumanization. By analysing the rise of totalitarianism and the destruction of the Jewish people from a phenomenological perspective, Arendt not only offers an understanding of European history, she also provides instruments to understand more recent political questions related to processes of dehumanization; for example, growing neo-nationalism and fear of Others, Islamophobia and the rise of right-wing parties in Europe. However, Arendt also provides theoretical suggestions for the way in which the world can be recreated through political action. As she says: 'the instrumentalization of action and the degradation of politics into a means for something else has of course never really succeeded in eliminating action, in preventing its being one of the decisive human experiences, or in destroying the realm of human affairs altogether' (Arendt, 1958: 230).

This relevance, as well as the formulation of hope, is probably the background for the widespread renewed interest for her work today – including our own (see e.g. Kruks, 2006; Fassin, 2009; Häkli and Kallio, 2014; Topolski, 2015; Dikeç, 2016; Kallio, 2017; Last, 2017). The parallel between the 1930s and the first decades of the twenty-first century is, as argued by Topolski (2015), the dominance of technocrats and economists in political affairs, the increasing numbers of refugees in Europe and the extension of the so called 'refugee crisis' that raises urgent political and ethical questions. Politics and the present de-politicization is, as noted by Swyngedouw, characterized by 'the disappearance of the political, the erosion of democracy and of the public sphere, and the colonialization of the political space by a consensual mode of governance' (2014: 123; see also Swyngedouw, 2018). Contrary to this development, *the political* should not be a reflection of something else, but a capacity of each and all to act politically (Dikeç and Swyngedouw, 2017).

ACTION

The main principle for everyday politics is the *responsibility to act*. For Arendt, it is grounded in *human plurality*, which she sees specifically as *the* condition for politics. What has been neglected, she says, is that human beings have to be understood in the plural and that each human being has the capacity to bring into the world new perspectives and new actions that do not necessarily fit any predictable political model. As argued by Arendt, 'plurality is the condition of human action because we are all the same, that is, human, in such a way that nobody is ever the same as anyone else who ever lived, lives, or will live' (Arendt, 1958: 8). Plurality is the cornerstone in action and is grounded in a paradox between equality and distinction. If we were not distinct we would be identical, and there would be no need to act or communicate. Distinction, particularity and uniqueness are conditions for the political to exist. This means that the political cannot exist without pluralism. In political terms there is no sameness, only difference. Therefore, 'we must recognize our inequality and celebrate our difference' (Topolski, 2015: 59). Politics is exactly what lies between people in what Arendt calls the *web of human relationships*. It arises directly out of acting together and creates a space of human interaction:

> In acting and speaking, men show who they are, reveal actively their unique personal identities and thus make their appearance in the human world, while their physical identities appear without any activity of their own in the unique shape of the body and sound of the voice. This disclosure of 'who' in contradistinction to 'what' somebody is – his qualities, gifts, talents, and short-comings, which he may display or hide – is implicit in everything somebody says and does. (Arendt, 1958: 179)

To show who we are suggests a shift from the self towards the Other. The conditioning of reality and plurality is *spaces of appearance*, meaning being seen or heard by others as well as ourselves. That is what constitutes reality, the common world and the public realm. 'The presence of others who see what we see and hear what we hear assures us of the reality of the world and ourselves' (Arendt,

1958: 50). The political realm is the space in which we co-create the shared world as a realm of difference and distinction. Political experience offers each person the chance to appear as particular individual in a shared public space and to distinguish herself through word and deed (Topolski, 2015). Arendt distinguishes between 'who' someone is and 'what' they are. What somebody *is* is relevant for activities related to labour and work – qualities, talents and shortcomings. In contrast, the 'who' somebody is can remain hidden from the persons themselves – but in politics the 'who' is the actor, unique and irreplaceable. The promise of political action does not derive from the identity of the actor before she steps into action, but from and through her action with others (Dikeç, 2016). It is a *politics of relationality*, in the words of Arendt:

> This revelatory quality of speech and action comes to the fore where people are *with* others and neither for nor against them – that is, in sheer human togetherness. Although nobody knows whom he reveals when he discloses himself in deed or word, he must be willing to risk the disclosure, and this neither the doer of good works, who must be without self and preserve complete anonymity, nor the criminal, who must hide himself from others, can take upon themselves. (Arendt, 1958: 180)

Declaring relationality and plurality the basic condition for political action is not a question of consensus. It involves a productive agonistic tension between equality and distinction – or plurality and particularity. Everyday politics challenges us and is full of disagreement, debate and strife. 'Political agonism confronts anonymity and is thus fundamental to the political. Action requires initiatives in that people must choose to appear and disclose "who they are" under the scrutiny of others' (Topolski, 2015: 59). Everyday politics is about *agonistic plurality*, meaning that the political is differentiated with conflicts, disagreements and many different perspectives but with the ultimate respect for one another's right to exist. This is in contrast to antagonism, which is based in a friend/enemy relation and becomes the struggle for the destruction of the enemy. The main challenge is 'to find ways of transforming inherent tendencies towards antagonism into peaceable relations of agonism, in which relations of identity and difference are experienced as relations between adversaries rather than enemies' (Barnett, 2004: 511).

> The characteristic of human action is that it always begins something new, and this does not mean that it is ever permitted to start *ab ovo*, to create *ex nihilo*. In order to make room for one's own action, something that was there before must be removed or destroyed, and things as they were before are changed. Such change would be impossible if we could not mentally remove ourselves from where we physically are located and *imagine* that things might as well be different from what they actually are. (Arendt, 1972: 5)

The political is rooted in the *beginning*; the impulse to act means to take initiatives to set something into motion on our own initiative. It presupposes that we imagine that things can be different. As argued by Arendt, this beginning is not the same as the beginning of the world; it is in the nature of the beginning that something new is started on our own initiative. 'It is not the beginning of something but of *somebody,* who is a beginner himself' (Arendt, 1958: 177). This is a capacity to act in the world which means that the unexpected can be expected. The political is always open, unpredictable and contingent – we will never know its outcome and we cannot predict or plan the possible futures. For Arendt, the new always appears in the guise of a miracle. We are not here to die, but to begin something. We are not here to blindly follow the standard, but for the possibility of the emergence of something new in the midst of ordinary routines and established norms characterizing our everyday lives (Dikeç, 2016: 21).

POWER AND EMPOWERMENT

> *Power* corresponds to the human ability not just to act but to act in concert. Power is never the property of an individual: it belongs to a group and remains in existence only so long as the group keep together. When we say of somebody that he is 'in power' we actually refer to his being empowered by a certain number of people to act in their name. The moment the group, from which the power originated to begin with (*potestas in populo,* without a people or group there is no power), disappears, 'his power' also vanishes. (Arendt, 1970: 44)

We should, says Arendt, distinguish between 'power', 'authority', 'strength', 'force' and 'violence' not just linguistically but for historical reasons. Strength is not power. It belongs to the singular; the individual entity or an object. The strength of even the strongest persons can always be overpowered by the many acting in concert (1970: 43–4). Power is always a potential and not a measurable and reliable entity like force. Authority can be vested in a person or office – between parents and children – but the greatest enemy of authority is contempt and the surest way to undermine it is laughter. Violence is distinguished by its instrumental character. 'Phenomenologically, it is close to strength, since the implements of violence, like all other tools are designed and used for the purpose of multiplying natural strength until, in the last stage of their development, they can substitute for it' (Arendt, 1970: 46).

Arendt's concept of power extends the concept of action as a protection of the spaces of appearance that arises in humans acting and speaking together. 'Power is what keeps the human realm, the potential space of appearance, between acting and speaking men in existence' (1958: 200). It is rooted in plurality. Power is politics from below:

> Empowerment is what we experience by means of action. This experience is an end in itself. Nonetheless, there are other potential 'by-products' such as a transformation of the political or a contingent and temporary empowering 'we' formation. Nonetheless, the political must remain a noninstrumental realm to preserve its principle of plurality. (Topolski, 2015: 66–7)

This has at least three implications in the way we characterize power in our phenomenological conceptualization of the political.

First, it has a spontaneous, unpredictable character – 'power springs up between men' (Arendt, 1958: 200). It has potentiality which corresponds to the character of action and the natality of the new beginning. Power cannot be stored as an item for the future: it must continually emerge anew. 'Power springs up between men when they act together and vanishes the moment they disperse' (Arendt, 1958: 200). Power therefore is a *potentiality* that can only be actualized but never fully materialized.

Secondly, power does not rest upon obedience, but upon consent. This non-hierarchical concept of power is, according to Peeters, 'echoed in Arendt's concept of the law. The laws of the political community must be thought of as *directives* that are "accepted," rather than as *imperatives* that are "imposed." The "obedience" to laws is comparable to the manner in which people who wish to play a game agree with the rules' (2008: 174).

Thirdly, power can only be thought of as an egalitarian and non-hierarchical relation between people. 'Power is actualized only where word and deed have not parted company, where words are not empty and deeds not brutal, where words are not used to veil intentions but to disclose realities, and deeds are not used to violate and destroy but to establish relations and create new realities' (Arendt, 1958: 200). Power answers to what Arendt calls 'sheer human togetherness', a life '*with* others and neither for or against them' (1958: 180). It does not exist without particularity where every actor is a distinct and irreplaceable human being, and where one discovers who one is by learning from the other and at the same time, through participation, helps to create a shared world. The potential *power of plurality*, which is the source of revolution and social movements, has greater permanence in the world because 'it brings about lasting change by transforming both people and the world' (Topolski, 2015: 66).

SPACES OF POLITICAL FREEDOM (THE COMMON WORLD)

In addition to plurality, action and empowerment, Arendt's contribution to everyday politics also has a spatial dimension, rooted in her phenomenological heritage and taking its starting point in her 'space of appearance' – in this way introducing a political space:

> What politics does is to open a space where matters of a shared world can be inscribed, debated and contested. This space is opened not in the name of private interests and by a capacity for rational calculation to promote them, but in the name of politics as transformative action and by a capacity to initiate new beginnings. (Dikeç, 2016: 58)

'Space of appearance' is a contingent public realm produced by action. It provides a common domain for experiences where we can appear to each other and share worldly concerns, debate and contest. As Arendt put it, 'the space of appearance comes into being wherever men are together in the manner of speech and action' (Arendt, 1958: 199). It is exactly in this space of appearance that we insert our self into the world and produce something not necessarily already given in speech and action. Everyday politics has transformative potential; it can open up new spaces and challenge the existing order of things – but only *potentially*, not necessarily and not forever. Here we should distinguish between the interrelation of acting, thinking and judging. We act and make sense of the world in the plurality of others, but we are also capable of stepping back from action in the public realm. 'We share a capacity not only to act but to stop and think as well' (Dikeç, 2016: 23). Thinking is the other side of action. Thinking is not done in isolation from the world; it is, rather, a reflexive capacity that can interrupt ordinary or routine ways of acting in the world. Not to think is the foundation for political disaster and dark times. The understanding of thoughtlessness is covered in Arendt's study of the relationship between the banal and the evil in *Eichmann in Jerusalem: A Report on the Banality of Evil* (1963), showing how banal routine and implicit obedience at its extreme can turn out a condition of possibility of radical evil. To stop and think is as politically important as action, and here 'judgement needs the presence of others "in whose place" it must think, whose perspectives it must take into consideration' (Arendt, 1977, cited in Dikeç, 2016: 25). The capacity to judge means that one is able to see things from the perspective of others. In a common world, acting and judging demands engagement with manifold others without necessarily having consensus or agreement. As Dikeç puts it, 'the creation of common worlds is a key to Arendt's politics, but her notion of common world does not imply a single vision of the world to which everyone subscribes' (2016: 27). Everyday politics is not related to unity, one world or consensus but to *differentiated worlds* and differentiated visions of the future.

Political freedom is, then, an intersubjective phenomenon. It does not belong to individuals but to the *space* between them. It is not an inner disposition, but a character of human existence in the world (Arendt, 1958). Freedom cannot be thought of in the singular as an inner motivation or will – an individual is not free, only 'we' are free. Freedom is, in this sense, an intersubjective phenomenon that finds its meanings in human relations rooted in action (Topolski, 2015).

Finally, spaces of political freedom are *world-oriented*. 'In addition to being free from oppression, freedom needs a direction – that of the world' (Topolski,

2015: 65). 'To live together in the world means essentially that a world of things is between those who have it in common as a table is located between those who sit around it; the world like every in-between, relates and separates men at the same time' (Arendt 1958: 52). Spaces of politics simultaneously separate and relate us. We relate to the world and are provoked into speech and deed by how the world appears to us. The worldly character of politics is related to how Arendt views power and action. It is boundless and connects to other spaces. The only precondition is the existence of other people and plurality to begin with.

This unfolding of everyday politics, consisting of action in the interspace between sameness and distinction, power manifested as empowerment, and spaces of political freedom, has provided us with tools for understanding not only the lived world of political action, but also the potential dangers of the implicit thoughtlessness of banal routine. In the following sections we will try to put some of this insight into use.

EVERYDAY NATIONALISM

In the following we explore the upsurge of nationalism in Denmark, simultaneously showing a plurality of nationalisms and an increasing Orientalism within the dominant form (Koefoed, 2006; see also Koefoed and Simonsen, 2007; Koefoed, 2015). The approach we take to nation and nationalism is rooted in the practice and narrative of everyday life. As argued by Billig (1995) in relation to his notion of *banal nationalism* in established nations like those in Europe, everyday practices reproduce national identities in ways so ordinary, so commonplace, that they escape attention altogether. This may happen in speech acts, routinely and unconsciously using homeland-making phrases; small unnoticed words such as 'we', 'the' people, 'this' country, 'here', 'society', or media announcements such as 'the' weather, 'home' news and 'foreign' news. Or it may occur through the use of symbolic material items such as coins, banknotes or flags, hanging unnoticed from public buildings or used at birthday parties and other informal celebrations. When using these linguistic and material markers regularly, 'we' are unmindfully reminded who we are and where we are. National identity becomes a routine way of talking and acting, a form of life. Banal nationalism is 'the ideological habits which enable the established nations of the West to be reproduced' (Billig 1995: 6). It operates as a particularly strong social and political force right at the heart of Western society, creating the continuous background for powerful political discourse. It equips us with an identity and ideological consciousness, encompassing and internalizing us in a complex series of themes about 'us' and 'them', about the homeland and the world at large.

The empirical analysis of everyday nationalism is grounded in a case study with fieldwork conducted in Hundested, a provincial town situated 65 km from Copenhagen. The study is based on qualitative in-depth interviews collecting narratives on national identity from informants representing different social groups and selected with variation in terms of gender, age, education, employment and political orientation. The purpose was to reveal diversity in the ways of signifying the Danish nation in the everyday narratives of the informants (Koefoed, 2006).

THE ORIENTALIZATION OF WELFARE STATE NATIONALISM

In a Scandinavian context, welfare as a concept is full of positive connotations, which in the myth of Danish civilization symbolizes wealth, progress, community and a good life. In the Danish context, 'our' welfare state is often set in contrast to other societies and nations and perceived as something unique and valuable for the imagined community. This view is connected to a comprehensive set of *rights,* public services, education, health and income distribution. But the narrative of welfare nationalism is also a story about great *challenges*, either from above, through globalization and the European Union, that is, through a re-scaling of political and economic power, or from below, through labour mobility and immigration. These challenges are articulated partly through expressions of anxiety, and partly through an unnoticed slide towards orientalist discourses and stereotypes. The story of the Danish welfare community becomes the story of the threatening Other:

> They are only moving up here because they want us to support them, right? They are not coming because they want to help us. They are coming because they want something. It is our values. They want our benefits, right? that our older generation has created. They want their bloody part of the cake. (Karen, 50)

> Our welfare society has deteriorated. In the hospitals we have waiting lists and people die like flies. I saw it with my mother-in-law. She was lying there with a bad heart and needed help. And she was lying there for such a long time nearly getting really ill. She had her operation and that gave her ten good years. That was a good thing. But I mean it's exactly in such a case that one says: 'They should just have all the resources that they need'. Yes, but where would they get the money from? And in this case we notice that we have used too many resources on foreigners that we could have used in the Danish society instead. (Søren, 54)

Welfare nationalism is a strong and shared narrative related to freedom, good life, solidarity and equality. What we experience in Denmark (and other Nordic countries) is that crisis and challenges to the welfare state are articulated through an invisible glide towards orientalist discourses and stereotypes. The story of the welfare community becomes the story of the threatening Other. It is narratives that focus on the external Other that is constructed as a mobile figure which not only intends to exploit the Danish welfare state, but also undermines it. In the above narratives, the mobility of the Other represents a threat to the productive and imaginative welfare community. The external Other in the narrative is a mobile group of people attracted by 'our resources'. The restructuring in the health sector is directly linked to the threatening mobility of immigrants and refugees. They become part of the same story. The internal Other becomes the explanation for any kind of difficulty or crisis in the service sector. The informant explains that the 'welfare system has deteriorated'. On the other hand, the person says that 'we have used too many resources on the foreigners'. In this story the internal Other is implicitly preventing the welfare system from saving lives. The narrative stages this as a conflict or a choice between 'us' and 'them'.

The social reproduction of the welfare community is thereby dominated by an Orientalism (see Said, 1985) that appeals to a cultural racism naturalizing and essentializing cultural difference. According to this, immigrants are bound to cultures that are alien to the 'Danish' one and resist integration into Danish society (see also Simonsen, 2004). Immigrants are a threat to Danish society, not only because they are supposed to 'pollute' Danish culture, but also because they allegedly intend to 'exploit' the Danish welfare system. According to this discourse, 'Danishness' is characterized by tolerance, enlightenment and equality. These alleged qualities are mobilized to support xenophobia by representing Muslims as intolerant fundamentalists who should not be tolerated in a tolerant society and Danes as a naïve people trying to do good for everybody, but merely opening themselves up to exploitation.

The orientalization of welfare state nationalism uncovers a negative affective cultural pessimism bound to the feeling of *ontological insecurity*: 'What will happen to our small country in this changing world of Europe-wide and global developments?', with political affect based on economic chauvinism: 'The wealth is ours and we do not want to share it with any-body' (Gingrich and Bank, 2006: 37–8). This narrative fantasy that the Other will steal something from us (Žižek, 1993) is also connected to the growth in national populism, right-wing nationalism, xenophobia and racism that has penetrated into everyday life and what it is acceptable to say and suggest (Simonsen, 2015). At the same time, orientalization of the Danish welfare state is not only a 'colonial present' (Gregory, 2004) on a small scale; it also has wider and more structural connections to the general transition of neoliberal governance from welfare state to security state and fragmented citizenship with, for example, different kinds of restrictions for immigrants and minorities. With the securitization of immigration, we have a situation like the one Lentin and Titley describe: 'if the neo-liberal state's function is to ensure citizens' security rather than their welfare, it must protect the desirables from the undesirables by either locking them up or locking them out' (2011: 172).

This Orientalist everyday nationalism is not what Billig (1995) characterizes as a 'hot' nationalism of 'exotic, rare and often violent specimens'. When it comes to the presence of extreme right-wing nationalist, racist and violent groups, Denmark is probably better off than many other countries. What we experience instead is a 'small' (and in a way more insidious) everyday racism, showing itself in a gradual slide in what it is socially acceptable to say and suggest – in political discourse and everyday talk – in relation to 'foreign' Others. On the other hand, the new nationalism is not 'banal' in the sense of unnoticed either; it is definitely articulated, penetrating into different spheres of everyday life. We here see a connection between the banal and the extreme that originates from Hannah Arendt's study *Eichmann in Jerusalem: A Report on the Banality of Evil* (1963), showing how banal routine and obedience at its extreme can render possible radical evil. What we face here is, of course, a very different situation, but still we see the connection between banal everyday prejudices performed in gestures and speech and the advance of populist anti-immigrant views gradually being normalized and gaining strong influence on the agenda on 'foreigners'. In Denmark, the extreme does not so much take the form of physical violence conducted by small radical groups. It is more a *symbolic violence* continuously shifting the limits of what it is possible to say about Other groups of humans. Besides the harm done to domestic minorities, in the dominant discourse it also evokes a merciless indifference to human suffering among refugees and asylum seekers and among captured opponents in the 'wars on terror' in which Denmark participates.

NATIONALISM IN THE PLURAL

However, everyday nationalism has many voices and, consequently, should be treated as a plurality. Notwithstanding the strength of the hegemonic Orientalist perspective on the nation, the scope of nationalism is much more differentiated and blurred than it suggests (Koefoed, 2006). Focusing on Orientalism alone means overlooking otherwise significant voices, practices and perspectives on the nation. It is important to bring out the complexity and ambiguity in nationalism by revealing other narrative actions which give rise to alternative/supplementary modes of negotiating and making sense of the nation in everyday life. They are not only produced and articulated by radical and regressive forces, but are an integrated part of everyday life. On a deeper level they reflect practices and discourses producing other types of nationalism. Each of these different nationalisms should be seen as part of a complex and contested narrative that together construct the everyday nation as imagined community.

The first of these alternative nationalisms we call a *social and critical nationalism*:

> But we also have a responsibility for ourselves, the people in Denmark, haven't we? Politicians are busier with the world outside than with what is going on here. They don't even know what is going on in Danish society. Among other things, the schools are run down. And they are cutting down on the hospitals, right? And they are so busy with what all the others are doing. (Karen, 50)

If you drive from here to Copenhagen, you will pass five or six McDonald's restaurants. And they are not especially Danish in my opinion. Multinational companies, right? You don't even notice it. Coca-Cola among other things. It tastes damned good, but it kind of occupies and takes up an incredible lot of space. There is nothing less Danish than that. I don't like these tendencies. But it's very hard to fight against it. It's capital that rules. We can take our own case here. When the ferry was closed down [...] It was capital that decided to close down the ferry. It was solely economic considerations. And that is what's happening, unfortunately: the Danish Steelwork among other things [closed down in 2002]. It was also economic considerations, right? So, these kinds of things [...] I don't like it. But you can't do anything about it. So, the world is already arranged. It is the capitals that govern, right? (Svend, 58)

Class inequalities and social conflicts are part of everyday life experiences and connect to what we call social nationalism, which organizes the nation as a social space with different social positions. Class division is here articulated in hierarchical positions between the elite and the ordinary people, upper and lower class, which not only produces abstract positions, it symbolizes concrete spatial conflicts, inequalities and differences among social groups. The differences between the people and the elite are articulated and produced as a set of meaningful categories in practice in three different ways. First, it is a class division that demonstrates that the nation state is a class society marked by economic and social inequalities. Secondly, it is articulated as a division between expert systems and people's democracy. Thirdly, the axis is produced as a conflict between global capital and local workers.

This everyday perspective on the nation can be found in two different versions constituting different trajectories. The *populist* track appears in stories describing how the (political) elite do not care about the ordinary people, and how they make alliances instead with the international, rootless, cosmopolitan elite and the immigrants against the 'people'. Members of the elite are seen here as the forerunners of the multicultural society. In the narrative, they not only betray the people in a social sense, but also in terms of culture. They betray the ordinary people who are imagined as the true bearers of the nation. As the respondent says the elite has been too busy with what is going on *outside* the nation and therefore has failed to protect the people *inside* the national territory where cuts in central national welfare institutions like public schools are part of everyday ordinary life.

The other trajectory criticizes the *class* division in society and the conflicts between capital and the everyday necessity of social reproduction. This narrative is concerned with the apparent division of the nation into two parts. The people and the elite are not able to communicate, it says, because they speak two different languages. Therefore, the social division in society is seen as weakening the community and as undermining the social cohesion of the nation. It connects to a critique of international and global capitalism and neoliberalism. As the respondent explain 'there is nothing less Danish than multinational companies'. This links directly to the global expansion of capital that is weakening local and national community, illustrated by the loss of jobs and the restructuring of the labour market. It is a story about domination of space that illustrates the conflict between vagabond capitalism and the necessity of social reproduction (Katz, 2001). What this narrative suggests and dreams of is a place characterized by social justice that is free from external control and capital domination. But as the informant concludes: *how* and from *where* can we act against global capitalism? The narrative implicitly finds its own solution in the national community. The critical perspective is also found as a left-wing critique of global capitalism, cultural imperialism and transnational governance articulated in relation to the integration into the European Union. Here the European Union has been seen as an external control that undermines national sovereignty, democracy and the welfare state.

A *spatial and temporal nationalism* rests upon the way in which spatial and temporal configurations are fundamental in the production of the everyday nation. The nation is habitually produced and reproduced by spatial and embodied practices. The nation comes into existence through *movement* and *bodily experience*. In this way, everyday narratives organize the changing relationship of places and spaces. They organize places and produce spaces. As de Certeau (1984) argued, stories carry out the labour of transforming places into spaces and spaces into places. The temporal involves activities that combine and give meaning to the nation in the complex of past–present–future (see Ricoeur, 1984). However, this is also combined with attempts to negotiate present spatial conflicts and dividing lines within the nation. In everyday life, the temporal aspect of nationalism does not reproduce a linear history of the nation. Instead, through the negotiation of multiple temporalities it constructs how, in everyday life, we understand ourselves as part of a larger imagined community. The central driving force is *orientation*: where do we come from, where are we now, and where are we going?

> I think that Danishness always will persist. I don't think that we should be afraid that Danishness will disappear because of immigration. It is something rooted deep inside us. (Lene, 32)

> I think that Danes will be something that you only read about in 100 or 200 years from now. The Danes will be someone that you read about in the universities or libraries. (Lene, 32)

In everyday nationalism we find two significant temporal perspectives on the nation. First a *generation* perspective that expresses the more universal side of the rhythm of human lives, the one that stages conflicts as well as continuity. It makes it possible to ground the narrative in between the 'new' and the 'old', by talking about conflicts related to generations. In the extract the respondent says that she believes that, in the future, the nation will be transformed into something we read about in the library and thereby produce a story about loss and nostalgia. Secondly, the *life perspective* suggests that there is no clear distinction between life stories and national stories; they are very closely mixed together. How the self makes sense of life in time is very closely related to how we make sense of different passages and changes in the national history. The narrative construction of national history in everyday life is created through intimate connections between the self and the imagined community. The life perspective thus connects two different temporalities: life-time and nation-time. Life-time is characterized by the fact that life has a direction going from life to death, while nation-time stretches out in a long duration (Anderson, 1991; Smith, 1999). However, narratives of the nation inscribe into our identities links to both the dead and the yet unborn. As the respondent formulates it, she is not afraid that 'Danishness will disappear because of immigration. It is something rooted deep inside us.' It imaginatively bridges, making our identity immortal through mythical connections. Or, with Anderson (1991: 12), nations 'always loom out of an immemorial past, and still more important, glide into a limitless future'. It is a double story (embedded in the same woman) telling how 'everything changes' through generations and in a strange way simultaneously emphasizing that 'nothing has changed' at all.

> If you are looking for the origins, then it is clear that the city is only a façade. It is absolutely not here that you find the origins of the Danish national spirit, if you can call it that. You will find it in the provinces, not in the big cities. The typical Danish landscape is grain fields, country roads and farms. This I understand as the deepest culture in Denmark. Yes, it is us. (Helle, 51)

Here the spatial (or material) aspect is related to the temporal. The respondent produces an image of a nation grounded in an image of a romantic landscape where the nation is represented by 'grain fields', 'country roads' and 'farms' thereby mythologizing a romantic landscape that hardly exists any more in Denmark (and only has done so for a relatively short period). Interestingly, the narrative also rests on a spatial distinction: it relates to a narrative that grounds the nation and the imaginative community in the countryside, signifying authentic Danishness in contrast to the superficiality and façade of the big city. It thus draws on a myth of Babylon of town and country, signifying the rural idyll and urban evil, and constituting a kind of 'provincial nationalism'.

Finally, we identified a *cosmopolitan nationalism* according to which the nation cannot be defined exclusively, and immigrants are not necessarily a burden on Danish society. They can just as well be enriching as regards both culture and the economy. The major argument here is about humanism, tolerance and equality, concepts that are therefore not reserved for one discourse. Instead they are 'floating signifiers' (Laclau and Mouffe, 1985), contested concepts fought for and decisive in the discursive struggle over 'Danishness'. In contrast to the

Orientalist nationalism where equality is articulated with similarity, and the values referred to are seen as pregiven, inherent qualities of 'Danishness' that the Others do not have, in humanist discourse they are something that ought to exist but does not necessarily. They therefore have to be nurtured and reproduced through decency in practice. If they are threatened, it is not by the immigrants but by the proponents of the Orientalist discourse.

This struggle is not only fought in the public sphere but also in everyday life:

> The fact that the world has become smaller, it's actually also a gigantic thing, isn't it? But it also takes some effort by each one of us. For example, that Hundested, it isn't the hub of the Universe; that we in some way need to learn something about other people. For instance, I need to learn something about Islam. I have a friend who has started to take classes on the history of religions because she thinks that she should 'damned well know something about Islam, because she can't just sit there and listen to all the shit they are telling her, can she?' She wants to know something about what it really is. (Janne, 56)

For this person, cosmopolitanism, the issue of inhabiting cosmos and polis, is not just some abstract spatial feeling, but something that concerns her everyday life and the place where she lives. Her hometown is, as she metaphorically formulates it, not 'the hub of the Universe'. The fact of living in a smaller world is something that concerns her as a human being. If the world is no longer out there at a safe distance but right here in the form of other religions and other ways of thinking, then we have to break with self-centredness and become cosmopolitans. The alternative makes us passive consumers of negative stereotypes ('shit') about the Other. Each human being has to navigate in that 'smaller world' by acquiring knowledge about the things that are represented as Other (in this case, Islam) in order to understand and avoid excluding it. It is, as mentioned in the beginning of the chapter, related to Arendt's argument about the human responsibility to act and to stop and think. This woman has a cosmopolitan attitude that, in her words, is 'gigantic', demanding and placing a responsibility on each and every human being.

POLITICS OF HOSPITALITY

Edward Casey discusses in his essay 'Strangers at the edge of hospitality' (2011) how strangers are located at the edge. Strangers have their place at the edge – or rather their 'non-place', since the edge is no place to be. There is no room at the edge where you can settle, identify yourself or become a citizen. This discussion is somewhat connected to what we in Chapter 4 discussed as 'the figure of the stranger'. However, the essay also, as the title says, connects the figure of the stranger to the notion of hospitality. It does so by digging a bit deeper into the notion of edge. The edge can take different forms. Besides spatial edges (those that occur at a gate or a border), we can talk about bodily edges (connected to bodily encounters) and cultural edges (connected to traditions or imaginations). Common to them all are that they, paradoxically, can both separate and bring together. Together with boundaries and bridges, which we discussed in Chapter 4, they belong to a family of concepts that constitutes a complex relationship of contradiction and connection, or distance and proximity. In other words, the edge is also where the strangers are received. It is where hospitality happens, where it is enacted. The non-place might open up and become an emergent place (called home, country or nation) where it is possible to settle in a more or less stable way.

In the twenty-first century a renewed interest in the theme of hospitality has occurred within both the humanities and the social sciences. It has arisen from the experience of a globalized social life, not least connected to migration as generator of beneficent as well as hostile 'welcome' practices, and it is in that way closely connected to issues of belonging, otherness and strangers that have been central in this book.

The debate on hospitality has become widespread, interdisciplinary and multicultural and, as Dikeç et al. (2009) observe, it is growing into a translation point between continental philosophy and empirical research agendas within the humanities and social sciences. Many authors, independent of disciplinary affiliations, approach the concept through the later work of Jacques Derrida in this exercise (see e.g. Rosello, 2001; Dikeç, 2002; Dikeç et al., 2009; Casey, 2011; Candea and da Col, 2012; Bulley, 2017). One conspicuous element of this work is Derrida's coining of the neologism *hostipitality* in order to demonstrate how hospitality is a term that carries its own contradiction incorporated into it (Derrida, 2000). Hospitality and hostility are inseparable; it is the necessary ethical requirement of absolute openness to the Other paired with the equally necessary exclusionary sovereignty, which simultaneously renders the former possible and negates its aspirations. Derrida develops this initial statement about the contradictory and paradoxical character of hospitality in four points (Derrida, 2000; Dikeç, 2002): (1) He repeatedly says that 'we do not know what hospitality is' – a statement in which he is focusing on the word 'know'. Obviously, it does not mean that the concept does not exist, but it is beyond any objective knowledge by being an 'intentional experience', directed towards the other as absolute stranger – as unknown. (2) The second point develops further by adding that we do not know what hospitality is because it is not a 'present being'. By this he means that this experience or intentional act often proclaims itself as a law, a duty or an obligation, that is, as a should-be rather than a being. It is an imperative involving a temporal contradiction, since the experience of offering or receiving hospitality cannot last; it is performed only 'in imminence of what is about to happen and only lasts an instant' (2000: 8). (3) In a third point which he calls the 'not yet' of our knowledge of hospitality, he refers to the European knowledge system on the concept which is limited by its reliance on Kant and his ideas of universally European right. On the other hand, he also sees the 'not yet' as an opening to what might come. (4) Finally, he refers to the contradiction or the 'double bind' of hospitality coming out of the fact that the 'host', in order to be able to offer hospitality to the stranger, must be master in his/her house, 'he must be assured of his sovereignty over the space and goods he offers or opens to the other as stranger' (2000: 14). In this regard Derrida also emphasizes the necessity for hospitality of the simultaneous existence of a threshold and a door to open, in this way returning to his initial statement on the existence of an unavoidable incorporated hospitality/hostility contradiction.

More concretely, this understanding endows hospitality with both *spatiality* and *temporality*. We can follow Bulley when he describes hospitality as 'a spatial relational practice with affective dimensions' (2017: 7), which involves the interplay between ethics and politics but, first of all, a (sensitive) practice of engagement with the stranger. The fundamental spatial dimension of hospitality is border, threshold or edge (to use Casey's notion from above). The threshold is the place for the stranger (as Casey says), but it is also where hospitality is enacted and strangers are received. As a necessary condition for this to happen, however, the threshold must be breached by an opening or a door that allows crossing and the enactment of a welcoming practice of 'giving place'. In this sense, 'thresholds are the very scenes for the drama of responsiveness, hospitality, and responsibility' (Dikeç et al., 2009). The temporal dimension takes the form of localizable historical contexts and the more or less durable moments of hospitality on the one hand, and on the other, the futurity of unforeseeable encounters, giving rise to charitable actions. The attention to the spatiality and temporality of the concept has also led to questioning of what Candea (2012) calls the 'scale-free abstraction' of Derrida's treatment of hospitality.[2] The questions concern the particular characteristics and practices of hospitality moving through scales such as intercorporeality of bodies, households, communities, nation states, all the way to the international organizations and 'hospitality industries'.

An interesting outcome of this urge for analysis of the complexity of different practices of hospitality is Dan Bulley's book *Migration, Ethics and Power* (2017), in which he examines a range of practices of hospitality and their production of 'homes' on a number of different scales. In the book, he identifies five modes of hospitality, each relating to particular practices: (1) 'Genocidal hospitality', here analysed in its idealized form in films, is about how individuals or groups when faced with the most appalling emergency can react with hospitality as an ethical action on the interpersonal level, for example by hiding or protecting others in your own 'home'. (2) 'Humanitarian hospitality' examines the 'humanitarian government' of international organizations that establish refugee camps as diverse, temporary spaces for 'saving' displaced people. (3) 'Flourishing hospitality' explores the hospitality afforded by urban spaces. It emphasizes security like the camps, but also an urban ethos of freedom, flourishing and coexistence. A particular form is 'Cities of Sanctuary' aiming to develop a particular culture of welcome (see also Derrida, 2001), but in most places the ethical form is as much about an 'ethics of indifference' as it is a welcoming embrace of plurality. (4) 'Unconditional hospitality' was the original border-conception of Levinas and Derrida. Here it is used to characterize the postcolonial state of Jordan, whose practices in relation to both Palestinian and Syrian refugees is considered by Bulley to be the closest we can find to deserve that term. (5) Finally he turns to Europe and its current 'hospitality crisis', which he calls '(Auto)Immunizing hospitality'. While the metaphor of Europe as a 'home' with the necessity of welcoming the outside world is common in European discourse, this is increasingly practised by a biopolitics where the protection of vulnerable refugees and asylum seekers is offered by supporting other spaces and territories – by an 'outsourcing of protection' (Gammeltoft-Hansen, 2011, see also Bialasiewicz and Maessen, 2018). It rests on a logic of caring for the stranger while at the same time immunizing Europe against threats from outside that cannot help to undermine both its self and those it nominally welcomes and protects. It is a self-destructive contradiction in Europe's ethos grown out of its practices of (auto)immunizing hostipitality.

ON HOSPITALITY IN PRACTICE

The case we will discuss next is about a broad movement emerging in Halsnæs, a small municipality (30,000 inhabitants) in northern Zealand in Denmark. The movement started with spontaneous local protest against the decision to close down a local refugee centre housing 700 asylum seekers. The main argument from the centre-right-dominated city council was that the asylum centre was spreading insecurity, fear and crime in the area. On 19 September 2014 a small group of around 100 people gathered and marched in the street from the railway station to the mayor's office, with banners saying 'Hospitable Halsnæs'. Arriving at the town hall, the group announced with a loudspeaker a protest including the message: 'it is with shame and frustration that we learn that the City Council has decided to close the asylum centre and by that move left us with a feeling of being cut off from the outside world, deprived of the possibility of being part of the world community'.[3]

Soon after, the group announced, as a political initiative and an act to put pressure on the political establishment, that if the municipality cannot find a safe place for the asylum seekers, we, the local citizens, will do so. We can open our homes and offer them housing. The idea immediately gained support from the local community via social digital media and the initiative was debated passionately, with intense media attention from local and national media. The idea that was initiated and fostered around a dinner table soon stood its test. A refugee family from Bosnia with two sons, which was applying for humanitarian asylum with reference to a background in which the father had been imprisoned during the Balkan wars and was suffering from severe traumas and various psychiatric disorders, was asking for protection. This was communicated by a Red Cross worker with the message that 'there is a family who needs protection'. That moment can be characterized as a turning point. Faced with the story of emergency a small group of people decided to act and to simply do it. They drove to the asylum centre, packed the family's things and opened their home to them, without knowing anything about the consequences. This was the beginning of something very intense, unpredictable and sometimes dramatic. The act was not planned or negotiated with anyone. It was born out of the impulse to act and to set something into motion on our own initiatives. Not long after, the movement was established under the name *Gæstfrie i Halsnæs* (Hospitable Halsnæs).

Hospitable Halsnæs, which was active for four years (2014–2018) with a strong support in the local community, has to be understood in the context of a rather hostile political climate around immigration in Denmark. It is related to what Bulley (2017) calls the 'hospitality crisis' in Europe, when the protection offered to vulnerable refugees came to mean supporting their resettlement in 'closer' spaces and territories (e.g. in Jordan, see Bulley, 2017). The year 2014 saw the very beginning of what later was later called the 'refugee crisis in Europe' that created a 'state of emergency' with temporary border control. In Denmark, restrictions on migration and issues of 'integration' have been a top priority since 2001. Restrictions have been increasing step by step. This includes restrictions on marriage with non-European citizens and on family unification, point-based residency systems, cuts in welfare benefits for refugees and ever stricter citizenship and Danishness tests. Anti-immigrant politics has become mainstream, adopted throughout almost the entire political spectrum. Fundamental rights of immigrants and asylum seekers have been systematically eroded by drafting new laws. Cuts in welfare benefits of 45 per cent, specifically targeting refugees, as well as other restrictions, were advertised in newspapers in Lebanon during the 'refugee crisis' to ensure that the message was clearly received. Other restrictions included the so-called jewellery bill, adopted in January 2016. The law empowers Danish authorities to seize any assets from asylum seekers in order to help pay for the migrants' subsistence in the country. The government later introduced tent camps for hosting asylum seekers, and the temporary border control has been extended several times with the approval of the European Union due to the alleged 'state of emergency'. A centre-right government that was formed in June 2015 has introduced 100 restrictions, and it has a tracker on the homepage of the Ministry of 'Foreigners' proudly informing the number and content of these restrictions. In 2019 the Danish government introduced a controversial deal to move unwanted migrants to a remote uninhabited island (Lindholm) once used for contagious animals. With regard to this new policy of isolation of asylum seekers, the Danish immigration minister Inger Støjberg wrote on Facebook that certain people 'are unwanted and they will feel it'. This includes moving asylum seekers with 'tolerated stay' status, meaning they do not have a residence permit but cannot be deported for other reasons – for example, stateless Palestinians. This anti-immigrant politics is legitimatized by and finds its support in 'everyday nationalism' – especially welfare nationalism. The concept of *Domopolitics* suggested by Walters (2004) can help us to understand the situation in Denmark and other parts of Europe with a national agenda of 'securing the border and keeping immigrants at a distance'. It refers to the government of the state as a *home,* and is capturing tendencies within the political meaning and governance of security today. It is strongly related to the idea of a (national) home as a place in the international order and to the necessity of every people to have a protected safe place. As argued by Walters, domopolitics embodies a tactic which juxtaposes the '"warm words" [...] of community, trust and citizenship, with the danger words of a chaotic outside – illegals, traffickers, terrorists' (2004: 241).

It is in this context and political landscape that Hospitable Halsnæs should be understood as a case showing different forms of hospitality. Here we find inspiration in Bulley's differentiated understanding of the complexity of different practices of hospitality, even if the practices in Denmark work in a different context from some of the ones he describes. For example, housing a refugee family for nearly two years relates to his idea of 'genocidal hospitality'. It is about how, in a specific situation, you are faced with an emergency that encourages you to react with hospitality as *ethical action* on the interpersonal level, by hiding and protecting them in your own 'home'. The importance here is being faced with the Other in a very concrete sense, and the opening of the door to 'strangers' is a temporary thing based in a specific situation. The concrete action was motivated by more than one factor. First, the emergency situation was related to the father's background in the Balkan wars, his imprisonment, and his suffering various forms of trauma and severe schizophrenia, and therefore for humanitarian reasons he was applying for asylum in Denmark together with his family. The emergency was related to everyday experiences of systematic lack of protection from the Danish state, which was in violation of international law by refusing to protect refugees for humanitarian reasons. Secondly, housing this family was motivated by a wish to protect the two sons in the family, who after four years in Denmark, had become Danes. 'Living on the edge' children are vulnerable and affected by immigration in a way that can be a traumatic experience in itself. One of the sons recounts that he had spent the first year staring into a white wall in the refugee centre, but as he said four years later 'We have invested everything. We are Danes now. This is where we belong.' Speaking fluent Danish, attending school, and having friends and social relations in Denmark for many years, the shared experience is that the Danish state did not live up to its responsibility under international law and the European understanding that 'children affected by migration, remain one of the most vulnerable groups in Europe today' and must be protected for humanitarian reasons. Thirdly, this was an ethical action but also, more broadly, a political act rooted in everyday life experiences in two ways. It was directing the discussion to another level from the abstract and ideological debates on numbers of refugees to concrete living people of flesh and blood. It was about a particular family, but politically it was directed towards a more general problem. It made a particularly strong case because it was based in everyday life experiences.[4]

In a broader sense Hospitable Halsnæs focused on developing a culture and a place of welcome that can be related to what Bulley called 'flourishing hospitality'. 2015 was the year of the so-called 'refugee crisis' and the arrival of new immigrants fleeing from the wars in Syria by crossing the Mediterranean. In the local context that meant the arrival of new refugees, and here the movement was working on welcoming and being friendly towards newcomers in the local community. The actions here were characterized by a lot of different initiatives and activities like creating *meeting places* in the local community with activities such as monthly cafés, with the possibility of talking, eating, dancing and creating music together, or creating a language café where people could learn Danish and Arabic in a language exchange. Other activities included 'visiting friends', which could create more intimate relations, friendships and helping hands: for collecting clothes and supporting children's participation in sports and cultural events. The general focus was on creating a place of coexistence. It is important to say that the renewed activism and action became part of an emerging nationwide movement from below, developing particularly in 2015 with the arrival of a large number of refugees. It was characterized by different more or less loosely organized initiatives that grew rapidly. Volunteers at the central station of Copenhagen were welcoming refugees, and 'Friendly Neighbours' was an initiative that spread rapidly across Denmark and received increasing attention as an alternative approach to meeting refugees. 'Refugees Welcome' was having an impact in Europe; in September 2015, in more than 85 cities in 30 countries across Europe, hundreds of thousands of protesters marched under banners saying 'Refugees Welcome' and 'Europe Says Welcome'.

Finally, with the reopening of the local refugee camp in 2016, the practices moved towards a *humanitarian hospitality*. The 'humanitarian government' of international organizations like the Red Cross, which produces refugee camps as diverse, temporary spaces for 'saving' displaced people, is dependent on local volunteers who can help with social activities, supporting with language training, collecting clothes and other necessities. Many of the activities in 2016 were concentrated around the refugee camp that was initiated by volunteers from Hospitable Halsnæs.

One important condition for Hospitable Halsnæs was that it was grounded in *human plurality,* meaning that the active group of people was very diverse. Some of the group members were politically active on the left, others came from a conservative background, and being 'accused of being a convergence of the extreme left', a conservative former major in the army appeared in national media and told his story. Some had experienced being 'a stranger' themselves; others had never spoken to a refugee before. Some had a background in the hospitality industry; others were motivated by political actions like demonstrating on a local and national level. Some had been refugees from Syria and Afghanistan, others from Africa or Eastern Europe. This also meant that the movement did have a plurality of perspectives and initiatives. Since the movement was organized non-hierarchically with no central organizing committee, the slogan was 'just do it' or 'try it out' in a strong shared expectation that things can be done differently.

The politics of hospitality is grounded in everyday politics in three different ways.

First, welcoming and being friendly towards the unknown Other is in opposition to failed governmental politics. In Denmark, the act of being friendly and welcoming the stranger is political because it disturbs and implicitly challenges consensus politics, where the scripted narratives is about preventing immigrants from coming by being tough and by creating a space of exclusion. It shows in practice that alternative ways of doing things are possible. It is not a dream or ideological statement, but something grounded in shared human experiences. It can arise out of frustration – or from a desire to be friendly. It has a common ground in the idea that we can do it differently and that we can show it in words and deeds. In everyday life, the politics of hospitality comes from below. It does not start out with a political plan – it is grounded in plurality where each brings their own perspectives into action. It springs up like many other resistance movements and can be unexpectedly powerful.

Secondly, in this regard, we can – to use an expression derived from Smith (1992) – talk about 'jumping scale'. For Smith, the power of jumping scale lies in the ability to overcome spatial difference and extend the geographical reach beyond the everyday locally bounded context in which political resistance is situated. It describes a political strategy and a practice whereby political claims and power established in one spatial scale can be expanded to another. Hospitable Halsnæs, like other movements, was operating politically in this in-between space between the local and national. In 2014, local demonstrations a week later were elevated to the national scale by announcing a national demonstration against restrictions in asylum politics in front of the Danish parliament and in the press declaring: 'At a time when up to 51 million people are fleeing war, violence, persecution and hunger, our prime minister speaks of asylum tightening. It is obscene.' This was soon followed by an incident in the parliament where a small group of people from Hospitable Halsnæs broke into the discussion in parliament on asylum tightening with a self-composed poetic song. These people were then arrested, but the idea of offering asylum seekers housing was rapidly spreading from the local to the national political agenda and was intensely debated among grassroots and parliamentary politicians. During a local organized concert in support of the family that had just been moved out of the refugee camp, the Minister for Finance and Domestic Affairs was asking to participate and to meet the family. Later in the same week, KL, the association and interest organization of the 98 Danish municipalities, contacted Hospitable Halsnæs to learn more about the idea and local experiences.

Thirdly, the political act of offering hospitality takes the form of a *new beginning*. It is based in the everyday spaces in which humans interact and take responsibility for the shared world. In some ways it was very simple, like a voice coming from ordinary people saying that we have had enough and we need to do something. This is transformative in the sense that the very act disrupts reality and creates a disturbance in the system, at least for a moment. It is linked to the hope that even in this situation, another world is possible. The power of everyday politics of hospitality is not granted or given by anyone. It springs up among ordinary people and corresponds to the human ability not just to act alone, but to act in concert. It is founded on our own ability to act, think and judge, using, for example, civil disobedience, such as driving asylum seekers from Denmark to Sweden under specific circumstances (as in 2015), being friendly to a stranger or disrupting the public (dis)order.

This reflects the approach we take to critical phenomenology. For us critical phenomenology is a philosophical/theoretical practice, but even more importantly, it is at the same time a political practice of restructuring the world in order to generate new and liberatory possibilities for meaningful experiences and existence. The borderland stands as the starting point for the sensitive analysis of difference that is grounded in everyday life experiences and the common world. It involves a political thinking that emphasizes coexistence and is characterized by a renewed critique of the current directions in politics, as well as different forms of everyday resistance, experiments and disruptions. And it is rooted in an ethic of responsibilities that can perhaps open up for a 'new humanism' and for the hope that the world can be recreated through common political action.

NOTES

1. For a thorough discussion and a direct further development of Merleau-Ponty's political thinking, see Kruks (1981) and Coole (2007a).
2. This criticism might be slightly unfair. If you look at Derrida's more concrete discussions in *On Cosmopolitanism and Forgiveness* (2001), he is precisely contrasting hospitalities at state and urban scale. What is at stake is probably rather a question of connecting the abstract philosophical level and the one of concrete social analysis.
3. The Hospitable Halsnæs case is grounded in participant observation in the period 2014–2018. It involved being an active part of the movement by sharing many of its activities like demonstrations, events, meetings, decision-making processes and concrete actions. We are aware that being an active member of the organization you are analysing can pose some methodological challenges.
4. Even though harbouring asylum seekers in private homes is rare in Denmark, the example given is not alone on the public scene. The priest Leif Bork Hansen, for example, spontaneously welcomed a group of refugees from Eastern Slovenia to his home when they were denied asylum in 1998. He did this in the belief that the asylum seekers had received unfair treatment from the Danish state.

References

Adey, P. and Bissell, P. (2010) 'Mobilities, meetings, and futures: An interview with John Urry', *Environment and Planning D, Society and Space*, 28 (1): 1–16.

Adey, P., Bissell, P., McCormack, D. and Merriman, P. (2012) 'Profiling the passenger', *Cultural Geographies*, 19 (2): 169–93.

Ahmed, S. (2000) *Strange Encounters. Embodied Others in Post-Coloniality*. London and New York: Routledge.

Ahmed, S. (2006) *Queer Phenomenology. Orientations, Objects, Others*. Durham, NC, and London: Duke University Press.

Ahmed, S. (2010) 'Orientations matter', in D. Coole and S. Frost (eds) *New Materialisms. Ontology, Agency, and Politics*. Durham, NC, and London: Duke University Press. pp. 234–58.

Alcoff, L.M. (1999) 'Towards a phenomenology of racial embodiment', *Radical Philosophy*, 95: 8–14.

Alcoff, L.M. (2006) *Visible Identities. Race, Gender and the Self*. Oxford: Oxford University Press.

Allport, G.W. (1954) *The Nature of Prejudice*. Cambridge, MA: Perseus Books.

Amin, A. (2002) 'Ethnicity and the multicultural city: Living with diversity', *Environment and Planning A*, 34 (6): 959–80.

Amin, A. (2012) *Land of Strangers*. Cambridge: Polity.

Amin, A. (2013) 'Land of strangers', *Identities: Global Studies in Culture and Power*, 20 (1): 1–8.

Amin, A. and Thrift, N. (2002) *Cities: Rethinking the Urban*. Cambridge: Polity.

Anderson, B. (1991) *Imagined Communities: Reflections on the Origin and Spread of Nationalism*. London: Verso.

Anderson, B. (2009) 'Affective atmospheres', *Emotion, Space and Society*, 2: 77–81.

Anderson, B. (2014) *Encountering Affect: Capacities, Apparatus, Conditions*. Farnham: Ashgate.

Anderson, B. and Harrison, P. (2006) 'Questioning affect and emotion', *Area*, 38: 333–35.

Anderson, B. and Harrison, P. (eds) (2010) *Taking-Place: Non-Representational Theories and Geography*. Farnham: Ashgate.

Anderson, B. and Tolia-Kelly, D. (2004) 'Matter(s) in social and cultural geography', *Geoforum*, 35: 669–75.

Andreassen, R. and Lettinga, D. (2012) 'Veiled debates: Gender and gender equality in European national narratives', in S. Rosenbaum and B. Sauer (eds) *Politics, Religion and Gender. Framing and Regulating the Veil*. Milton Park: Routledge. pp. 17–36.

Arendt, H. (1958) *The Human Condition*. Chicago, IL: Chicago University Press.

Arendt, H. (1970) *On Violence*. Orlando, FL: Houghton Mifflin Harcourt.

Arendt, H. (1972) *Crises of the Republic: Lying in Politics. Civil Disobedience. On Violence. Thoughts on Politics and Revolution.* New York, NY: Houghton Mifflin Harcourt.

Arendt, H. (1973) *The Origins of Totalitarianism.* New York, NY: Harcourt, Brace, Jovanovitch.

Arendt, H. (2006) *Eichmann in Jerusalem: A Report on the Banality of Evil.* London: Penguin Classics.

Arendt, H. (2007) *The Jewish Writings.* New York, NY: Schocken.

Auger, M. (2002) *In the Metro.* Minneapolis, MN: University of Minnesota Press.

Bakhtin, M.M. (1984 [1968]). *Rabelais and his World.* Bloomington, IN: Indiana University Press.

Barnett, C. (2004) 'Deconstructing radical democracy: Articulation, representation, and being-with-others', *Political Geography*, 23 (5): 503–28.

Bauman, Z. (1991) *Modernity and Ambivalence.* Ithaca, NY: Cornell University Press.

Beaumont, J. and Baker, C. (eds) (2011) *Postsecular Cities. Space, Theory and Practice.* London: Bloomsbury.

de Beauvoir, S. (2010) *The Second Sex.* New York, NY: Knopf.

Berg, A.M. (2011) 'Byen på den anden ende – en undersøgelse af folkelige festivaler og kultur i dansk planlægning'. PhD dissertation, University of Copenhagen.

Bernasconi, R. (1996) 'Casting the slough: Fanon's new humanism for a new humanity', in L.R. Gordan, T.D. Whiting and R.T. White (eds) *Fanon: A Critical Reader.* Oxford: Blackwell. pp. 113–2.

Bessone, I. (2017) 'Social circus as an organized cultural encounter. Embodied knowledge, trust and creativity at play', *Journal of Intercultural Studies*, 38 (6): 651–64.

Bialasiewicz, L.A. and Maessen, J.M.A.H. (2018) 'Scaling rights: The "Turkey Deal" and the divided geographies of European responsibility', *Patterns of Prejudice*, 52 (2): 210–30.

Bille, M. (2015) 'Hazy worlds: Atmospheric ontologies in Denmark', *Anthropological Theory*, 15 (3): 257–74.

Bille, M. and Sørensen, T.F. (eds) (2016) *Elements of Architecture. Assembling Archaeology, Atmosphere and the Performance of Building Spaces.* London: Routledge.

Bille, M. and Simonsen, K. (2019) 'Atmospheric practices: On affecting and being affected', *Space and Culture*, doi: 10.1177/1206331218819711

Bille, M., Bjerregaard, P. and Sørensen, T.F. (2015) 'Staging atmospheres. Materiality, culture and the texture of the in-between', *Emotion, Space and Society*, 15: 31–38.

Bille, T. (2014) 'Politielevers levede erfaringer i praktikken'. PhD dissertation, Roskilde University, DK. Available from https://www.ucviden.dk/portal/en/publications/politielevers-levede-erfaringer-i-praktikken(ba13626c-9aaf-451d-9415-0a91433ea10b).html [accessed 30 May 2019].

Billig, M. (1995) *Banal Nationalism.* London: Sage.

Binnie, J., Holloway, J. and Millington, S. (eds) (2006) *Cosmopolitan Urbanism.* London: Routledge.

Bissell, D. (2010) 'Passenger mobilities: Affective atmospheres and the sociality of public transport', *Environment and Planning, D, Society and Space*, 28 (2): 270–89.

Bladt, M. (2013) 'De unges stemme: Udsyn fra en anden virkelighed', PhD dissertation, Roskilde University, DK.

Blunt, A. (2007) 'Cultural geographies of migration: Mobility, transnationality and diaspora', *Progress in Human Geography*, 31: 682–94.

Böhme, G. (1993) 'Atmosphere as the fundamental concept of a New Aesthetics', *Thesis Eleven*, 36: 113–26.

Bondi, L. (2005) 'Making connections and thinking through emotions: Between geography and psychotherapy', *Transactions of the Institute of British Geographers*, 30: 433–48.

Borren, M. (2008) 'Towards an Arendtian politics of in/visibility: On stateless refugees and undocumented aliens', *Ethical Perspectives: Journal of the European Ethics Network*, 15 (2): 213–37.

Bourdieu, P. (1977) *Outline of a Theory of Practice*. Cambridge: Cambridge University Press.

Bourdieu, P. (1990) *The Logic of Practice*. Cambridge: Polity Press.

Braun, B. (2004a) 'Querying posthumanisms', *Geoforum*, 35: 269–73.

Braun, B. (2004b) 'Modalities of posthumanism', *Environment and Planning A*, 36: 1352–56.

Brenner, N. and Schmid, C. (2011) 'Planetary urbanization', in M. Gandy (ed.) *Urban Constellations*. Berlin: Jovis. pp. 10–13.

Brenner, N. and Schmid, C. (2015) 'Towards a new epistemology of the urban?', *City*, 19 (2–3): 151–82.

Brighenti, A. (2007) 'Visibility. A category for the social sciences', *Current Sociology*, 55 (3): 323–42.

Bruner, J. (1991) 'The narrative construction of reality', *Critical Inquiry*, 18: 1–22.

Bulley, D. (2017) 'Migration, ethics and power', *Spaces of Hospitality in International Politics*. London: Sage.

Butler, J. (1989) 'Sexual ideology and phenomenological description: A feminist critique of Merleau-Ponty's *Phenomenology of Perception*', in J. Allen and I.M. Young (eds) *The Thinking Muse: Feminism and Modern French Philosophy*. Bloomington, IN: Indiana University Press. pp. 85–100.

Calhoun, C. (2003) '"Belonging" in the cosmopolitan imaginary', *Ethnicities*, 3 (4): 531–68.

Candea, M. (2012) '*Derrida en Corse?* Hospitality as scale-free abstraction', *Journal of the Anthropological Institute*, 18: 34–48.

Candea, M. and da Col, G. (2012) 'The return to hospitality', *Journal of Royal Anthropological Institute*, 18 (1): 1–19.

Casey, E.S. (1993) *Getting Back into Place. Toward a Renewed Understanding of the Place-world*. Bloomington, IN: Indiana University Press.

Casey, E.S. (2011) 'Strangers at the edge of hospitality', in R. Kearney and K. Semonovitch (eds) *Phenomenologies of the Stranger. Between Hostility and Hospitality*. New York, NY: Fordham University Press. pp. 39–48.

Cataldi, S.L. (1993) *Emotion, Depth, and Flesh: A Study of Sensitive Space: Reflections on Merleau-Ponty's Philosophy of Embodiment*. New York, NY: SUNY Press.

Cataldi, S.L. (2008) 'Affect and sensibility', in R. Diprose and J. Reynolds (eds) *Merleau-Ponty: Key Concepts*. Stocksfield: Acumen. pp.163–73.

de Certeau, M. (1984) *The Practice of Everyday Life*. Berkeley, CA: University of California Press.

de Certeau, M. (1997) *Culture in the Plural*. Minneapolis, MN: University of Minnesota Press.

de Certeau, M. (1998) 'Ghosts in the city', in M. de Certeau, M. Giard and P. Mayol (eds) *The Practice of Everyday Life. Volume 2: Living and Cooking*. Minneapolis, MN: University of Minnesota Press. pp. 133–44.

Christiansen, L.B., Galal, L.P. and Hvenegaard-Lassen, K. (2017) 'Organised cultural encounters: Interculturality and transformative practices', *Journal of Intercultural Studies*, 38 (6): 599–605.

Churchill, S. (2008) 'Nature and animality', in R. Diprose, and J. Reynolds (eds) *Merleau-Ponty. Key Concepts*. Stocksfield: Acumen. pp. 174–84.

Cloke, P. and Beaumont, J. (2012) 'Geographies of postsecular rapprochement in the city', *Progress in Human Geography*, 37 (1): 27–51.

Collins, M. (2010) 'Conflict and contact: The "humane" city, agonistic politics, and the phenomenological body', *Environment and Planning D: Society and Space,* 28 (5): 913–30.

Cook, I. and Crang, P. (1996) 'The world on a plate: Culinary culture, displacement and geographical knowledges', *Journal of Material Culture*, 1 (2): 131–53.

Cook, I. et al. (2008) 'Geographies of food: Mixing', *Progress in Human Geography*, 32 (6): 821–33.

Cook, I. and Tolia-Kelly, D. (2010) 'Material geographies', in D. Hicks and M. Beaudry (eds) *Oxford Handbook of Material Culture Studies*. Oxford: Oxford University Press. pp. 99–122.

Coole, D. (2001) 'Thinking politically with Merleau-Ponty', *Radical Philosophy*, 108: 17–29.

Coole, D. (2005) 'Rethinking agency: A phenomenological approach to embodiment and agentic capacities', *Political Studies*, 53: 124–42.

Coole, D. (2007a) *Merleau-Ponty and Modern Politics after Anti-humanism*. Plymouth: Rowman and Littlefield.

Coole, D. (2007b) 'Experiencing discourse: Corporeal communicators and the embodiment of power', *British Journal of Politics and International Relations*, 9: 413–33.

Coole, D. and Frost, S. (eds) (2010) *New Materialisms. Ontology, Agency, and Politics*. Durham, NC, and London: Duke University Press.

Crang, M. (2000) 'Relics, places and unwritten geographies in the work of Michel de Certeau (1925–86)', in M. Crang and N. Thrift (eds) *Thinking Space*. London: Routledge. pp. 136–54.

Crossley, N. (2013) 'Habit and habitus', *Body & Society*, 19 (2–3): 136–61.

Dalton, J. (2005) 'Man is indestructible: Blanchot's obscure humanism', *COLLOQUY text theory critique,* 10: 150–70.

Darling, J. and Wilson, H.F. (eds) (2016) *Encountering the City: Urban Encounters from Accra to New York*. London: Routledge.

Deleuze, G. (1994) *Difference and Repetition*. London: Athlone.

Derrida, J. (2000) 'Hostipitality', *Angelaki: Journal of the Theoretical Humanities*, 5 (3): 3–18.

Derrida, J. (2001) *On Cosmopolitanism and Forgiveness*. London: Routledge.

Dikeç, M. (2002) 'Pera Pera Poros. Longings for spaces of hospitality', *Theory, Culture & Society*, 19 (1–2): 227–47.

Dikeç, M. (2016) *Space, Politics and Aesthetics*. Edinburgh: Edinburgh University Press.

Dikeç, M. and Swyngedouw, E. (2017) 'Theorizing the politicizing city', *International Journal of Urban and Regional Research*, 41 (1): 1–18.

Dikeç, M., Clark, N. and Barnett, C. (2009) 'Extending hospitality: Giving space, taking time', *Paragraph*, 32 (1): 1–14.

Diken, B. (1998) *Strangers, Ambivalence and Social Theory*. Århus: Dansk center for migration og internationale studier.

Diprose, R. (2017) 'The body and political violence. Between isolation and homogenization', in L. Dolezal and D. Petherbridge (eds) *Body/Self/Other. The Phenomenology of Social Encounters*. Albany, NY: State University New York Press. pp. 21–46.

Dolezal, L. and Petherbridge, D. (eds) (2017) *Body/Self/Other. The Phenomenology of Social Encounters*. Albany, NY: State University New York Press.

Donald, J. (1997) 'This, here, now. Imagining the modern city', in S. Westwood and J. Williams (eds) *Imagining Cities. Scripts, Signs, Memory*, London: Routledge. pp. 181–201.

Donald, J. (1999) *Imagining the Modern City*. London: Athlone.

Douglas, R. (1994) *Purity and Danger. An Analysis of the Concepts of Pollution and Taboo*. London: Routledge.

Duffy, M. (2005) 'Performing identity within a multicultural framework', *Social & Cultural Geography*, 6(5): 677–92.

Duruz, J. (2005) 'Eating at the borders: Culinary journeys', *Environment and Planning D: Society and Space*, 23 (1): 51–69.

Dyer, R. (1997) *White Essays on Race and Culture*. London: Routledge.

Edensor, T. (2010) (ed.) *Geographies of Rhythm: Nature, Place, Mobilities and Bodies*. Farnham: Ashgate.

Edensor, T. (2012) 'Illuminated atmospheres: Anticipating and reproducing the flow of affective experience in Blackpool', *Environment and Planning D: Society and Space*, 30: 1103–22.

Elden, S. (2009) *Terror and Territory: The Spatial Extent of Sovereignty*. Minneapolis, MN: University of Minnesota Press.

Evans, D. (2008) 'Chiasm and flesh', in R. Diprose and J. Reynolds (eds) *Merleau-Ponty. Key Concepts*. Stocksfield: Acumen. pp. 184–96.

Falassi, A. (ed.) (1987) *Time Out of Time: Essays on the Festival*. Albuquerque, NM: University of New Mexico Press.

Fanon, F. (1967a) *Black Skin White Masks*. New York, NY: Grove Press.

Fanon, F. (1967b) *A Dying Colonialism*. New York, NY: Grove Press.

Fassin, D. (2009) 'Another politics of life is possible', *Theory, Culture & Society*, 26 (5): 44–60.

Fassin, D. (2013) *Enforcing Order: An Ethnography of Urban Policing*. Cambridge: Polity.

Finnegan, R. (1998) *Tales of the City. A Study of Narrative and Urban life*. Cambridge: Cambridge University Press.

Finstad, L. (2003) *Politiblikket*. Oslo: Pax Forlag.

Foucault, M. (1970) *The Order of Things: An Archeology of the Human Sciences*. New York, NY: Random House.

Foucault, M. (1978) *The History of Sexuality. Vol. I*. New York, NY: Vintage Books.

Fyfe, N. (1998) *Images on the Street: Planning Identity and Control in Public Space*. London: Routledge.

Gadamer, H. G. (1995) *Truth and Method*. New York, NY: Continuum.

de Galambert, C. (2005) 'The city's "nod of approval" for the Mantes-la-Jolie mosque project: Mistaken traces of recognition', *Journal of Ethnic and Migration Studies*, 31 (6): 1141–59.

Gale, R. (2005) 'Representing the city: Mosques and the planning process in Birmingham', *Journal of Ethnic and Migration Studies*, 31 (6): 1161–79.

Gale, R. and Naylor, S. (2002) 'Religion, planning and the city: The spatial politics of ethnic minority expression in British cities and towns', *Ethnicities*, (2): 387–409.

Gammeltoft-Hansen, T. (2011) 'Outsourcing asylum: The advent of protection lite', in L. Bialasiewicz (ed.) *Europe in the World: EU Geopolitics and the Making of European Space*. Aldershot: Ashgate.

Gilligan, C. (1982) *In a Different Voice: Psychological Theory and Women's Development*. Cambridge, MA: Harvard University Press.

Gilroy, P. (1991) *There Ain't No Black in the Union Jack: The Cultural Politics of Race and Nation*. Chicago, IL: The University of Chicago Press.

Gilroy, P. (2006) *Postcolonial Melancholia*. New York, NY: Columbia University Press.

Gingrich, A. and Banks, M. (2006) *Neo-nationalism in Europe and Beyond: Perspectives from Social Anthropology*. New York, NY: Berghahn.

Goffman, E. (1963) *Behavior in Public Places*. New York, NY: The Free Press.

Goffman, E. (2010) *Relations in Public: Microstudies of the Public Order*. New Brunswick, NJ: Transaction Publishers.

Goldberg, D.T. (1993) *Racist Cultures: Philosophy and the Politics of Meaning*. Oxford: Blackwell.

Goldberg, D.T. (2009) *The Threat of Race: Reflections of Racial Neoliberalism*. Oxford: Wiley/Blackwell.

Göle, N. (2011) 'The public visibility of Islam and European politics of resentment: The minarets-mosques debate', *Philosophy and Social Criticism*, 37 (4): 383–92.

Goonewardena, K. (2018) 'Planetary urbanization and totality', *Environment and Planning D: Society and Space*, 36 (3): 456–73.

Graham, S. (2008) 'Cities as strategic sites: Place annihilation and urban geopolitics', in S. Graham (ed.) *Cities, War, and Terrorism: Towards an Urban Geopolitics*. Malden, MA: Blackwell. pp. 31–53.

Green, K. (2011) 'It hurts so it is real: Sensing the seduction of mixed martial arts', *Social and Cultural Geography*, 12 (4): 377–96.

Gregory, D. (1994) *Geographical Imaginations*. Oxford: Blackwell.

Gregory, D. (2004) *The Colonial Present*. Oxford: Blackwell.

Gregory, D. (2011) 'The everywhere war', *The Geographical Journal*, 177 (3): 238–50.

Griffero, T. (2014). *Atmospheres: Aesthetics of Emotional Spaces*. Farnham: Ashgate.

Grosz, E. (1995) *Space, Time, and Perversion: Essays on the Politics of Bodies*. New York, NY: Routledge.

Grosz, E. (2001) *Architecture from the Outside: Essays on Virtual and Real Space*. Cambridge, MA: MIT Press.

Guenther, L. (2011) 'Resisting Agamben: The biopolitics of shame and humiliation', *Philosophy and Social Criticism*: 1–21. doi: 10.1177/0191453711421604

Guenther, L. (2017) 'A critically phenomenology of solidarity and resistance in the 2013 California prison hunger strikes', in L. Dolezal and D. Petherbridge (eds) *Body/Self/Other: The Phenomenology of Social Encounters*. Albany, NY: State University of New York Press. pp. 47–74.

Habermas, J. (2006) 'Religion in the public sphere', *European Journal of Philosophy*, 14: 1–25.

Habermas, J. (2008) 'Notes on a postsecular society', *Signs and Sight.com* 18 June: 1–23.

Häkli, J. and Kallio, K.P. (2014) 'Subject, action and polis: Theorizing political agency', *Progress in Human Geography*, 38 (2): 181–200.

Haldrup, M., Koefoed, L. and Simonsen, K. (2006) 'Practical orientalism: Bodies, everyday life and the construction of otherness', *Geografiska Annaler: Series B, Human Geography*, 88 (2): 173–84.

Hamington, M. (2008) 'Resources for feminist care ethics in Merleau-Ponty's Phenomenology of the Body', in G. Weiss (ed.) *Intertwinings. Interdisciplinary Encounters with Merleau-Ponty*. New York, NY: State University of New York Press. pp. 203–20.

Harding, S. (1998) *Is Science Multicultural? Postcolonialisms, Feminisms, and Epistemologies*. Bloomington, IN: Indiana University Press.

Harrison, P. (2008) 'Corporeal remains: Vulnerability, proximity, and living on after the end of the world', *Environment and Planning A*, 40: 423–45.

Harvey, D. (2008) 'The right to the city', *New Left Review* 53: 23–40.

Hass, L. (2008) 'Elemental alterity: Levinas and Merleau-Ponty', in G. Weiss (ed.) *Intertwinings. Interdisciplinary Encounters with Merleau-Ponty*. New York, NY: State University of New York Press. pp. 31–44.

Hasse, J. (2014) 'Atmospheres as expression of medial power. Understanding atmospheres in urban governance and under self-guidance', *Lebenswelt. Aesthetics and Philosophy of Experience*, 4 (1): 214–29.

Hasse, J. (2016) 'Traffic architecture: Hidden affections', in M. Bille and T.F. Sørensen (eds) *Elements of Architecture. Assembling Archaeology, Atmosphere and the Performance of Building Spaces*. London: Routledge. pp. 177–94.

Hatziprokopiou, P. and Evergeti, V. (2014) 'Negotiating Muslim identity and diversity in Greek urban spaces', *Social and Cultural Geography*, 15 (6): 603–26.

Heidegger, M. (1962) *Being and Time*. Oxford: Blackwell.

Heidegger, M. (1997) 'Building, dwelling, thinking', in N. Leach (ed.) *Rethinking Architecture. A Reader in Cultural Theory*. London and New York: Routledge. pp. 100–24.

Hensley, S. (2011) '"It's the sugar, the honey that you have": Learning to be natural through rumba in Cuba', *Gender, Place and Culture*, 18 (2): 195–215.

Hesse, B. (2007) 'Racialized modernity: An analytics of white mythologies', *Ethnic and Racial Studies*, 30 (4): 643–63.

Holmberg, L. (2000) 'Discretionary leniency and typological guilt: Results from a Danish study of police discretion', *Journal of Scandinavian Studies in Criminology and Crime Prevention*, 1: 179–94.

Honneth, A. (1995) *The Struggle for Recognition: The Moral Grammar of Social Conflicts*. Cambridge: Polity Press.

hooks, b. (2006) 'Eating the Other: Desire and resistance', in M.G. Durham and D.M. Kellner, (eds) *Media and Cultural Studies: Keyworks* (revised edition). Oxford: Blackwell. pp. 266–80.

Hvorslev, B. (2014, 11 June) 'Moskeer er uundgåelige i et demokrati', *Jyllands-Posten*. https://jyllands-posten.dk/debat/kronik/article6793894.ece [accessed 11 June 2019].

Ingold, T. (2012) 'The atmosphere', *Chiasma International*, 14: 75–87.

Ingold, T. (2016) 'Lighting up the atmosphere', in M. Bille and T.F. Sørensen (eds) *Elements of Architecture. Assembling Archaeology, Atmosphere and the Performance of Building Spaces*. London: Routledge. pp. 163–76.

Jamieson, K. (2004) 'Edinburgh: The festival gaze and its boundaries', *Space and Culture*, 7 (1): 64–76.

Jenkins, R. (1996) *Social Identity*. London: Routledge.

Jenkins, R. (2000) 'Categorization: Identity, social process and epistemology', *Current Sociology*, 48 (3): 7–25.

Jensen, H.L. (2012) 'Emotions on the move: Mobile emotions among train commuters in the south east of Denmark', *Emotion, Space and Society*, 5 (3): 201–6.

Jensen, O.B. (2006) '"Facework", flow and the city: Simmel, Goffman, and mobility in the contemporary city', *Mobilities*, 1 (2): 143–65.

Jensen, O.B. (2009) 'Flows of meaning, cultures of movements: Urban mobility as meaningful everyday life practice', *Mobilities*, 4 (1): 139–58.

Jensen, O.B. (2010) 'Negotiation in motion: Unpacking a geography of mobility', *Space and Culture*, 13 (4): 389–402.

Johnson, G. (2008) 'Merleau-Ponty, reciprocity, and the reversibility of perspectives', in G. Weiss (ed.) *Intertwinings. Interdisciplinary Encounters with Merleau-Ponty*. New York, NY: State University of New York Press. pp. 169–88.

Journal of Ethnic and Migration Studies 31 (6) (2005) Special issue: Mosque Conflicts in European Cities.

Juul, K. (2014) 'Performing belonging, celebrating invisibility? The role of festivities among migrants of Serbian origin in Denmark and in Serbia', *Nordic Journal of Migration Research*, 4 (4): 184–91.

Kallio, K.P. (2017) 'Shaping subjects in everyday encounters: Intergenerational recognition in intersubjective socialisation', *Environment and Planning D: Society and Space*, 35 (1): 88–106.

Katz, C. (2001) 'Vagabond capitalism and the necessity of social reproduction', *Antipode*, 33 (4): 709–28.

Katz, C. (2007) 'Banal terrorism', in D. Gregory and A. Pred (ed.) *Violent Geographies. Fear, Terror, and Political Violence*. New York, NY: Routledge. pp. 349–63.

Kazig, R. (2008) 'Typische Atmosphären städtischer Plätze. Auf dem Weg zu einer anwendungsorientierten Atmosphärenforschung', *Die Alte Stadt*, 35 (2): 147–60.

Kearney, R. and Semonovitch, K. (eds) (2011) *Phenomenologies of the Stranger. Between Hostility and Hospitality*. New York, NY: Fordham University Press.

Kearney, R. and Semonovitch, K. (2011a) 'At the threshold. Foreigners, strangers, others', in R. Kearney, and K. Semonovitch, (eds) (2011) *Phenomenologies of the Stranger. Between Hostility and Hospitality*. New York, NY: Fordham University Press. pp. 3–36.

Keith, M. (2005) *After the Cosmopolitan? Multicultural Cities and the Future of Racism*. London and New York, NY: Routledge.

Keller, K.D. (2005) 'The corporeal order of things: The *Spiel* of usability', *Human Studies*, 28: 173–204.

Keller, K.D. (2010) 'Institution – A generative structure of meaning', in K. Novotný, S.H. Taylor, A. Gléonec and P. Specián, P. (eds) *Thinking in Dialogue with Humanities. Paths into the Phenomenology of Merleau-Ponty*. Prague: Zeta Books. pp. 259–69.

Kipfer, S. (2007) 'Fanon and space: Colonization, urbanization, and liberation from the colonial to the global city', *Environment and Planning D: Society and Space*, 25: 701–26.

Kipfer, S. and Goonewardena, K. (2007) 'Colonization and the New Imperialism. On the meaning of urbicide today', *Theory & Event*, 10 (2). doi: 10.1353/tae.2007.0064

Knott, K. (2010) 'Cutting through the postsecular city: A spatial interrogation', in A.L. Molendijk, J. Beaumont, C. Jedan, (eds) *Exploring the Postsecular: The Religious, the Political and the Urban*. Boston, MA/Leiden: Brill. pp 19–38.

Koefoed, L. (2006) 'Glokale nationalismer: Globalisering, hverdagsliv og fortællinger om dansk identitet'. PhD dissertation, Department of Environmental, Social and Spatial Change, Roskilde University.

Koefoed, L. (2015) 'Majority and minority nationalism in the Danish post-welfare state', *Geografiska Annaler: Series B, Human Geography*, 97 (3): 223–32.

Koefoed, L. and Simonsen, K. (2007) 'The price of goodness: Everyday nationalist narratives in Denmark', *Antipode*, 39 (2): 310–30.

Koefoed, L. and Simonsen, K. (2010) *Den fremmede, byen og nationen – om livet som etnisk minoritet*. Fredriksberg: Roskilde Universitetsforlag.

Koefoed, L. and Simonsen, K. (2011) '"The stranger", the city and the nation: On the possibilities of identification and belonging', *European Urban and Regional Studies*, 18: 343–57.

Koefoed, L. and Simonsen, K. (2012) '(Re)scaling identities: Embodied Others and alternative spaces of identification', *Ethnicities*, 12 (5): 623–42.

Koefoed, L., Christensen, M.D. and Simonsen, K. (2017) 'Mobile encounters: Bus 5A as a cross-cultural meeting place', *Mobilities*, 12 (5): 726–39.

Koefoed, L., Neergaard, M.D. and Simonsen, K. (forthcoming) 'Multicultural festivals: Between performance, pleasure and politics', *Space and Culture*.

Kruks, S. (1977) 'Merleau-Ponty: A phenomenological critique of liberalism', *Philosophy and Phenemological Research*, 37 (3): 394–407.

Kruks, S. (1981) *The Political Philosophy of Merleau-Ponty*. Brighton: The Harvester Press.

Kruks, S. (2006) 'Spaces of freedom': Materiality, mediation and direct political participation in the work of Arendt and Sartre', *Contemporary Political Theory*, 5 (4): 469–91.

Kruks, S. (2012) *Simone de Beauvoir and the Politics of Ambiguity*. Oxford: Oxford University Press.

Kruks, S. (2014) 'Women's "Lived Experience": Feminism and phenomenology from Simone de Beauvoir to the present', in Evans, M., Hemmings, C., Henry, M., Johnstone, H., Madhok,, S., Plomien, A. and Wearing, S. (eds) *The SAGE Handbook of Feminist Theory*. London: Sage. pp. 75–92.

Laclau, E. and Mouffe, C. (1985) *Hegemony and Socialist Strategy: Towards a Radical Democratic Politics*. London: Verso.

Lapina, L. (2017) '"Cultivating integration"? Migrant space-making in urban gardens', *Journal of Intercultural Studies*, 38 (6): 621–36.

Larsen, T.S. (2018) 'Advanced marginality as a comparative research strategy in praxis: The Danish "Grey Belt" in conversation with the French "Red Belt"', *Urban Geography*, 39 (8): 1131–51.

Larsen, T.S. and Delica, K.N. (2017) *Historicizing the production of territorial stigmatization: A review of literature*', Paper presented at 7th Nordic Geographers Meeting, Stockholm, June 2017.

Last, A. (2017) 'Re-reading worldliness: Hannah Arendt and the question of matter', *Environment and Planning D: Society and Space*, 35 (1): 72–87.

Laurier, E., Lorimer, H., Brown, B., Jones, O., Juhlin, J., Noble, A., Perry, M., Pica, D., Sormani, P. and Strebel, I. (2008) 'Driving and 'passengering': Notes on the ordinary organization of car travel', *Mobilities*, 3(1): 1–23.

Lefebvre, H. (1970) *Le manifeste différentialiste*. Paris: Galimard.

Lefebvre, H. (1984) *Everyday Life in the Modern World*. New Brunswick, NJ: Transaction Books.

Lefebvre, H. (1991a) *The Production of Space*. Oxford: Blackwell.

Lefebvre, H. (1991b) *Critique of Everyday Life*. Vol. I. London: Verso Books.

Lefebvre, H. (1996a) 'The right to the city', in E. Kofman, and E. Lebas (trans. and eds) *Writings on Cities*. Oxford: Blackwell. pp. 63–184.

Lefebvre, H. (1996b) 'Seen from the window', in E. Kofman, and E. Lebas (trans. and eds) *Writings on Cities*. Oxford: Blackwell. pp. 219–27.

Lefebvre, H. (2003) *The Urban Revolution*. Minneapolis, MN: University of Minnesota Press.

Lefebvre, H. (2004) *Rhythmanalysis: Space, Time and Everyday Life* (S. Elden and G. Moore, eds). London: Continuum.

Lefebvre, H. and Regulier, C. (1996) 'Rhythmanalysis of Mediterranean cities', in E. Kofman, and E. Lebas (trans. and eds) *Writings on Cities*. Oxford: Blackwell. pp. 228–240.

Leinonen, J. and Toivanen, M. (2014) 'Researching in/visibility in the Nordic context: Theoretical and empirical views', *Nordic Journal of Migration Research*, 4 (4): 161–67.

Leitner, H. (2012) 'Spaces of encounters: Immigration, race, class, and the politics of belonging in small-town America', *Annals of the Association of American Geographers*, 102 (4): 828–46.

Lentin, A. and Titley, G. (2011) *The Crisis of Multiculturalism: Racism in a Neoliberal Age*. London: Zed.

Levinas, E. (1987) 'Philosophy and the idea of infinity', in *Collected Philosophical Papers*. New York, NY: Springer. pp. 47–59.

Levinas, E. (1991) *Otherwise Than Being or Beyond Essence*. Dordrecht: Kluwer.

Ley, D. (2011) 'Preface: Towards the postsecular city?', in J. Beaumont and C. Baker (eds) *Postsecular Cities. Space, Theory and Practice*. London: Bloomsbury. pp. xii–xiv.

Lipsky, M. (1980) *Street-level Bureaucracy. Dilemmas of the Individual in Public Services*. New York, NY: Russel Sage Foundation.

Lofland, L.H. (1973) *A World of Strangers. Order and Action in Urban Public Space*. Prospect Heights, IL: Waveland Press.

Loftsdottir, K. and Jensen, L. (2012) *Whiteness and Post-colonialism in the Nordic Region: Exceptionalism, Migrant Others and National Identities*. Farnham: Ashgate.

Lægaard, S. (2010) 'Religiøse symboler, religionsfrihed og det offentlige rum: 'stor-moskeer' i København', *Tidsskriftet Politik*, 13 (4): 6–14.

Löfgren, O. (2008) 'Motion and emotion: Learning to be a railway traveller', *Mobilities*, 3 (3): 331–51.

Mahendran, D. (2007) 'The facticity of blackness. A non-conceptual approach to the study of race and racism in Fanon's and Merleau-Ponty's phenomenology', *Human Architecture: Journal of the Sociology of Knowledge*, 5 (3): 191–204.

Marselis, R. (2017) 'Bridge the gap: Multidirectional memory in photography projects for refugee youths', *Journal of Intercultural Studies*, 38 (6): 665–78.

Massey, D. (1994) *Space, Place and Gender*. Oxford: Polity Press.

Massey, D. (2005) *For Space*. London: Sage.

Matejskova, T. and Leitner, H. (2011) 'Urban encounters with difference: The contact hypothesis and immigrant integration projects in eastern Berlin', *Social and Cultural Geography*, 12: 717–43.

McCann, R. (2008) 'Entwining the body and the world: Architectural design and experience in the light of "Eye and Mind"', in G. Weiss (ed.) *Intertwinings: Interdisciplinary Encounters with Merleau-Ponty*. Albany, NY: State University of New York Press. pp. 265–82.

McCormack, D. (2006) 'For the love of pipes and cables: A response to Deborah Thien', *Area*, 38: 330–32.

McCormack, D.P. (2008) 'Engineering affective atmospheres on the moving geographies of the 1897 Andrée expedition', *Cultural Geographies*, 15(4): 413–30.

Melançon, J. (2014) 'Thinking corporeally, socially, and politically: Critical phenomenology after Merleau-Ponty and Bourdieu', *Bulletin d'analyse phénoménologique*, X 8, 1782–2041.

Mendieta, E. (2001) 'Invisible cities. A phenomenology of globalization from below', *City*, 5 (1): 7–26.

Merleau-Ponty, M. (1960) *Signes*. Paris: Les Éditions Gallimard.

Merleau-Ponty, M. (1962) *Phenomenology of Perception*. London: Routledge and Kegan Paul.

Merleau-Ponty, M. (1964) *The Primacy of Perception*. Evanston, IL: Northwestern University Press.

Merleau-Ponty, M. (1968) *The Visible and the Invisible*. Evanston, IL: Northwestern University Press.

Merleau-Ponty, M. (1969) *Humanism and Terror*. Boston, MA: Beacon Press.

Merleau-Ponty, M. (1973) *The Prose of the World*. Evanstone, IL: Northwestern University Press.

Merleau-Ponty, M. (1974) *Adventures of the Dialectic*. London: Heinemann.

Merleau-Ponty, M. (2003) *Nature. Course Notes from Collège de France*. Evanston IL: Northwestern University Press.

Merrifield, A. (2013) *The Politics of the Encounter: Urban Theory and Protest Under Planetary Urbanization*. London: University of Georgia Press.

Merrifield, A. (2014) *The New Urban Question*. London: Pluto Press.

Meyer, K. (2008) 'Rhythms, streets, cities', in K. Goonewardena, S. Kipler, R. Milgrom and C. Schmid (eds) *Space, Difference, Everyday Life. Reading Henri Lefebvre*. New York and London: Routledge. pp. 147–60.

Mitchell, D. (2003) *The Right to the City: Social Justice and the Fight for Public Space*. New York, NY: Guilford Press.

Mitchell, D. and L.A. Staeheli (2009) 'Public space', in R. Kitchin and N. Thrift (eds) *International Encyclopedia of Human Geography*. Vol 8. London: Elsevier. pp. 511–16.

Mohr, E.J. (2014) 'Max Scheler's critical theory: The idea of critical phenomenology', PhD dissertation, Duquesne University. https://dsc.duq.edu/etd/939 [accessed 22 May 2019].

Moi, T. (1999) *What is a Woman?* Oxford: Oxford University Press.

Molendijk, A.L., Beaumont, J. and Jedan, C. (eds) (2010) *Exploring the Postsecular: The Religious, the Political and the Urban*. Boston, MA/Leiden: Brill.

Molz, J.G. (2007) 'Eating difference. The cosmopolitan mobilities of culinary tourism', *Space and Culture*, 10 (1): 77–93.

Morris, D. (2008) 'Body', in R. Diprose, and J. Reynolds (eds) *Merleau-Ponty Key Concepts*. Stocksfield: Acumen. pp. 111–21.

Mørck, Y. (1998) *Bindestregs-danskere: Fortællinger om køn, generationer og etnicitet*. København: Forlaget Sociologi.

Nava, M. (2002) 'Cosmopolitan modernity: Everyday imaginaries and the register of difference', *Theory, Culture & Society*, 19 (1–2): 81–99.

Naylor, S. and Ryan, J.R. (2002) 'The mosque in the suburbs: Negotiating religion and ethnicity in South London', *Social and Cultural Geography*, 3 (1): 39–59.

Neergaard, M. de. Koefoed, L. and Simonsen, K. (2017) 'Purpose-built mosques in Copenhagen: Visibility, publicity and cultural dispute', *Nordic Journal of Architectural Research*, 29 (1): 61–84.

Nørregaard-Nielsen, E. and Rosenmeier S.L. (2007) *Nydanskere i nattelivet*. København: Nørregaard-Nielsen og Rosenmeier.

Olwig, K. (2011) 'All that is landscape is melted into air: The "aerography" of ethereal space', *Environment and Planning D: Society and Space*, 29 (3): 519–32.

Pain, R. (2009) 'Globalized fear? Towards an emotional geopolitics', *Progress in Human Geography*, 33: 466–86.

Pain, R., Smith, S.J. and Graham, S. (eds) (2008) *Fear: Critical Geopolitics and Everyday Life*. Aldershot: Ashgate.

Peake, L. (2016) 'The twenty-first century quest for feminism and the global urban', *International Journal of Urban and Regional Research*, 40 (1): 219–27.

Peeters, R. (2008) Against violence, but not at any price, Hannah Arendt's concept of power. *Ethical Perspectives*, 15 (2): 169–92. doi: 10.2143/EP.15.2.2032366

Pettigrew, T.F., Tropp, L.R., Wagner, U. and Christ, O. (2011) 'Recent advances in inter-group contact theory', *International Journal of Intercultural Relations*, 35 (3): 271–80.

Pinder, D. (2005) *Visions of the City: Utopianism, Power and Politics in Twentieth-Century Urbanism*. New York, NY: Routledge.

Pred, A. (1990) *Lost Words and Lost Worlds: Modernity and the Language of Everyday Life in Late Nineteenth Century Stockholm*. Cambridge: Cambridge University Press.

Radhakrishnan, R. (2005) 'Globality is not worldliness', *Gamma: Journal of Theory and Criticism*, 13: 183–98.

Raj, D.S. (2003) *Where Are You From? Middle Class Migrants in the Modern World*. Berkeley, CA: University of California Press.

Revill, G. (2015) 'How is space made in sound? Spatial mediation, critical phenomenology and the political agency of sound', *Progress in Human Geography*, doi:10.1177/03 09132515572271

Reynolds, J. (2004) *Merleau-Ponty and Derrida: Intertwining Embodiment and Alterity*. Athens, OH: Ohio University Press.

Ricoeur, P. (1984) *Time and Narrative* Vol. 1. Chicago, IL: University of Chicago Press.

Riis, H.B. (2017) 'It doesn't matter if you're black or white: Negotiating identity and Danishness in intercultural dialogue meetings', *Journal of Intercultural Studies*, 38(6): 694–707.

Robinson, J. (2014) 'New geographies of theorizing the urban. Putting comparison to work for global urban studies', in S. Parnell and S. Oldfield (eds), *The Routledge Handbook on Cities of the Global South*. London: Routledge. pp. 57–70.

Rosello, M. (2001) *Postcolonial Hospitality*. Stanford, CA: Stanford University Press.

Rosenberg, S. and Sauer, B. (2012) *Politics, Religion and Gender. Framing and Regulating the Veil*. London/New York, NY: Routledge.

Roy, A. (2014) 'Worlding the South. Towards a post-colonial urban theory', in S. Parnell and S. Oldfield (eds) *The Routledge Handbook on Cities of the Global South*. London: Routledge. pp. 9–20.

Ryan, A. and Wollan, G. (2013) 'Festivals, landscapes and aesthetic engagement: A phenomenological approach to four Norwegian festivals', *Norsk Geografisk Tidsskrift – Norwegian Journal of Geography*, 67 (2): 99–112.

Røgilds, F. (1995) *Stemmer i et grænseland: En bro mellem unge indvandrere og danskere?* København: Politisk Revy.

Said, E.W. (1978) *Orientalism. Western Conceptions of the Orient.* London: Routledge and Kegan Paul.

Said, E.W. (1997) *Covering Islam. How the Media and the Experts Determine How We See the Rest of the World.* New York, NY: Vintage Books.

Said, E.W. (2004) *Humanism and Democratic Criticism.* New York, NY: Columbia University Press.

Sandercock, L. (1998) *Towards Cosmopolis. Planning for Multicultural Cities.* Chichester: Wiley.

Sandercock, L. (2003) *Cosmopolis II: Mongrel Cities in the 21st Century.* New York, NY: Continuum.

Schatzki, T. (2002) *The Site of the Social: A Philosophical Account of the Constitution of Social Life and Change.* University Park, PA: The Pennsylvania State University Press.

Scheper-Hughes, N. and Bourgois, P. (2004) 'Introduction: Making sense of violence', in N. Scheper-Hughes and P. Bourgois *Violence in War and Peace: An Anthology*, 4. Malden, MA: Blackwell. pp. 1–13.

Schmidt, G. (2011) 'Understanding and approaching muslim visibilities: Lessons learned from a fieldwork-based study of muslims in Copenhagen', *Ethnic and Racial Studies*, 34 (7): 1216–29.

Seamon, D. (1979) *A Geography of the Lifeworld. Movement, Rest and Encounter.* London: Croom Helm.

Sennett, R. (1994) *Flesh and Stone. The Body and the City in Western Civilization.* London: Penguin.

Sennett, R. (2012) *Together.* London: Allen Lane.

Serban, C. (2010) 'La Chair chez Merleau-Ponty, entre affection et auto-affection', in Novotný, K., Hammer, T.S., Gléonec, A. and Specián, P. (eds) *Thinking in Dialogue with Humanities. Paths into the Phenomenology of Merleau-Ponty.* Bucharest: Zeta Books. pp. 69–83.

Sheller, M. (2004) 'Mobile publics: Beyond the network perspective', *Environment and Planning D*, 22 (1): 39–52.

Simmel, G. (1950a [1903]) 'The metropolis and mental life', in K. Wolff (trans.) *The Sociology of Georg Simmel.* New York, NY: Free Press, pp. 409–424.

Simmel, G. (1950b [1908]) 'The stranger', in K. Wolff (trans.) *The Sociology of Georg Simmel.* New York, NY: Free Press. pp. 402–408.

Simonsen, K. (1993) *Byteori og Hverdagspraksis.* København: Akademisk Forlag.

Simonsen, K. (2004) 'Europe, national identities and multiple others', *European Urban and Regional Studies*, 11 (4): 357–62.

Simonsen, K. (2005a) 'Bodies, sensations, space and time: The contribution from Henri Lefebvre', *Geografiska Annaler*, 87B: 1–15.

Simonsen, K. (2005b) *Byens mange ansigter – konstruktion af byen i praksis of fortælling.* Frederiksberg: Roskilde Universitetsforlag.

Simonsen, K. (2007) 'Practice, spatiality and embodied emotions: An outline of a geography of practice', *Human Affairs*, 17: 168–82.

Simonsen, K. (2008a) 'Place as encounters: Practice, conjunction and co-existence', in J.O. Bærenholdt and B. Granås (eds) *Mobility and Place: Enacting Northern European Peripheries.* Aldershot: Ashgate. pp. 13–27.

Simonsen, K. (2008b) 'Practice, narrative and the "multicultural city": A Copenhagen case', *European Urban and Regional Studies*, 15 (2): 145–58.

Simonsen, K. (2010) 'Encountering O/other bodies: Practice, emotion and ethics', in B. Anderson and P. Harrison (eds) *Taking-Place: Non-Representational Theories and Geography*. Farnham: Ashgate. pp. 221–240.

Simonsen, K. (2012) 'In quest of a new humanism: Embodiment, experience and phenomenology as critical geography', *Progress in Human Geography*: 37 (1): 10–26.

Simonsen, K., Koefoed, L. and de Neergaard, M. (2017) 'Festival as embodied encounters: On Kulturhavn in Copenhagen', *Journal of Intercultural Studies*, 38 (6): 637–50.

Simonsen, K., de Neergaard, M. and Koefoed, L. (2019) 'A mosque event: the opening of a purpose-built mosque in Copenhagen', *Social & Cultural Geography*, 20(5): 649–70.

Smith, A. (1999) *Myth and Memories of the Nation*. Oxford: Oxford University Press.

Smith, N. (1992) 'Geography, difference and the politics of scale', in I.J. Dorety, E. Graham and M. Mallek (eds) *Postmodernism and the Social Science*. London: Macmillan. pp. 57–79.

Smith, M., Davidson, J., Cameron, L. and Bondi, L. (eds) (2009) *Emotion, Place and Culture*. Farnham: Ashgate.

Sollund, R. (2006) 'Racialization in police stop and search practice – the Norwegian case', *Critical Criminology*, 14 (3): 265–92.

Spencer, D.C. (2009) 'Habit(us), body techniques and body callusing: An ethnography of mixed martial arts', *Body & Society*, 15 (4): 119–43.

Staeheli, L.A. and Mitchell, D. (2007) 'Locating the public in research and practice', *Progress in Human Geography*, 31 (6): 792–811.

Swanton, D. (2010) 'Flesh, metal, road: Tracing the machinic geographies of race', *Environment and Planning D, Society and Space*, 28 (3): 447–66.

Swyngedouw, E. (1997) 'Neither global nor local: "Glocalization" and the politics of scale', in K. Cox (ed.) *Spaces of Globalization*. New York, NY: Guilford Press. pp. 137–66.

Swyngedouw, E. (2014) 'Where is the political? Insurgent mobilisations and the incipient "return of the political"', *Space and Polity*, 18(2): 122–36.

Swyngedouw, E. (2018) *Promises of the Political: Insurgent Cities in a Post-political Environment*. London: MIT Press.

Thibaud, J.P. (2011) 'Sensory design. The sensory fabric of urban ambiances', *Senses and Society*, 6 (2): 203–15.

Thrift, N. (1996) *Spatial Formations*. London: Sage.

Thrift, N. (2008) *Non-Representational Theory. Space, Politics, Affect*. London and New York, NY: Routledge.

Tolia-Kelly, D. (2006) 'Affect – an ethnocentric encounter?: Exploring the "universalist" imperative of emotional/affectual geographies', *Area*, 38: 213–17.

Tonkiss, Fran (2003) 'The ethics of indifference: Community and solitude in the city', *International Journal of Cultural Studies*, 6 (3): 297–311.

Topolski, A. (2015) *Arendt, Levinas and a Politics of Relationality*. London/New York, NY: Rowman & Littlefield.

Tuan, Y.-F. (1974) 'Space and place: A humanistic perspective', *Progress in Human Geography*, 6: 233–46.

Valentine, G. (2008) 'Living with difference: Reflections on geographies of encounter', *Progress in Human Geography*, 32 (3): 323–37.

Walters, W. (2004) 'Secure borders, safe haven, domopolitics', *Citizenship Studies*, 8 (3): 237–60.

Waquant, L. (2004) *Body & Soul: Notebooks of an Apprentice Boxer*. Oxford: Oxford University Press.

Waquant, L. (2008) *Urban Outcasts: A Comparative Sociology of Urban Marginality*. Cambridge: Polity.

Waquant, L., Slater, T. and Pereira, V.B. (2014) 'Territorial stigmatization in action', *Environment and Planning A*, 46 (6): 1270–80.

Weate, J. (2001) 'Fanon, Merleau-Ponty and the difference of phenomenology', in R. Bernasconi (ed.) *Race*. Oxford: Blackwell. pp. 169–83.

Weiss, G. (1999) *Body Images: Embodiment as Intercorporeality*. New York, NY, and London: Routledge.

Weiss, G. (2008) *Refiguring the Ordinary*. Bloomington and Indianapolis, IN: Indiana University Press.

Whyte, Z. (2017) 'Meetings of the art: Cultural encounters and contact zones in an art project for asylum-seeking minors in Denmark', *Journal of Intercultural Studies*, 38 (6): 679–93.

Williams, R. (1975) *The Country and the City*. Oxford: Oxford University Press.

Wilson, H.F. (2011) 'Passing propinquities in the multicultural city: The everyday encounters of bus passengering', *Environment and Planning A*, 43 (3): 634–49.

Wilson, H.F. (2017a) 'On geography and encounter: Bodies, borders, and difference', *Progress in Human Geography*, 41 (4): 451–71.

Wilson, H.F. (2017b) 'On the paradox of "organised encounter"', *Journal of Intercultural Studies*, 38 (6): 606–20.

Wylie, J. (2010) 'Non-representational subjects?', in B. Anderson and P. Harrison (eds) *Taking Place: Non-representational Theories and Geography*. Farnham: Ashgate. pp. 99–117.

Young, I.M. (1990a) *Throwing Like a Girl and Other Essays in Feminist Philosophy and Social Theory*. Bloomington, IN: Indiana University Press.

Young, I.M. (1990b) *Justice and the Politics of Difference*: Princeton, NJ: Princeton University Press.

Young, I.M. (2005) *On Female Body Experience*. New York, NY: Oxford University Press.

Žižek, S. (1993) *Tarrying with the Negative: Kant, Hegel, and the Critique of Ideology*. Durham, NC: Duke University Press.

Žižek, S. (2008) *Violence: Six Sideways Reflections*. New York, NY: Picador.

Index

References to Footnotes contain the letter 'n', followed by the Note number.

www.ingramcontent.com/pod-product-compliance
Lightning Source LLC
Chambersburg PA
CBHW070933030426
42336CB00014BA/2660